# Start-Up Factories

# Start-Up Factories
## High Performance Management, Job Quality, and Regional Advantage

Peter B. Doeringer
*Boston University*

Christine Evans-Klock
*Boston University*

David G. Terkla
*University of Massachusetts Boston*

2002

**OXFORD**
UNIVERSITY PRESS

and

**W.E. Upjohn Institute**
for Employment Research

Oxford University Press

Oxford New York
Athens Auckland Bangkok Bogotá Buenos Aires Cape Town Chennai Dar es Salaam
Delhi Florence Hong Kong Istanbul Karachi Kolkata Kuala Lumpur Madrid
Melbourne Mexico City Mumbai Nairobi Paris São Paulo Shanghai Singapore Taipei
Tokyo Toronto Warsaw and associated companies in Berlin Ibadan

Published by Oxford University Press, Inc.
198 Madison Avenue, New York, New York, 10016
www.oup.com
Oxford is a registered trademark of Oxford University Press
and by the
W.E. Upjohn Institute for Employment Research
Kalamazoo, Michigan 49007
www.upjohninstitute.org

**Library of Congress Cataloging-in-Publication Data**

Doeringer, Peter B.
   Start-up factories : high performance management, job quality and regional
advantage / Peter Doeringer, Christine Evans-Klock, David G. Terkla.
     p. cm.
   Includes index
     ISBN 0–19–514747–2 (hardcover : alk. paper)
     1. Factory management—Case studies. 2. New business
enterprises—Management—Case studies. I. Evans-Klock, Christine
   II. Terkla, David G. III. W.E. Upjohn Institute for Employment Research. IV. Title
TS155 .D62 2002
658.5—dc21

                 2002005104

Printing number: 9 8 7 6 5 4 3 2 1
Printed in the United States of America on acid-free paper

Cover design by J.R. Underhill.
Index prepared by Nancy Humphreys.

# Contents

# Figures

# Tables

# Preface

This book is the product of almost a decade of study of what new manufacturing plants reveal about future trends in the workplace practices and management strategies of U.S. manufacturing. The project began as a study of the location decisions of Japanese transplants in the United States. The decade of the 1980s had seen an enormous inflow of Japanese direct investment into the United States, rising from about $600 million in 1980 to almost $20 billion in 1990 (U.S. Dept. of Commerce 1992). While California was initially the state of choice for Japanese investment, accounting for almost 40% of the jobs in Japanese-owned manufacturing plants prior to 1980, a much wider range of states was attracting Japanese capital during the investment spurt of the 1980s. By the end of 1989, there were 679 new Japanese-owned manufacturing facilities operating in the United States.

Needless to say, there was aggressive competition among states for these new plants and considerable controversy over what mattered to their location choices. We initially sought to identify what factors made states attractive to Japanese transplants through a carefully designed set of matched case studies of Japanese transplants and corresponding new branch plants of domestic manufacturing companies. Two corollary aspects of the location study were to determine the number and quality of the jobs being generated by these factories as they started up in their new locations, and to compare job creation rates of the Japanese plants with those of counterpart domestic start-ups.

It quickly became apparent during the field research, however, that start-up factories provide an unusual window of opportunity for studying a broader range of issues about the adoption and effectiveness of advanced management practices. During our pilot interviews, we found that new manufacturing plants shared common characteristics of using state-of-the-art technologies, new types of work organization, and innovative human resources practices, as well as making carefully informed location decisions. Managers of all the start-ups saw themselves as being at the leading edge of both technological and managerial strategies within their parent corporations, and they were expected to set the company-wide pattern for future productivity and efficiency gains.

As the study progressed, our interest turned toward understanding the new management practices adopted by start-up factories and how these practices might affect their productivity growth as well as their jobs and location decisions. At the same time, we observed some puzzling differences between Japanese transplants and domestic start-ups. For example, we noted that comparable Japanese transplants and domestic start-ups were making similar location choices, but for different reasons. We further learned that underneath the common technologies and common nomenclature of management strategies, Japanese transplants were often managed very differently from their domestic counterparts. Finally, we were struck by the case study evidence showing that when Japanese transplants and domestic start-ups were matched by product, technology, and location, the Japanese transplants seemed to experience faster rates of growth in output and employment and received additional investments in plant and equipment more quickly than the domestic start-ups.

The original focus on plant location and regional economic development gave way to a broader research agenda, which focuses on the high performance management strategies adopted by new factories and on how these strategies influenced the quality of work, the choice of plant location, and the overall growth in productivity and jobs. The result is a book that integrates three themes: high performance management strategy (including the economics of efficiency wages and compensation incentives), the quality of jobs created by high performance management practices combined with new manufacturing technologies, and regional economic development.

These themes are normally treated as separate areas of study. Instead, they must be analyzed as components of a single system of high performance production management. Efficiency wages and compensation incentives are only one element of a larger set of high performance strategies for controlling labor costs and raising productivity. High performance management strategies result in good jobs at high wages, but the effectiveness of high performance strategies depends upon firms tapping into distinctive types of regional advantage.

While we cannot claim to have found a single set of management or policy prescriptions that fits all cases, there is a clear chain of evidence showing that the adoption of high performance management strategies can contribute substantially to productivity improvement and the growth of high-wage jobs in a wide range of industries. The intensity with which high performance management practices are adopted is systematically related to the choice of state locations with workforce characteristics that support such practices. Regions that attract such firms derive an unusual level of benefits in terms of long-term growth in jobs of very high quality. These are powerful findings for both regional development policy and national economic competitiveness.

This project was supported by a research grant from the W.E. Upjohn Institute for Employment Research. A grant from the Alfred P. Sloan Foundation supported exploratory research on Japanese transplants in Georgia and Kentucky and much of the material on organizational aspects of efficiency was compiled under a grant from the National Science Foundation. Christine Evans-Klock participated in this research as a doctoral student at Boston University, prior to joining the International Labour Oganization (ILO). The responsibility for opinions expressed in this book rests solely with the authors and publication does not constitute an endorsement by the International Labour Office of the opinions expressed herein.

We are grateful to Eli Berman, Tim Bartik, Ross Gittell, Susan House-man, Harry Katz, Kevin Lang, Paul Osterman, Michael Piore, Ray Vernon, and a number of anonymous referees for their valuable comments on various parts of the manuscript. Seminar presentations at Massachusetts Institute of Technology, Harvard University, the University of Massachusetts, the International Labor Organization, the Federal Reserve Bank of Boston, the W.E. Upjohn Institute For Employment Research, and the University of Paris, XIII, were also helpful in shaping our ideas. Jean Poitras and Mary F.P. O'Neill provided helpful research assistance. Finally, we wish to thank all of the plant managers, front-line workers, and union representatives who generously donated their time to participate in this study.

Boston, Massachusetts
Geneva, Switzerland
December 2001

# 1
# Introduction

The conventional wisdom among economists and business analysts is that new and more dynamic business organizations are replacing those of the "old" economy. The old economy specialized in the mass production of standardized products using narrowly skilled labor and machinery that were often dedicated to particular products. That economy was characterized by bureaucratic management practices and strong unions that raised wages and reduced workforce flexibility. The "new" economy produces a more diverse range of goods with shorter product cycles. Workers are more skilled and flexible and equipment is more adaptable. The new economy is relatively free of unions and is managed more nimbly. The old economy provided relatively high-wage and secure jobs for high school graduates. As these high school jobs are being phased out, the new economy is generating jobs with higher real wages, particularly for those with college degrees.

Unfortunately, this description of the declining old economy and the booming new one is not fully supported by the facts. What we see instead are a set of disturbing economic trends that span both the old and new economies. One element of concern is the sluggish growth in productivity. National growth in productivity (as measured by increases in output per hour in the business sector) rose at an annual rate of 3.2% between 1960 and 1973, but this rate of growth fell to 1.7% per year between 1973 and 1996 (Council of Economic Advisers 2000, Table B-47).[1] At the same time, the growth in real wages slowed from an annual rate of 2.7% between 1960 and 1973 to 1.2% per year from 1973 to 1996 (Council of Economic Advisers 2000, Table B-47). Along with a slowdown in real wage growth, workers were also receiving a shrinking share of national productivity growth and experiencing less employment stability. Only 35% of the workforce was in career jobs (jobs lasting at least 10 years) in 1996, compared with 41% in 1979, and 20% fewer workers reported a strong attachment to their employers in the 1980s than in the 1970s (Mishel, Bernstein, and Schmitt 1999).

Productivity growth partly rebounded after 1996, growing at 2.6% per year through 1999, and real wages began to grow faster as well (Mishel, Bernstein, and Schmitt 2001; Economic Policy Institute 2000). However, as the early years of the new millennium are showing, the sustainability of this turnaround is uncertain. The implications of the new economy for career employment and the sharing of productivity gains between workers and employers remains unclear.

It has always been difficult for economists to account for trends in productivity. The major long run sources of productivity growth—research and development and investments in physical and human capital—do not seem to have slackened significantly since the early 1970s, nor did they show a sharp acceleration during the recovery in productivity growth during the late 1990s (Denison 1985; Mohr 1983; Council of Economic Advisers 2001). Similarly, none of the disruptions caused by the OPEC oil crises, increased import penetration, shifts in the composition of output from goods to services, or cyclical factors seems to explain much of the trends in productivity growth.

Growth in information technologies has recently been cited as the source of the recovery in productivity growth during the late 1990s (Council of Economic Advisers 2001). However, economic progress through new technologies also depends on the skills and motivation of workers. There is a growing sentiment that high productivity growth requires appropriate organizational strategies and performance incentives (Chandler 1992; Williamson 1975; Simon 1991; Cappelli 1999; Caroli and Van Reenen 2001).

Outmoded workplace practices have been singled out to explain why U.S. productivity growth has lagged (Dertouzos, Lester, and Solow 1989; Ouchi 1984; Kochan, Katz, and McKersie 1986; Aoki 1990; Milgrom and Roberts 1990; Kochan and Osterman 1994; Daft 1998; Cappelli 1999; Appelbaum et al. 2000). This organizational interpretation sees a need for "innovative" management practices and performance incentives that will raise labor productivity and improve business performance.

While the definition of what constitutes such new "high performance" management practices varies from study to study, several recent reviews of the high performance management literature suggest an emerging consensus around a set of key practices. These include intensive training on-the-job and in technical subjects (such as statistical quality control), the use of production teams with fluid job assignments, and the encouraging of workers to collaborate with supervisors to help in solving production and quality-control problems (Becker and Gerhart 1996; Huselid 1995; Appelbaum and Batt 1994; Osterman 1994, 2000; Mohrman, Galbraith and Lawler 1998; Black and Lynch 1999).

The adoption of these core high performance management practices by U.S. business has increased over the last decade.  According to one national survey, only about one-third of U.S. manufacturing plants made substantial use of such practices in 1992 (Osterman 1994), but adoption rates had increased by the late 1990s to 50% or more for most key practices (quality circles, job rotation, and total quality management [TQM]) and over 70% of the firms surveyed adopted two or more of such practices (Osterman 2000).  There is also a growing body of evidence that these practices have positive effects on business performance (Ichniowski, Shaw, and Prennushi 1997; MacDuffie 1995; Kruse 1993; Bartel 1995; Kleiner and Bouillon 1988; Katz, Kochan and Gobeille 1983; Black and Lynch 1999; Osterman 2000).

As the efficiency advantages from adopting high performance organizational practices have become so widely documented, however, two puzzles remain.  One is why has it taken over two decades for these practices to become widely adopted by American industry?  The second is why are not the documented gains in plant-level productivity associated with these practices being more widely shared with workers through higher wage gains and more job security (Osterman 2000)?[2]

More intensive investment in workforce training should result in higher wages being paid for higher skills.  The growing use of teams implies an increase in the firm-specific component of skills that should further encourage employers to raise wages and increase long-term employment.  The adoption of quality circles and other problem-solving mechanisms could be expected to require added financial incentives to secure the cooperation of workers in solving quality control and production problems.  Yet, the divergence between productivity and real earnings growth continues.

## NEW EVIDENCE FROM START-UP FACTORIES

This book helps to explain these puzzles by addressing six key questions about high performance management practices in the American workplace:

1) To what extent do the newest and technologically most advanced manufacturing plants adopt high performance management practices?

2) Are there complementarities among these practices?

3) Is there a single "best practice" model of high performance management being used by these plants?

4) Do high performance management practices contribute to jobs of high quality?

5) Are there unique regional characteristics that reinforce high performance workplace practices? and

6) How large a competitive advantage can be generated by factories that combine state-of-the-art technologies with comprehensive high performance management strategies?

Like other studies, this book confirms that "best practice" manufacturing companies are raising productivity and lowering unit costs by introducing innovative high performance management practices. The catch for many companies, however, is that the full benefits of these practices are not being captured because they are not being accompanied by corresponding adjustments in other management strategies and because they are not combined with appropriate incentives for their employees to cooperate with change.

This study breaks new ground by showing that high performance management practices are most effective when they are embedded in a larger set of management strategies, ranging from taking workforce attitudes into account when choosing business locations to the sharing of managerial power and authority with employees. It also demonstrates that high performance management and good jobs go hand in hand, and it offers concrete proposals for how to accelerate productivity growth while raising earnings and job security.

Unlike previous studies that have looked at the experience of established firms, we analyze only new plants. New plants have unfettered choices of technologies, organizational structures, management practices, compensation incentives, and locations. As a result, they offer a leading indicator of what will become best-practice management in the next decade or so.

Our sample consists of 48 new branch plants of large manufacturing companies in the United States that began operating between 1978 and 1990. These plants are in three industries that cover a wide range of technologies, products, and production processes. They are located in three different geographic regions that were chosen to reflect differences in education levels of workers, workforce attitudes, and labor–management environments. The sample was selected with the expectation that it would contain a high proportion of plants that are actively and successfully adopting innovative management practices. Japanese-owned start-ups were oversampled to further ensure a rich mix of plants using such practices.

We conducted extensive case study interviews with these start-up factories in the early 1990s using a combination of structured and open-ended interviews. Through these interviews, along with substantial shop-floor visits, we have assembled a detailed description of the high performance organizational strategies, compensation practices, and location decisions of these start-up plants. Quantitative data were collected from each plant on the high performance management practices adopted, the characteristics of jobs created, and the experience with increasing the plant's production during the period from the date of start-up through the early 1990s.

The plants sampled were typically designated by their parent corporations to represent the next generation of technology and management practices. As such, they received intensive, across-the-board corporate assistance with strategic business decisions. They universally adopted advanced technologies, typically involving computerized manufacturing and quality monitoring. They almost always sought to match these technologies with high performance management practices. They typically pay high wages and often offer incentives for raising productivity and gaining additional skills. They also try to optimize their business locations by choosing sites where the education, skills, and aptitudes of workers will be the most compatible with their technologies and organizational practices.

We attribute this strong orientation towards technological and organizational optimization as emblematic of the special advantages available to start-up branch plants. New plants have no prior organizational history or established work practices that have to be accommodated. They therefore provide a relatively unrestricted opportunity for introducing new technologies and organizational practices, which explains why they are seen as the flagship branches of their parent corporations. Moreover, the managers interviewed report that their start-ups were achieving high rates of growth in productivity and output, and they attribute this success to their organizational practices.

These conclusions from the case studies are confirmed by econometric analysis of data collected from the start-ups during our interviews. They are further supported by similar analyses of a unique national panel database of start-up factories that we compiled from Dun and Bradstreet records and the Japan Economic Institute's directories of Japanese affiliates in the United States. These data, covering approximately the same period (1978–1988) as the case studies, allow us to broadly test the effect of high performance workplace organizations on employment and productivity growth.

The national data also allow us to identify the regional location advantages that are most likely to contribute to the success of start-ups adopting different types of management strategies. Although other research has examined the location decisions of new manufacturing plants (Carlton 1983; Schmenner, Huber, and Cook 1987), this is the first study to explore the impact of management practices on business location.

## MAJOR THEMES

The book develops a series of themes about the economics of high performance management, both in theory and in practice. These themes include the types of high performance practices adopted by start-ups, the quality of jobs provided, and the interaction between management strategies and business location. The effects of these practices on business performance are analyzed using a "ramp-up production function" that captures employment growth and productivity improvement.

## The Adoption of High Performance Practices

Most managers of our start-up plants are adopting the types of management practices that are frequently identified by economists and management experts as contributing to strong business performance. They use such practices more frequently and apply them to a larger fraction of their employees than was the case in the average U.S. manufacturing plant during the same time period. However, we often find a gap between the adoption and the effectiveness of such practices. The contribution to productivity growth of high performance practices is far greater among start-ups that integrate specific practices into a more comprehensive system of high performance organizational practices than among start-ups that adopt these strategies piecemeal.

This is particularly evident among Japanese transplants, which create hybrid organizational systems that deliberately adapt Japanese-style management practices to the labor market and industrial relations environments of the United States (Liker, Fruin, and Adler 1999; Pil and MacDuffie 1999; Jenkins and Florida 1999; Doeringer, Evans-Klock, and Terkla 1998). This process of creating hybrid organizational systems most often involves a cluster of high performance practices that include intensive training, widespread opportunities for employee participation in workplace decisions, teamwork, and compensation practices that reward productivity improvement. These practices are then integrated with total quality management approaches, lean operations management, just-in-time logistics arrangements, and plant location decisions.

Consistent with other studies, we find these practices confer a sizeable advantage in terms of productivity and employment growth. This advantage is greatest in those start-ups that incorporate these practices into their larger management frameworks. Complementarities among practices are very important, including those associated with both worker voice and employee empowerment. These high performance practices are found to be effective in a wide range of industries.

## High Performance Practices and Good Jobs

The typical established manufacturing plant that adopts high performance management practices does not share the resulting productivity gains with its employees (Osterman 2000). The reverse is true for the high performance start-ups in our sample: almost all of these start-ups pay high wages, offer career job ladders, and provide ample opportunities for employee voice. Most also offer their core workforces high job security through explicit employment guarantees, widespread use of buffer stocks of temporary workers, and relatively high rates of employment growth. These various aspects of job quality are reminiscent of the types of organizational practices that were adopted during the old economy of the 1950s and 1960s, when productivity gains and wage increases moved together.

Some have argued that these good job characteristics might also reflect benefits that are necessary to compensate for the intensified work effort, added job responsibilities, and management by stress that have been reported in some case studies of Japanese factories (Parker and Slaughter 1988; Raysey, Scholerious, and Harley 2000). However, we found little evidence in our interviews and plant tours of these kinds of negative job characteristics among either domestic or Japanese-owned start-ups.

To the contrary, the work organization and employment relationships in these start-ups are generally very positive. In addition to high pay, we typically encountered various mechanisms, such as quality circles and high levels of employee involvement, that strengthened employee autonomy and control over the organization and conduct of work. Even though our location analyses reveal that start-up factories typically prefer to site their facilities where the probability of unionization is low, and relatively few plants in our sample are unionized, we were surprised by the extent to which employees could exercise power. In many of the start-ups, workers had substantial opportunities for contributing voice, controlling production processes and quality, and exercising authority to evaluate co-workers through peer review procedures.

### Business Location and Regional Advantage

Choosing a location is one of the most important strategic decisions made by start-up plants.  Our data reveal sharp differences in
location choices between start-ups that integrate specific high performance practices with their overall organizational strategies and those
that do not.  While the same location options are presumably available
to all start-ups, and all of the start-ups use many of the same criteria for
choosing an optimal location, those that most frequently use the hybrid
high performance model value different locations and interpret location
criteria differently than other start-ups.

The start-ups that most frequently adopt high performance management practices place greater priority on the presence of large pools
of high school–educated labor and on workforce attitudes that favor
cooperation and problem resolution.  Start-ups that adopt high performance practices in a more piecemeal way tend to place relatively less
weight on workforce factors compared with other regional cost factors,
such as wages and proximity to markets.  Even where the location criteria are identical, such as the preference for locating in regions where
unions are weak, the most frequent adopters of high performance management practices associate unions with adversarial labor–management relationships and difficulties in developing a collaborative workforce.  The other start-ups avoid unions because they think there will be
less upward pressure on wages and the workforce will be more willing
to accept employer authority.

## NEW POSSIBILITIES FOR ENHANCING
## U.S. MANUFACTURING

The experience of start-up factories in adopting high performance
management practices provides new insights into how U.S. manufacturing can improve labor productivity and job quality in the coming
years.  The analyses in subsequent chapters develop unambiguous evidence that adopting high performance management practices can
enhance productivity growth in U.S. manufacturing.  These same practices that raise productivity appear to work best when they are com-

bined with high-wage, relatively secure, and otherwise good jobs, at least in our sample of start-ups. Industry by industry, these high performance start-ups generate good jobs at a faster rate than the average firm generates average jobs.

High performance management practices are not simply one more management fad that, at best, provides one-time performance improvements (Carson et al. 2000). They contribute substantially to productivity growth over periods as long as a decade or more. With the exception of industries using labor-intensive technologies and mass-producing low-value-added products, high performance management practices appear to be successful across a wide range of technologies and products.

The experience with start-up factories reported in this book is an encouraging indicator of the prospects for raising productivity in manufacturing while also rebuilding a base of good jobs for high school graduates. As new high performance plants replace older, traditionally managed plants, there should be corresponding increases in productivity, wages, and jobs for front-line manufacturing workers with no more than high school degrees.

However, we also see cautionary signs amidst the general diffusion of high performance management practices. One problem is that some established companies that are shedding their traditional management systems are replacing them with systems that rely more on market relationships rather than with high performance practices that enhance employee skills and motivate high productivity. The second problem is that the potential productivity gains from high performance management practices are being diluted by firms that refuse to share productivity gains with their employees. Both national surveys and case study evidence suggest that the relatively equal sharing of productivity gains between employers and workers is no longer the norm, even for plants that are adopting high performance organizational practices. The goal of this book is to demonstrate to economists, labor and management professionals, and policymakers that there is a set of general principles about how to rebuild management systems in ways that simultaneously provide higher rates of growth in business productivity and a greater sharing of these productivity gains with workers.

## PLAN OF THE BOOK

Chapter 2 provides a brief review of theories of organizational performance that are relevant to understanding how high performance management practices should affect business performance and employment relationships. A detailed description of the sample of the start-up factories and an overview of their management practices are presented in Chapter 3. Chapter 4 describes the pattern of adoption of specific high performance workplace practices by different types of start-ups and identifies the most common set of hybrid practices. Chapter 5 examines the characteristics of jobs in start-up factories and analyzes the relationship between higher performance management practices and various dimensions of job quality. The sixth and seventh chapters explore the relationship between the use of high performance practices and business location decisions, using both case study information and formal models of business location. The consequences for productivity and job growth of adopting high performance workplace practices and choosing high performance business locations are examined in Chapter 8. The final chapter summarizes the findings and presents proposals for managers, labor organizations, and policymakers on how to improve business productivity and enhance state and local economic development.

## Notes

1. This adverse trend in productivity growth is far more pronounced in the United States than in most of the other industrialized countries with which it competes (Baily and Chakrabarti 1988; Mishel, Bernstein, and Schmitt 2001).
2. The exceptions to this conclusion are the national studies that report earnings gains for a limited subset of high performance practices (Black and Lynch 1999 and Cappelli and Neumark 1999) and a set of case studies showing a correlation between high performance practices and wage gains in steel and apparel plants, but not in medical electronics imaging plants (Appelbaum et al. 2000). The positive results of the latter study may be influenced by sample selection bias, because participating plants had to agree to allow their employees to be surveyed.

# Part I
## The Theory of High Performance Management

# 2
# Theories of High Performance Management

Various theories have been proposed to explain why different types of high performance workplace organizations arise and how they can contribute to aggregate trends in productivity growth (Westney 1999). Economic theories see workplace organizations as instruments for correcting market failures that would otherwise undermine the efficiency with which labor inputs are employed. Behavioral science theories emphasize social and psychological motivators of effort and commitment as sources of increased productivity. Power theories explain many workplace organizations as emerging from a "labor process" in which employers develop organizational practices to extract quasirents from workers and where unions are a countervailing force to employers in shaping organizational practices and distributing quasirents (Edwards 1979; Goldberg 1980; Raysey, Scholerious, and Harley 2000).

All three theories agree that the most important productivity-enhancing workplace organizational practices—accurate matching of worker abilities and job requirements, intensive workplace training, strong incentives for productivity, and effective supervision—are most often found among large firms in capital-intensive industries that have relatively high levels of value added. These are also the kinds of firms that traditionally pay relatively high wages and tend to have hierarchical organizational structures based on internal labor markets and promotion ladders (Doeringer and Piore 1971; Williamson 1985; Frazis et al. 1998; Cappelli 1999; Lazear 1998).

The major differences among these theories lie in their assumptions. Economic theories assume that technology plays a major role in determining the need for organizational practices that can raise efficiency by correcting market failures. According to this view, workers will opportunistically take advantage of employers when market failures allow them to, and economic incentives are the primary means of offsetting opportunistic workforce behavior. Behavioral science theories assume that workers are not inherently opportunistic, that social and psychological incentives can be as powerful as economic incentives, and that these incentives can be applied constructively across a wide range of technologies. Power theories assume that employers will use economic, social, and psychological incentives to generate quasi-rents (profits), which may be combined with organizational practices that weaken the individual and collective power of workers to affect the distribution of these rents.

Much of the evidence in support of these different assumptions, however, is either circumstantial or inconclusive (Raysey, Scholerious, and Harley 2000). For example, the assumption that production technologies determine whether or not efficiency practices are needed is often justified by the systematic differences among industries in the adoption of efficient organizational practices and "efficiency wage" incentives (Dickens, Katz, and Lang 1986; Katz and Summers 1989; Aoki 1990; Lincoln and Kalleberg 1990). Others accord greater prominence to factors such as nationality and culture, economic class, unionization, and public policy (Cole 1971; Dore 1973; Maurice, Sellier, and Silvestre 1984; Braverman 1974; Maurice, Sorge, and Warner 1980). They often see opportunistic behavior as the result, rather than the cause, of the workplace organizations that were adopted (McGregor 1960). Because of these differences, each theory provides a different interpretation of the sources of productivity change and suggests different policies for increasing the growth of labor productivity.

## ECONOMIC THEORIES OF MARKET FAILURE

Economic theories of workplace organizations attribute the adoption of organizational practices to failures of competitive labor markets, e.g., transaction costs, imperfect information, and the loss of firm-specific assets (Williamson 1985; Delery and Doty 1996; Lazear 1998; Gibbons and Waldman 1999a). Market imperfections allow workers to increase their utility or well-being by taking opportunistic advantage of employers in ways that raise the cost of production whenever their abilities or productivity are difficult for employers to observe. Workers exaggerate their qualifications, threaten to quit after employers have invested in firm-specific hiring or training costs, or take time off and work less hard when they are unlikely to be caught shirking. Conversely, if workers face high transaction costs of job changing or if information on their productive qualities is difficult to communicate to other firms, employers may opportunistically take advantage of these costs by paying workers less than their productive contribution to the firm. Workplace organizations represent substitutes for competitive markets and help to offset the efficiency losses resulting from market failures.

The extent to which these market failures lead to efficiency losses varies among technologies. Therefore, the extent to which organizational practices are substituted for markets will vary among firms. Some technologies only require information that is easily obtained and skills that are general and paid for by workers, so that efficiency losses are low and profit-maximizing employers will be able to rely on competitive labor markets. Other technologies require costly information and high levels of training investment by employers. Firms with these technologies will rely less on competitive markets and will increasingly internalize market functions by developing organizational practices that minimize efficiency losses (MacLeod and Malcomson 1998; Huselid 1995).

The efficiency gains from adopting organizational practices result in firms receiving quasi-rents that can increase their profits, without relying on imperfectly competitive labor markets. Since organizational substitutes for markets also have costs and their effectiveness is presumably subject to diminishing returns, profit-maximizing employers will always balance the costs of reducing market failures against their efficiency benefits. The resulting organizational choices will optimize profits, but they are not likely to completely eliminate competitive market failures.

Some economic theories focus on compensation incentives, known as "efficiency wages," to correct market failures (Lang, Leonard, and Lilien 1987; Katz and Summers 1989). Others develop more comprehensive theories of workplace organizations that include hierarchical internal labor markets (Doeringer and Piore 1971; Williamson 1975; Williamson, Wachter, and Harris 1975; Gibbons and Waldman 1999b) and personnel management systems (Lazear 1998; Blakemore 1987; Kleiner et al. 1987; Winship and Rosen 1988).

## Efficiency Wages

Efficiency wages involve the payment of compensation premiums above competitive market rates of pay. There are several different versions of efficiency wage theory: selection and matching, turnover, and monitoring and motivation. Each assumes that the payment of wage premiums will generate positive quasi-rents from correcting labor market failures, but they posit different explanations of the sources of these quasi-rents (Katz and Summers 1989; Weiss 1990).

Selection and matching theories postulate certain abilities that are particularly productive in some technological settings but are hard to observe by employers. Workers with these special abilities should command a higher market value than otherwise comparable workers, but only if they are successfully matched with those employers who can benefit most from these abilities. If workers know more about their own abilities than do employers and if there are transaction costs to job search by workers and to recruitment and hiring by employers, efficiency gains can be realized by having employers and workers exchange lower-cost signals of a productive match.

The employer signal, in this case, is a higher wage offer that is commensurate with the expected higher productivity of the workers having the requisite abilities. Workers with these hard-to-observe abilities will selectively apply only for jobs with these high wages in anticipation of an efficient job match. Workers without these abilities will be at risk of subsequently being discharged if they are hired by high wage employers and will economize on their search costs by applying only to lower wage employers who do not value these abilities (Weiss 1980, 1990; Katz and Summers 1989; Weitzman 1989). An alternative version of this matching theory is that wages above market levels are needed to generate large pools of job applicants, which will allow employers to reduce the direct costs of recruitment and selection costs (Katz and Summers 1989).

Turnover theories assume that there are technologies that require firm-specific recruitment and training investments. Because such investments raise labor productivity within the firms that provide such training, but not in other firms, the costs of these investments are at least partly borne by the firm and the employer collects at least some of the investment returns. If workers quit their jobs after being trained, however, the period of time over which employers can realize a return on their training investments is curtailed, and employers must also incur the additional costs of training replacement workers. Where job-changing costs to employees are low, employers who must make firm-specific skill investments will pay efficiency-wage premiums as an incentive to reduce the probability that a trained employee will quit. Any surplus above the normal returns on the firm's investments that is generated by firm-specific training represents a quasi-rent that increases profits (Salop 1979; Stiglitz 1974).

Monitoring and motivation theories argue that a principal–agent problem will arise where technologies make it difficult or costly for employers to observe individual effort. If opportunistic workers are paid only their competitive market wage and the costs of job changing are low, they will have no incentive to work hard because it is unlikely that their low effort will be observed and there are few costs to being discharged.[1] The payment of an efficiency-wage premium under these circumstances reduces the agency problem by raising the opportunity cost to workers of disciplinary terminations (Katz and Summers 1989; Leonard 1987; Bulow and Summers 1986; Gibbons and Waldman 1999a).[2]

## Internal Labor Markets and Personnel Management Systems

The principles of efficiency wage theory have also been incorporated into more-comprehensive explanations of workplace organizations and the employment relationship. Traditionally, the predominant workplace organizational practices in the United States have been those embodied in internal labor markets, or what are sometimes called organizational "hierarchies" (Williamson 1975; Williamson, Wachter, and Harris 1975) or the "New Deal" employment model (Kochan, Katz, and McKersie 1986). Following Doeringer and Piore (1971), these theories emphasize the importance of skills that are idiosyncratic to the firm and the need to address information and monitoring problems that can arise from opportunistic worker behavior (Williamson 1975; Williamson, Wachter, and Harris 1975; Gibbons and Waldman 1999a).

Williamson (1975) provided a detailed description of how efficient recruitment and selection practices, job and promotion ladders, and efficiency wages and compensation premiums that favor long-service workers are all organizational devices designed to maximize profits by changing the economic incentives for workers in situations where labor markets have failed. For example, one traditional source of productivity growth in internal labor markets is the simplification of jobs and the use of highly specialized labor. The division and specialization of labor results in job skills being firm-specific, but it also reduces the cost to employers of training investments by reducing the skill content of jobs. Efficiency wages help employers to recruit workers who are quick and efficient learners.

Because many skills are firm-specific, jobs in internal labor markets tend to be organized into skill ladders that can efficiently build skills on-the-job in an efficient training sequence. To capture the efficiencies of progressive training sequences, internal labor markets typically fill most job vacancies by promotion from within the firm. Efficiency wages help to reduce quit rates among trained workers, and the pay increases that come from promotion along a job ladder provide deferred efficiency incentives that are only paid to those workers who remain with the firm for long periods of time.

Seniority, as well as merit, is often used as a criterion for promotion and layoff. One advantage of seniority is that it protects more senior workers from competition from less senior workers, thereby encouraging senior workers to cooperate in training their successors. Promotion and layoff by seniority also reflect the efficiencies of targeting the highest amount of firm-specific training investments on those workers who have most clearly demonstrated their willingness to remain with the firm. It also provides a formula for retaining these trained workers for the longest time if there is an adverse shift in labor demand.

Productivity in these internal labor market firms is further strengthened by governance processes within the firm. Typically, the employer has broad authority to define productivity standards and to discharge employees for failure to meet these standards. The payment of efficiency wages, deferred compensation, and seniority-based job security provide incentives for employees to be highly productive, because they substantially raise the cost of being discharged for inefficient job performance. Where workplace governance is shared with workers, as in the case where unions are present, productivity can also be increased through "effort contracts" that are either formally negotiated with unions or informally negotiated with front-line workers.

Other types of personnel management practices, such as the composition of fringe benefits, retirement practices, and job design, can be similarly understood in terms of improving the efficiencies of matching and increasing efficiency rents from training and effort motivation (Lazear 1998). Finally, internal labor market theories ascribe efficiency benefits to practices defined in personnel manuals, collective bargaining contracts, and bureaucratic work rules, because codified rules can economize on limited (or bounded) managerial decision-making capacity.

Some have argued, however, that these organizational arrangements are only efficient in the mass production of complex standardized products with relatively predictable demand. They are not sufficiently flexible for the production of more specialized complex products and services for which demand is variable and product cycles are often short (Piore and Sabel 1984; Aoki 1990; Milgrom and Roberts 1992; Daft 1998).

**Evidence of Economic Efficiency**

There is considerable indirect evidence to support these various theories of how to correct labor market failures. Matching efficiencies, for example, are suggested by the correlation between wage premiums and the number of applicants for job vacancies (see Dickens, Katz, and Lang 1986; Katz and Summers 1989) and by the tendency of large firms with internal labor markets to spend more on recruitment than smaller firms (Holzer, Katz, and Krueger 1988). Training and turnover theories are consistent with large firms providing more training and paying higher wages than smaller firms (Frazis et al. 1998; Brown, Hamilton, and Medoff 1990), and there is a well-established inverse correlation between the wages paid by these firms and quit rates (Dickens, Katz, and Lang 1986; Katz and Summers 1989). Differences in the payment of efficiency wages by type of industry and size of establishment are often interpreted as evidence that workplace organizations are rooted in production technologies that are most vulnerable to the opportunistic behavior of workers.

Direct measures of the relationship between efficiency wages and labor productivity are limited to small-scale surveys of workers and establishments (Ehrenberg and Milkovich 1987; Lawler 1971, 1981a; Hackman, Lawler, and Porter 1983; Hammner and Hammner 1983). These studies typically find high wages to be associated with increases in labor productivity of as much as 30% (Locke et al. 1980). However, this relationship holds most strongly for piece rates and other incentive pay systems where worker effort is easiest to monitor (Viteles 1953; Locke et al. 1980). The generally accepted view is that pay matters to worker performance, although the causality may run in both directions (Roethlisberger and Dickson 1939; Lawler 1971, 1981b, 2000).

## SOCIAL AND PSYCHOLOGICAL THEORIES OF LABOR PRODUCTIVITY

A second set of theories about how labor efficiency can be increased is based on the behavioral sciences (Kleiner et al. 1987; Lawler 1971; Doeringer et al. 1991; Doeringer 1991; Stajkovic and Luthans 1997). These theories focus on the social and psychological rewards of work and on the formation of work attitudes. They acknowledge a role for economic incentives in controlling behaviors of the kinds posited by efficiency wage theories, but they tend to minimize the importance of opportunistic behavior and often argue that wage incentives are secondary to other motivators of productive behavior.

Behavioral science theories of labor productivity fall into two broad categories, human relations and behavior modification. These theories characteristically focus on the motivation and retention of productive labor. and they often examine the collective behavior of peer work groups (Lewin 1947; Maslow 1954; Likert 1967; Herzberg, Mausner, and Snyderman 1959; Roethlisberger and Dickson 1939; Williamson 1975; Freeman and Medoff 1984; Kandel and Lazear 1992).

### Human Relations Theories

The distinction between the market failure and human relations approaches to labor productivity is summarized well in a classic study by McGregor (1960) that proposed two theories of human behavior, Theory "X" and Theory "Y". Theory X embodies the principles of economic theories of market failure and opportunistic worker behavior. Economically rational workers will increase their utility by taking advantage of employers whenever possible. This may mean asking for higher pay and threatening to quit after receiving firm-specific training or by shirking when their productivity cannot be observed. Theory X workers are largely motivated by economic rewards, but close supervision and disciplinary penalties are also necessary to deter opportunistic behavior.

Theory Y is about "social man," for whom work can be a positive and rewarding experience and whose opportunistic behavior depends on whether or not jobs are satisfying and pay is equitable. Theory Y is based largely on small-scale surveys, dating back to the 1930s, alleging a positive relationship between productivity and intrinsic sources of motivation—job satisfaction, job enrichment, and worker participation in managerial decisions (Roethlisberger and Dickson 1939; Mohrman, Galbraith, and Lawler 1998). A central conclusion that emerges from this research is that economic incentives matter to behavior, but intrinsic rewards at the workplace—social relationships at work, respect from supervisors and co-workers, and opportunities for responsibility, autonomy, and creativity—can also be powerful motivators of efficient workforce behavior.

Job satisfaction, for example, is often found to be a stronger deterrent to turnover and absenteeism and a stronger motivator of job performance than is high pay (Sutermeister 1976; Mowday, Porter, and Steers 1982: Lawler 1971, 1981b, 1996). Job satisfaction is affected by a wide range of variables. Difficult or stressful jobs, reliance on discipline to maintain effort, and arbitrary management decisions have negative effects on satisfaction, whereas job security, promotion opportunities, and positive personal relationships between workers and managers serve to increase job satisfaction.[3] Some studies find a correlation between wages and job satisfaction. However, no consistent relationship has been shown between job satisfaction and labor productivity, except through the indirect effects of satisfaction in reducing labor turnover (Bowey and Thorpe 1986; Hackman and Oldham 1980; Schneider 1984).

Opportunities for workers to exercise "voice" by participating in workplace decision making are a second source of productivity according to Theory Y. Workforce surveys repeatedly show that workers highly value the opportunity to exercise voice (Commission on the Future of Worker-Management Relations 1994; Freeman and Rogers 1999). One result of participation is increased job satisfaction (McGregor 1960; Lewin 1951; Lawler 1971; Mayo 1933; Argyris 1957, 1964). A second is that production efficiency may be improved by tapping the production knowledge and problem-solving capacities of workers (Appelbaum and Batt 1994; Commission on the Future of Worker-Management Relations 1994a).

A third aspect of human relations theories of labor productivity deals with supervision and monitoring. Monitoring of worker productivity, which is assumed in economic theory to be a key element in maintaining labor productivity, has a much more limited value under human relations theory. While there is evidence that close monitoring raises productivity, it does so only in the short term. Over the longer term, workers respond negatively to being supervised, and productivity falls (Likert 1958).

An alternative approach to closely monitoring workers is that supervisors should develop close social relationships with workers and build mutual trust and obligation by assisting in training, suggesting constructive ways to improve job performance, and encouraging individual and group participation in workplace decision-making (Davis 1987; Strauss 1977; Adler 2001). Productivity can also be motivated by ensuring that managers are perceived as "fair" and that workers are treated as respected members of the work community (Lawler 1971; Bendix 1956; Whyte 1955; Cartwright and Lippit 1976; Akerlof and Yellen 1990). Fairness, group participation, and positive supervisory attitudes towards workers can affect group (as well as individual) attitudes, and group work norms are thought to be a more powerful motivator of productivity than individual incentives (Roethlisberger and Dickson 1939; McGregor 1960; Kandel and Lazear 1992). The more recent emphasis on the use of teams and quality circles may also help to raise productivity by fostering peer motivation and peer pressures to meet output norms (Adler 2001).

Some elements of these human relations theories have also been incorporated into social theories of efficiency wages. One example is based on equity and fairness in wages. Workers in stable employment situations, such as those found in internal labor markets, often think in terms of a "fair day's pay for a fair day's work." They form standards for judging the characteristics of a fair relationship between effort and pay based on comparisons with the effort and pay of other workers. A number of studies confirm that shirking results when actual pay is set below what is perceived as fair pay, while higher levels of effort are stimulated by pay that is more than fair (Mathewson 1931; Coch and French 1948; Adams 1988; Lawler and O'Gara 1967). In formal models of fairness efficiency, effort is assumed to be a function of the relationship between the actual wage and the fair wage, or of the degree of wage inequality as measured by the variance in wages (Akerlof and Yellen 1990). There are also studies showing that fair pay can be as important as high pay in determining job satisfaction and reducing quits (Lawler 1981b).

Another social model of efficiency wages is based on the payment of "gift" incentives for which employees respond with reciprocal "gifts" of higher effort (Akerlof 1982, 1984). Because gifts signify employer generosity, they inspire reciprocal obligations of hard work, cooperation, and loyalty in the workforce. For such gift payments to inspire effort reciprocity, they must not be conditional upon productive behavior. Typical examples of gift incentives are the employee welfare programs adopted by large paternalistic firms in the 1920s (Brandes 1970; Newby 1977, 1979; Brody 1980; and Jacoby 1985, 1997) and the discretionary payments and time off from work which small paternalistic firms give to their employees on social occasions and in times of personal need (Doeringer 1984).

## Behavior Modification and Social Learning

A second type of behavioral theory of labor productivity involves behavior modification and draws heavily on the empirical findings of learning psychology (Hilgard and Marquis 1961; Skinner 1953; Bandura 1969). Behavior modification, or operant conditioning, is a process of stimulating and then reinforcing desired worker behaviors (Vroom 1964; Luthans and Lyman 1976; Luthans and Kreitner 1984; Stajkovic and Luthans 1997). Behavior modification eliminates principal–agent conflicts by inducing changes in the underlying preferences of workers. Rather than using wage incentives and the threat of discharge to reorder opportunistic preferences, behavior modification reduces the psychological inclination towards opportunism and strengthens workers' identification with the goals of the firm.

Behavior modification has been used successfully in a number of large non-union companies such as IBM, Texas Instruments, and Hewlett Packard. These firms historically paid wages that were among the highest in the economy and they were known for having workforces that were highly productive, "self-supervised," and "self-disciplined." While these characteristics appear to reflect the spirit of principal–agent theories of shirking, the foundations of self-discipline and motivation in these firms come more from psychological conditioning than from efficiency-wage incentives.

A typical application of behavior modification theory is for firms to recruit workers who are predisposed to equate their self-interest with the success of the firm. Managers then identify, or construct, situations that lead to productive behaviors such as high effort or cooperation. These productive work behaviors are repeatedly reinforced through participatory discussions with supervisors about job performance and career development until the desired behavior becomes ingrained.

Behavior modification in these firms is closely tied to a larger social and psychological context designed to motivate labor productivity by altering worker preferences. As in human relations theories, high wages are used less as an incentive for productivity than as a means for establishing perceptions of wage fairness among the workforce so that "fairness efficiencies" can be realized. Instead of reinforcing economic incentives of high wages by using the threat of discharge, as is the case under principal–agent theories of shirking and efficiency wages, these firms provide unusually strong employment guarantees (Foulkes 1980; Ouchi and Price 1983; Lee 1987). From the perspective of employees, high wages, employment guarantees, and one-on-one career development discussions with supervisors represent gifts that are not explicitly conditioned upon individual productivity, and these gifts can engender a reciprocal gift to the firm in the form of high labor productivity.

Finally, behavior modification in these firms relies heavily upon a type of "social learning" that is distinct from traditional human capital investments (Bandura 1977; Luthans and Kreitner 1984). Social learning uses day-to-day interactions among co-workers who serve as role models for one another and who provide peer reinforcement for good performance and high cooperation, to complement feedback from supervisors. Social learning is further strengthened by good interpersonal relations among workers and managers that both increase the intrinsic value of work and reduce principal–agent conflicts by enhancing the perceived legitimacy of management's objectives (Likert 1958; Gouldner 1954; Strauss 1977; Habermas 1970, 1975). Social learning combined with positive reinforcement provides strong performance incentives without the adverse effects on productivity that are associated with discipline and discharge (Hammner and Hammner 1983). As workers and supervisors train and reinforce one another's behavior, a largely self-perpetuating culture of productivity and cooperation is established (Schein 1985).

A frequent outcome of this conditioning process is a psychological "effort contract" reached between the firm and individual workers, which incorporates understandings about performance goals expected of employees and the career development investments by the firm that are required to achieve these goals (Lee 1987; Rousseau 1995; Cappelli 1999). The effort norms in these contracts represent performance thresholds, which the social incentives of the productivity culture encourage employees to surpass. Supervisors encourage employees to internalize responsibility for their own supervision so that performance under these effort contracts is self-monitored. Shortfalls in performance are self-disciplined and the rewards for performance come from self-reinforcement, as well as from reinforcement from supervisors and peers.

## THEORIES OF HIGH PERFORMANCE MANAGEMENT

The burgeoning interest in high performance management practices grows out of many of the same concerns with labor productivity that have also motivated previous economic and behavioral theories of productivity, and many of the key themes of these earlier theories are synthesized in the high performance management literature (Abernathy et al. 1999; Mowery 1999; Freeman and Kleiner 2000; Black and

Lynch 1997, Cappelli and Neumark 1999; Mohrman, Galbraith, and Lawler 1998; Ichniowski, Shaw, and Prennushi 1997). For example, job rotation and the use of production teams represent extensions of the on-the-job training previously provided for specialized jobs along job ladders with narrow skills.

Encouraging workers to collaborate with supervisors in solving production and quality-control problems is similar to earlier practices of using employee involvement to increase job satisfaction and reduce labor turnover. The benefits from such employee participation are also likely to be enhanced by having a workforce which is more broadly trained and which can draw on the experience of working in teams.

The growing use of bonuses and other compensation incentives that are linked to productivity and business performance can be seen as a recasting of efficiency wage premiums in a form that strengthens efficiencies in production, learning, and problem solving. The more intensive screening for worker qualities such as problem solving, teamwork skills, and commitment to the firm illustrates how the efficiencies of high performance management practices may require higher costs of workforce recruitment, selection, and matching. These various interactions among high performance practices also underscore the potential gains from combining these practices into a coherent high performance management system, rather than adopting them piecemeal.

## THEORIES OF LABOR CONTROL AND POWER

A final set of theories of labor productivity also synthesizes these various theories of efficiency, but reinterprets them in terms of the inherent conflict between the profit-maximizing goals of employers and the utility maximization goals of workers. "Efficient" theories of power argue that employers will maximize profits by seeking efficient organizational solutions to market failures and then seek to retain as large a share as possible of any efficiency rents created by these organizational practices. Workers should also favor efficient organizational practices because the efficiency rents that result from such practices can potentially be reallocated from employers to employees through the exercise of bargaining power.

However, this distinction between efficient organizational practices and power relationships between employers and their workers is somewhat artificial (Goldberg 1980). The choice among organizational practices can affect relative bargaining power between employers and workers, as well as efficiency rents. For example, if the largest efficiency gains come from organizing work into teams of broadly skilled workers, teams of workers may have greater power to bargain over efficiency rents than if jobs were simplified and workers did not have an opportunity to develop team solidarity. Similarly, in situations where efficiency gains are maximized by employers investing heavily in training workers in firm-specific skills, the costs of replacing such workers will rise. Where the transaction costs of replacing trained workers are high, the threat of quitting increases the bargaining power of individual workers. When unions can organize collective quits or strikes, these replacement costs can be even higher, because trained workers also represent part of the capacity of employers to train replacement workers.

These are examples of classic conflicts of interest between employers and workers over the control of productivity, as well as over the distribution of efficiency gains through bargaining. The typical result is a bargaining process in which the ultimate sanctions are the power of employers to discharge workers and of workers to quit or collectively strike. Such power relationships depend upon the transaction costs of worker replacement and job search, the costs of detecting shirking, and the extent to which employer or worker power can be reinforced through collective action.

In order to maximize profits, employers must consider the trade-off between efficiency gains from organizational practices and the effects of these practices on the power of workers to bargain for a larger share of the efficiency gains. In principle, this trade-off can mean that employers may generate larger profits by adopting second-best practices in terms of organizational efficiency, provided they weaken the power of workers to bargain over efficiency rents.

These theories of second-best organizational practices interpret efficiency wages, internal labor markets, human relations practices, and behavioral modification as organizational devices for reducing worker power by manipulating the transaction costs facing workers. They also see such practices as enhancing employer control over labor by changing individual preferences for shirking behavior in favor of a greater commitment to the profit-maximizing goals of the firm (Dalton 1959; Stone 1975; Edwards 1979; Burawoy 1979, 1985; Jacoby 1985; Goldberg 1980; Pfeffer 1982). The loss of bargaining power and commitment to the firm can be directed at weakening unions, which are seen as the primary organizations for enhancing the power of workers to resist employer control over labor effort and for gaining a larger share of efficiency gains generated by such practices.

The evolution of workplace practices and collective bargaining, according to power theories of efficiency, provides an indicator of shifts in the balance of power in labor markets. In the late 19th and early 20th centuries when unions were relatively weak, for example, employers introduced scientific management practices, deskilled jobs, relied on piece rates and discipline to control shirking, and sometimes paid wage premiums above prevailing market rates in order to diminish worker discontent (Taylor 1911; Aitken 1985; Montgomery 1987; Brody 1980; Raff 1991; Gordon 1997).

High labor turnover and the continuing risk of labor strife led to the development of a new and more complex set of labor control practices during the 1920s. These "welfare capitalism" systems included the provision of paternalistic gifts and services to deserving employees, the development of formal internal labor markets and of personnel offices to administer internal labor markets fairly, and various policies to block unionization (Hyman and Brough 1975; Jacoby 1985, 1997; Brandes 1970). When the high jobless rates of the Great Depression ended the need for these productivity incentives, however, employers reverted to using the threat of discharge to control labor power.

The New Deal labor policies of the 1930s and union involvement in the regulation of wages and working conditions during World War II shifted the balance of power in favor of workers. Collective bargaining in the postwar period introduced a contractual basis for career employment based on seniority, due process restrictions on discharges, and explicit labor contracts enforceable by arbitration. In addition to efficiency wages, and in place of gift-based compensation premiums, workers received union premiums that embodied a roughly equal division of efficiency rents between workers and employers (Jacoby 1985, 1997; Kaboolian 1990; Kochan, Katz, and McKersie 1986; Mishel, Bernstein, and Schmitt 1999).

While these changes in bargaining power and organizational practices could be interpreted in terms of union monopoly distortions and the introduction of organizational inefficiencies into the firm, there are studies showing that collective bargaining can also be a source of off-setting efficiencies. For example, union wage premiums that distribute efficiency rents from employers to workers also contribute to efficiency rents by allowing employers to recruit workers with greater amounts of human capital and by further reducing labor turnover (Freeman and Medoff 1984).

These types of efficiency wage gains, however, are dwarfed by the possibilities for fairness and voice effects on labor productivity. Unions increase workplace fairness by negotiating standardized wages, strengthening the use of objective criteria (such as seniority) in promotions and layoffs, insisting on due-process grievance procedures, and reducing wage dispersion (Freeman and Medoff 1984). Collective bargaining can also provide more secure and effective avenues for workers to exercise productivity-enhancing voice (Freeman and Medoff 1984). Because collective bargaining can protect job security, workers may be less hesitant to suggest ways of increasing labor productivity, and they may be less resistant to efficiency improvements proposed by management. Similarly, grievance procedures can be a means of identifying workplace problems that might otherwise be neglected by management.

These aspects of fairness and voice in unionized workplaces can have a large effect on quit rates, even after controlling for union wage effects (Freeman and Medoff 1984). In addition, there is case study evidence that effort bargains and collective voice can result in higher levels of productivity than in comparable non-union firms (Jacoby 1985; Kochan, Katz, and McKersie 1986; Allen 1984; Freeman and Medoff 1984; Commission on the Future of Worker-Management Relations 1994).

## DYNAMIC EFFICIENCY

These various economic, organizational, psychological, and power theories of labor efficiency provide micro-foundations for explaining how aggregate labor productivity can be increased. Market failure theories of efficiency wages and internal labor markets emphasize the one-time gains in labor productivity that come from substituting workplace organizations for imperfect markets. Social, psychological, and power theories of labor productivity, however, suggest organizational opportunities for continuous improvements in productivity growth.

For example, the development of individual effort contracts by companies like IBM during the 1970s and 1980s were intended to yield continuous improvements in individual productivity (Doeringer 1991). The expectation was that the effort norms embodied in individual effort contracts would be periodically reset at higher levels. These effort contracts were linked to a reward system based on career development and were negotiated in the context of workplace cultures that encouraged higher levels of effort. Similarly, various group participatory arrangements, such as quality circles, are designed to raise productivity through continuous problem solving. Because these attitudes are so embedded in the social fabric and social norms of the workplace, they are particularly important as a control device in just those situations where efficiency wages have been argued to be most needed. These include situations where procedures are not standardized, where there is a need for employee discretion, and where the measurement and monitoring of effort are most difficult (Aoki 1990; Pascal 1986).

In unionized workplaces, the traditional means of increasing productivity over time have involved renegotiating collective effort bargains through bargaining over work speeds and piece rates, as well as by the informal changes in shop-floor effort bargains. More recently, effort bargaining has taken the form of procedures for improving productivity by tapping into worker voice and problem-solving capacities. The most common mechanisms are labor–management committees (variously labeled quality circles, quality of work life, and employee involvement) designed to secure the individual and collective participation of workers in improving productivity (Kochan, Katz, and McKersie 1986; Cappelli 1999).

## RECENT CHALLENGES TO ORGANIZATIONAL
## SOURCES OF EFFICIENCY

Organizational theories of labor productivity posit various avenues for achieving efficiency gains. However, there is a widespread belief that a combination of factors—global competition, deregulation, technological change, shorter product cycles, and more volatile product demand—are making it more costly for firms to continue these organizational practices (Doeringer et al. 1991; Cappelli 1999). Some firms are turning to new forms of organizational practices, whereas others are dismantling organizational practices in favor of more market-based employment relationships.

Evidence of the latter view is provided by various studies of the decline of those sectors of the economy in which internal labor markets and social and behavioral incentives were prevalent, and their replacement with more flexible, but less permanent, "new economy" jobs (Bluestone and Harrison 1982; Burtless 1990; Freeman and Katz 1994; Harrison and Bluestone 1988; Farber 1998; Jacobson, LaLonde, and Sullivan 1993; Cappelli 1999). Other studies emphasize the decline of employment guarantees and career employment opportunities and the growing use of temporary and contingent jobs (Mishel, Bernstein, and Schmitt 1999, 2001). A third strand of analysis emphasizes how new technologies have raised the demand for workers with high levels of formal education relative to that for workers with less education (Bound and Johnson 1992; Berman, Bound, and Griliches 1994) and that immigration may be reinforcing this trend (Borjas, Freeman, and Katz 1997).

In addition, increased product proliferation and shorter product cycles may be undermining the efficiencies of labor specialization and the returns to firm-specific investments in on-the-job training (Piore and Sabel 1984; Abernathy et al. 1999), which are consistent with the modest decline observed in the length and stability of career jobs (Neumark, Polsky, and Hanson 1999). In the unionized sector, there is considerable evidence that concession bargaining has altered collective effort bargains and that there is a shift towards greater use of pay that is contingent on performance (Mitchell 1994; Mishel, Bernstein, and Schmitt 2001; Cappelli 1999).

Furthermore, where traditional internal labor markets are being replaced by more open employment structures, responsibility for skill preparation has been shifted from employers to workers (Mitchell 1994; Cappelli 1999). There is less of an emphasis within these firms on providing training for internal career development and more of an emphasis on the hiring of general skills, which are typically paid for by workers, and in substituting assistance in gaining employability on the external labor market for guarantees of job security.

Some of this shift from organizational to market sources of efficiency may be more apparent than real, since less stable employment and a higher probability of job loss can accomplish the same effort incentives and reductions in quit rates as efficiency wages and other organizational practices. Similarly, the alleged shift from employer-financed training in firm-specific skills to employee-financed training in general skills may be offset by the greater use of teams and the increased delegation of quality-control responsibilities to employees, both of which are likely to involve firm-specific learning and to encourage employers to retain trained workers.

What is clear, however, is that the strongest sources of productivity growth—those from intensive training financed by employers, psychological effort contracts and behavior modification practices, and commitment to problem solving—are unlikely to be sustained without the reinforcements of high and fair wages, the gift of strong employment guarantees, or some new set of functionally equivalent organizational practices. Similarly, efficiencies derived from worker voice are presumably diminishing as the fraction of workers in unions continues to decline, and these voice alternatives to worker exit can only be restored by reversing the decline of unions or developing alternative forms of worker participation.


## IMPLICATIONS FOR ECONOMIC EFFICIENCY, PRODUCTIVITY GROWTH, AND REAL WAGES

These changes in workplace organization and their overall consequences for economic efficiency and productivity growth are subject to different interpretations, depending upon one's theoretical perspective. Market failure theories see new technologies, greater competition, and diminished union power as eliminating some of the underlying conditions that once contributed to labor market failures and distortions. As labor markets have become more competitive, the need for efficiency-wage incentives and internal labor markets has lessened and traditional workplace organizations can be dismantled. Under this interpretation, the slow growth in productivity and real wages in the United States is a transitional problem in an economy that will henceforth be able to rely more heavily on the efficiencies of well-functioning competitive markets, in which wages will signal workers to invest in general human capital and market incentives will govern labor effort.

Social and psychological theories of labor productivity see such changes as undermining the extrinsic and intrinsic incentives and the psychological contracts that U.S. workplaces have adopted to motivate labor productivity (Mohrman 1999; Rousseau 1995). Productivity gains that depended on such practices will be adversely affected and labor markets without efficiency incentives will exhibit slow growth of labor productivity and real earnings.

Power theories see the decline of unions and the rise of employment insecurity as signalling a resurgence of employer power. The changing balance of power in the labor market allows employers to be less concerned about having to share efficiency rents with their employees. The decline in worker power should, therefore, allow employers to adopt the most efficient organizational practices. While productivity gains should result from this change in organizational practices, they are more likely to translate into increased profits than into increased real wages.

While economists generally applaud these changes as evidence of an apparent decline in market failures, management experts are typically more skeptical about the ability of competitive markets to encourage continuous growth in productivity. Instead, they see a need for developing new efficiency organizations to replace those that have become obsolete. If technology, competition, and the decline of unions have eroded the old arrangements for enhancing and continuously increasing labor productivity, the interest in high performance management practices represents the desire to find new sources of efficiency and productivity growth. Advocates of power theories argue that restoring previous levels of rent sharing and rates of increase in real wages will depend on policies that strengthen unions or some other form of representation that enhances worker power.

Much of the evidence to date supports the interpretations of all three theories. There appears to be a greater reliance on labor market competition among large employers who are increasing their use of contingent and contract labor, shifting their emphasis from career development to employability development and relying more on bonuses and other forms of contingent pay (Cappelli 1999). The growing diffusion of high performance organizational practices suggests the adoption of new types of practices that promote greater efficiencies than those that they are replacing (Cappelli 1999; Osterman 2000). The greater reliance on competitive markets, the adoption of new high performance practices, and the failure of real wages to keep up with productivity growth are all consistent with the kinds of organizational developments predicted by a shift in power from workers to employers.

As the following chapters will show, however, many start-up factories in the manufacturing sector are charting a different path from that predicted by either the economic or the power theories of organizations. They are adopting high performance organizational practices without markedly increasing their reliance on competitive labor markets. Moreover, these practices are associated with both high wages and relatively strong career employment guarantees, and they include new sources of voice and power for workers.

## Notes

1. The problem of shirking is probably not trivial. One study of nonunion manufacturing plants, for example, estimated that as many as half of all workers actually shirked by restricting their work effort (Mathewson 1931).
2. A variant of this shirking model theory uses efficiency wages and the threat of discharge to motivate higher productivity rather than simply to avoid shirking. There are also alternatives to efficiency-wage premiums, such as the posting of performance bonds by employees (Lazear 1981) or the use of promotions to high-wage jobs as a form of "rank order" tournament (Lazear and Rosen 1981) that rewards those workers who have demonstrated the very highest performance.
3. Standard economic theory, however, interprets these factors as positive or negative characteristics of jobs for which competitive labor markets compensate by adjusting wages to reflect job differences.

# Part II
# High Performance
# Management Strategies

# 3
# The Management Strategies
# of Start-Up Factories

The previous chapter discusses a number of changes in the business environment—increasing competition, new technologies, more general skill requirements, and weaker unions—that might be encouraging employers to replace traditional methods of workplace management with new high performance management practices. A variety of theories also argue for the superiority of high performance over more traditional management practices as a means of improving efficiency and raising productivity, and there is growing evidence to support this view.

Nevertheless, high performance management practices have diffused rather slowly through U.S. manufacturing, and only recently has a majority of employers adopted any of these practices (Osterman 2000). The standard explanation for this slow adoption rate is that innovative management practices are not always easy to implement. For example, one recent survey found that it was relatively easy for managers to introduce employee empowerment, but that total quality management and quality circles are far more difficult to implement (Carson et al. 2000).

Most of these studies, however, look at changing management practices in businesses that are already established. Whether it is new technologies that are being introduced, management cultures that are being changed, jobs that are being redesigned, or workers that are being retrained, second-best accommodations must inevitably be made with existing practices and workplace settings. New technologies are typically placed in existing physical structures, it is established work practices that are being reorganized or redesigned; new skills and work habits are grafted onto those already present in the incumbent workforce; and new workers are typically recruited from the same local labor pools.

Rather than examining efficiency changes in such existing plant environments, this book focuses exclusively on new (greenfield) plants. This chapter and those that follow examine the managerial practices, reward structures, and location decisions of new manufacturing plants. These manufacturing start-ups represent situations where management has far greater latitude in adopting innovative practices than is likely in established plants (Lawler 1978; Walton 1985).

However, the effectiveness of these practices cannot be analyzed independently from the larger management strategies governing choices of technology, production methods, and business location. The best-managed plants in our study approach productivity and efficiency as a systematic process in which high performance management practices are integrated with other management strategies so as to capture both the benefits from adoption of individual practices and those available from complementarities among practices.

Business start-ups are able to select the optimal combination of technology, plant and equipment layout, job configuration, internal labor markets, work methods, human resources practices, management cultures, and plant location from among a wide range of options. Modifications and adjustments in management strategies and fine-tuning of management practices are also easiest to accomplish in the early years of business start-ups, before habits and customs become more permanently established.

New plants, therefore, represent a much better window for looking at the future of high performance management practices in U.S. manufacturing than do established plants that are adopting such practices. The start-ups that are the most successful in identifying the productive combinations of new technologies and high performance strategies will gradually gain market share from established businesses that do not adopt such practices. High performance practices will gradually spread through the economy as inefficient plants are closed and as other firms imitate successful practices. This book documents which high performance strategies contribute to making start-ups successful and thus are most likely to be diffused widely throughout the economy.

## THE CASE STUDY SAMPLE

This book is based upon the in-depth analysis of the high performance management practices adopted by a sample of 48 new manufacturing plants. The sample covers three 2-digit industries—rubber and plastic products (SIC 30), electrical equipment (SIC 35), and non-electrical machinery (SIC 36)—so as to include a wide range of products, production methods, and technologies. The sample firms produce auto dashboards, plastic bottles, construction equipment, industrial saws, air conditioners, circuit boards, and video cassettes, to name a few (Table 3.1). The production processes in our sample range from relatively low-skilled, labor-intensive mass production (wire cable assembly) to intermediate-skilled, assembly-line technologies (circuit boards and automobile dashboards), to high-skilled, batch-production technologies (cutting tools).

The sample includes mainly large plants. The average starting employment of the sample is 265 and the range was from 15 to 1,800 workers. Most of the plants fall in the range of 100–500 employees, with only 13% having fewer than 50 employees and the same percentage having 500 or more employees (Table 3.2).

**Geographic Diversity**

The case study sample is drawn from a southern state (Georgia), a border state (Kentucky), and the northeastern region (Massachusetts, New York, and New Jersey). These locations were chosen to represent labor markets having different kinds of workers and different labor relations environments (Table 3.3). Incorporating such regional differences into the sample design is particularly important because start-ups tend to choose locations, in part, because of the match between their management practices and the characteristics of the available labor supply.

Georgia was selected because it is a state with a growing industrial base. Its most distinguishing labor market characteristic is that it is an "employment-at-will" state with a right-to-work law and a low rate of unionization. This relatively union-free environment was regarded as an attraction by many of the firms in our sample that chose a Georgia location. Its workforce also has below-average levels of education and relatively low average value added per worker hour. Given its relatively low education levels, low productivity, and weak unions, Georgia's manufacturing wages are relatively low.

**Table 3.1  Characteristics of the Field Research Sample**

| SIC[a] | State | Product | No. of workers | Start year | Compound annual avg. employment growth (%) |
|---|---|---|---|---|---|
| 30* | Ga. | Misc. plastic products | 129 | 1980 | 9.6 |
| 30* | Ga. | TV frames | 300 | 1989 | 26.0 |
| 30* | Ga. | Gaskets | 375 | 1980 | 11.6 |
| 30* | Ky. | Industrial belts | 120 | 1988 | 18.9 |
| 30* | Ky. | Rubber components | 100 | 1988 | 42.5 |
| 30* | Ky. | Auto dashboards | 340 | 1988 | 8.0 |
| 30* | N.J. | Plastic labels | 110 | 1985 | 27.6 |
| 30* | N.J. | Plastic labels/seals | 39 | 1986 | 14.7 |
| 30* | N.Y. | Auto parts | 600 | 1979 | 31.4 |
| 30 | Ga. | Plastic parts | 105 | 1983 | 9.1 |
| 30 | Ga. | Auto molding | 175 | 1985 | −1.9 |
| 30 | Ga. | Plastic food packaging | 216 | 1978 | 8.2 |
| 30 | Ky. | Plastic parts | 77 | 1987 | 17.8 |
| 30 | Ky. | Plastic parts | 131 | 1978 | 4.6 |
| 30 | Mass. | Misc. plastic products | 50 | 1978 | 1.5 |
| 30 | N.J. | Plastic bottles | 200 | 1978 | −5.0 |
| 35* | Ga. | PC monitors | 411 | 1985 | 22.4 |
| 35* | Ga. | Construction equip. | 52 | 1988 | 24.0 |
| 35* | Ga. | Construction equip. | 15 | 1987 | −27.9 |
| 35* | Ky. | Machine tools | 275 | 1982 | 23.1 |
| 35* | Ky. | Cutting tools | 21 | 1989 | 51.4 |
| 35* | Ky. | Metal products centers | 25 | 1987 | 3.8 |
| 35* | Mass. | Personal computers | 788 | 1983 | 16.5 |
| 35* | N.J. | Textile machinery | 27 | 1988 | 22.0 |
| 35* | N.J. | Computer peripherals | 60 | 1990 | 7.1 |
| 35 | Ga. | Industrial saws | 250 | 1978 | 2.6 |

**Table 3.1 (continued)**

| SIC[a] | State | Product | No. of workers | Start year | Compound annual avg. employment growth (%) |
|---|---|---|---|---|---|
| 35 | Ga. | Motors | 350 | 1983 | 12.6 |
| 35 | Ky. | Motor brushes | 64 | 1984 | 4.2 |
| 35 | Ky. | Precision machine parts | 70 | 1984 | 24.1 |
| 35 | Mass. | Industrial equip. | 65 | 1990 | −16.2 |
| 35 | Mass. | Industrial equip. | 160 | 1978 | 9.7 |
| 36* | Ga. | Auto and consumer electronics | 931 | 1987 | 20.3 |
| 36* | Ga. | Video cassettes | 300 | 1980 | 8.8 |
| 36* | Ga. | Compact disks | 300 | 1987 | 37.7 |
| 36* | Ga. | TVs, phones | 676 | 1984 | 17.6 |
| 36* | Ky. | Electronic auto parts | 534 | 1985 | 19.9 |
| 36* | Ky. | Wire cable assembly | 1,800 | 1988 | 34.5 |
| 36* | Ky. | Electronic auto parts | 125 | 1989 | 46.2 |
| 36* | Mass. | Micro diskettes | 215 | 1989 | 6.1 |
| 36* | Mass. | Micro diskettes | 350 | 1989 | 36.8 |
| 36* | N.J. | Elect. optical instruments | 44 | 1982 | 7.2 |
| 36 | Ga. | Circuit boards | 350 | 1989 | −11.2 |
| 36 | Ga. | Elect. auto part | 440 | 1978 | 9.7 |
| 36 | Ga. | Wire harnesses | 350 | 1978 | 7.6 |
| 36 | Ky. | Truck wire harnesses | 134 | 1985 | 4.3 |
| 36 | Ky. | Air conditioners | 300 | 1978 | 11.0 |
| 36 | Mass. | Circuit boards | 104 | 1987 | 26.8 |
| 36 | Mass. | Computer equipment | 54 | 1982 | 0.0 |

[a] An asterisk (*) in the SIC column indicates Japanese ownership.

**Table 3.2  Plant Size Distribution of Case Study Sample**

| No. of workers | % of sample |
|:---:|:---:|
| 1–49 | 12.5 |
| 50–99 | 16.7 |
| 100–249 | 29.2 |
| 250–499 | 29.2 |
| 500+ | 12.5 |

**Table 3.3  State Labor Market Characteristics, mid 1980s**

| State | % High school graduates | Median education (yrs.) | Mean manuf. wage ($) | % Union in manuf. | % Rural | Value-added per production worker/hr.[a] ($) |
|:---|:---:|:---:|:---:|:---:|:---:|:---:|
| Ga. | 65.3 | 12.2 | 8.10 | 13.6 | 36.1 | 27.25 |
| Ky. | 60.9 | 12.1 | 9.53 | 26.5 | 54.5 | 36.97 |
| Mass. | 77.6 | 12.6 | 9.00 | 19.1 | 9.1 | 33.94 |
| N.J. | 73.6 | 12.5 | 9.86 | 23.2 | 0.1 | 37.56 |
| N.Y. | 72.1 | 12.5 | 9.67 | 50.6 | 9.5 | 38.99 |
| U.S. avg. | 72.6 | 12.5 | 8.14 | 20.5 | 36.6 | 34.06 |

[a] For the manufacturing sector.
SOURCE:  U.S. Bureau of Labor Statistics; U.S. Department of Education; U.S. Bureau of the Census.

Kentucky was chosen as a border state sharing characteristics of both the south and the north. Unlike Georgia, it is a state where the fraction of the workforce that is unionized is above the U.S. average. Like Georgia, its education level is below average, but labor productivity is relatively high in Kentucky. Between high productivity and union bargaining, manufacturing wages are above the national average and close to the average for the northeastern states in which we studied start-ups.

The three states in the northeast region have average levels of education, labor productivity that is average or above, and above-average manufacturing wages. They are largely urbanized states with strong union movements, particularly New York and New Jersey.

## Sample Selection

The universe of start-ups from which our sample was selected was defined by business directories in each region and from directories of Japanese factories compiled by the Japan Economic Institute. Several restrictions were imposed on this universe in order to increase the probability of capturing plants that would be using high performance management practices. First, the sample was limited to plants that were branches of large companies, to eliminate start-ups where entrepreneurial organizational practices are likely to be important. Choosing branch plants also meant that strategic support from corporate headquarters would be available for assisting in location and technology decisions, facilitating operations set-up, and developing the plant's workforce. Second, the sample was restricted to plants with start-up dates between 1978 and 1990 in order to ensure that the start-ups would have been through a substantial period of increasing production ("ramp-up" period) when we visited them in the early 1990s.

After stratifying the branch plants by region, industry, and nationality of ownership, our sample was drawn randomly from each subgroup, with a deliberate oversampling of Japanese-owned plants. Other research has shown that Japanese transplants are particularly intensive adopters of high performance management practices (Fucini and Fucini 1990; Kenney and Florida 1993; Abo 1994; Jenkins and Florida 1999) and having a significant representation of new Japanese plants in our sample also allows us to examine whether the practices adopted by Japanese transplants are in any way different from those adopted by domestically owned start-ups.

The success of this study depended critically on the willingness of start-up plants to participate actively. Because Japanese transplants are far fewer than domestic start-ups, the sampling procedure began with the selection and recruitment of the Japanese transplants. In those instances where a transplant was unwilling to participate in the study, a replacement plant was randomly selected. Once the sample of Japanese transplants was identified, a similar procedure was used to select the sample of domestic start-ups that approximated as closely as possible the size, industry, location, and initial year of operation of the Japanese transplants. In the end, we received strong support from almost all the start-ups in our initial sample and were successful in implementing the overall sampling framework (Table 3.4).[1]

## Data Collection Procedures

The case study sites were visited by one or more members of the research team between 1991 and 1993.[2] Additional follow-up information was obtained from some sites by phone in 1994. Interviews were conducted with senior plant managers, human resources and personnel managers, and production supervisors. In a number of instances, interviews were also held with engineering and technical personnel managers. Plant visits typically lasted half a day.

The interviews were both structured and open-ended in order to probe fully the relationship between management practices and plant efficiency, but common information on management practices was collected across the sample. During the interviews, "triangulation" methods were used wherever possible to ensure that findings were confirmed by more than one manager and that any inconsistencies among the interviewees were resolved. While we did not have a systematic interview protocol for employees, we were able to conduct unstructured interviews with workers during shop-floor tours, and we also met with union officials whenever possible to cross-check the information provided by management.

**Table 3.4  Case Study Sample Start-Ups by Industry and Region**

| Industry | Georgia | | Kentucky | | Northeast | |
|---|---|---|---|---|---|---|
| | Japanese | Domestic | Japanese | Domestic | Japanese | Domestic |
| Rubber and plastics | 3 | 3 | 3 | 2 | 3 | 2 |
| Electrical equipment | 3 | 2 | 3 | 2 | 3 | 2 |
| Non-electrical machinery | 4 | 3 | 3 | 2 | 3 | 2 |

Retrospective data were collected on the decision to locate the facility, the choice of technology, and on the ramp-up process. Detailed data were collected on employment, compensation, training, work organization, employee participation, and a variety of other management practices affecting labor productivity. In discussing location decisions, plant managers were invited to explain which location factors had been important in their location selection. Questions about additional factors were asked after interviewees had an opportunity to volunteer their own responses, and respondents were explicitly asked what factors were relatively unimportant to the location decision.

The advantage of this relatively open interview method is that respondents' answers were not biased or limited by the interviewers' questions. The structured element of the interviews, however, ensured that the topics discussed across interviews were consistent and that some relevant factors were not omitted inadvertently by individual interviewees.

## AN OVERVIEW OF START-UP FACTORIES

Start-up factories are typically seen as flagship operations by their parent corporations, and they are intended to set the pattern for the next generation of manufacturing operations. Advanced technologies (often based on computer-controlled production processes) and modern management practices characterize all the plants in the sample.

Many of the initial management strategies—choice of technology, investment criteria, selection of plant sites, planning and budgeting procedures, and information systems used to evaluate business performance—are determined by corporate headquarters. The parent corporations also provide considerable technical assistance in plant design and equipment layout, work organization, and human resources practices. Once the start-ups open, they are required to meet relatively demanding targets of efficiency and productivity that are set by corporate headquarters, and they are offered continuing consulting assistance when problems arise in meeting these targets.

Senior managers of these plants typically come from other branch plants in the company. They are knowledgeable about state-of-the-art high performance management practices and are well versed in their corporations' approaches to operations management. When U.S. managers are hired in Japanese transplants or are promoted to replace Japanese managers, they are usually given training in Japanese management practices at one or more counterpart production facilities in Japan. Whenever Japanese managers are subsequently replaced by U.S. managers, this occurs under the tutelage of senior Japanese managers to ensure that Japanese planning and production practices remain the norm.

The final staffing patterns, work organization, and human resources and compensation practices, however, are determined by each start-up. These determinations are almost exclusively the prerogative of management, with only informal input from workers. In our sample, only three of the plants (only one of which is a Japanese transplant) are unionized, and, even in the unionized plants, managers retain strong prerogatives in the initialization of particular practices. However, employees often reshape the subsequent implementation of these practices through various consultative and participatory mechanisms.

Start-ups typically pay wages that are well above the average for their local labor markets. Almost half pay starting wage rates that are in the top 20% of the local wage distribution, and about one-fourth augment hourly pay with bonuses for group performance based on profits or productivity gains. Fringe benefit packages are also typically generous in these plants.

Over half of the sample attempts to enhance the job security of their core workforce. Some start-ups have explicit no-layoff policies, and many use a buffer stock of temporary workers to protect the job security of more-permanent workers during business downturns.

In addition to paying well and providing relatively secure employment, two in five have internal labor markets with promotion ladders. Since these start-ups tend to grow relatively rapidly (the compound average annual growth rate of employment for our sample is 14%, and only five plants have experienced an employment decline; see Table 3.1), promotion prospects are generally good.

As might be expected from generous compensation, secure employment, and opportunities for promotion, these start-ups are able to be very selective in their hiring process. They tend to have substantial queues of applicants, often as high as 20 or more qualified appli-

cants for each job. The start-ups recruit relatively well-educated workers (with at least a high school degree or its equivalent), and most
plants look for workers with at least two to three years of prior work
experience. Many engage in elaborate testing of prospective applicants, some have incumbent employees participate in interviewing and
evaluating job applicants, and some screen applicants through preemployment training that includes teamwork exercises in problem solving.

While there is considerable variation in the adoption of particular
management practices at the plant level (as will be seen in the next
chapter), the vast majority of the start-ups strive to increase productivity through various types of high performance practices including
training, performance incentives, and opportunities for worker participation. Specific practices include assigning primary responsibility for
quality control to individual production workers; organizing production into small work teams; giving these teams the resources (training,
release time) and incentives (merit raises and promotions) to resolve
problems and devise productivity-enhancing innovations; training
intensively (including teamwork skills, cross-job skill training, and on-
the-job training through job rotation); and being committed to sharing
productivity gains with the workforce and providing it with secure
employment. More than half the plants in our sample adopt two or
more of these practices.

The most common high performance practices center on training,
with almost 80% of the sample providing substantial job entry training
of three days or more and almost two-thirds also providing technical
training (Table 3.5). The return on these training investments is relatively secure because the high wages, good job security, and promotion

**Table 3.5  High Performance Management Practices Adopted by 50% or
More of Sample**

| Practice | Adoption (%) |
|---|---|
| Substantial job entry training | 79 |
| Technical training | 65 |
| Weekly or monthly shift meetings | 75 |
| Quality circles | 52 |

opportunities keep quit rates low in these plants. Worker voice and participation is also widely encouraged. Three-quarters of the plants hold weekly or monthly shift meetings, and over half have formal quality circles designed to promote continuous improvements in productivity (Table 3.5).

The frequency with which start-ups use high performance management practices appears to substantially exceed the average for U.S. manufacturing. While there are no data that allow us to make comprehensive comparisons between the management practices of our sample of start-ups and those of established U.S. manufacturing plants, a 1992 survey of innovative work practices in a representative sample of U.S. manufacturing plants (Osterman 1994) permits us to make comparisons for a limited set of practices at a similar point in time.[3]

This survey reported adoption frequencies for four high performance practices, i.e., teamwork, job rotation, total quality management, and quality circles. These data show that roughly one in three U.S. manufacturing plants adopted at least one of these four high performance practices.[4] The start-ups in our sample substantially exceeded that rate except in the case of job rotation (Table 3.6).

The greatest difference in adoption rates is for total quality management, with 75% of our sample adopting TQM management practices (defined as daily or weekly team meetings and/or reliance on production workers for quality control) compared with 32% for all of U.S. manufacturing. Similarly, over half of our start-ups have quality cir-

**Table 3.6  Case Study Sample and U.S. Adoption Rates of Selected High Performance Management Practices (%)**

| Practice | Case study sample | U.S. manufacturing |
|---|---|---|
| Teams | 41.7 | 32.3 |
| Job rotation | 27.1 | 37.4 |
| TQM | 75.0 | 32.1 |
| Quality circles | 52.1 | 29.7 |
| None of the above | 20.8 | 33.2 |

SOURCE: Case study column, authors' survey; U.S. manufacturing column, Osterman (1994).

cles, while quality circles are found in only 30% of the U.S. manufacturing firms. Only one-fifth of our sample uses none of these practices, compared with one-third of U.S. manufacturing plants.

These particular comparisons, however, understate the importance of high performance management practices in our sample. The national study of manufacturing plants did not report adoption rates for a number of high performance management practices such as intensive training and group compensation incentives, which managers in our sample consider to be critical to productivity and efficiency. Furthermore, as the following examples will show, it is the interactions and complementarities among practices that are most critical to the high performance equation.

## HIGH-END START-UPS

Many of the start-up plants that use high performance management practices systematically integrate them with other types of high performance management strategies. In addition, these plants often borrow and adapt practices that have been used elsewhere in their parent companies. While this process of creating hybrid combinations of management practices is explored in more detail in the next chapter, two examples from our sample will illustrate the ways in which these plants bundle their management practices.

### A Rubber-Products Japanese Transplant

One example of the intensive adoption of high performance management practices is a nonunion, Japanese transplant firm that produces rubber products, mainly for the automobile industry. It is located in a small city in southwest Kentucky, a site that was partly chosen to reduce the likelihood of union activity that might create an "us-against-them" attitude between workers and management.

Employment qualifications include high school degree or its equivalent, two years of experience in manufacturing, plus some type of post–high school course. These hiring standards, however, are not used to measure skill or knowledge. Rather, they are threshold hiring criteria that are typically used to identify groups of workers who are likely to be trainable, take initiative, have an aptitude for continuously improving their own performance, and be amenable to team relationships with management and co-workers.

For example, postsecondary education and training can be in any field and are used as evidence of the applicants' motivation to improve themselves. Manufacturing experience is used as an indicator that applicants have practical knowledge of what it is like to work in a manufacturing plant. However, applicants with work experience in the same industry are often rejected because management wants to "train people right the first time." Both managers and employees also intensively interview applicants for production jobs in order to identify workers having these hard-to-measure qualities.

Substantial resources are devoted to worker training. Three weeks is spent on orientation training to familiarize new employees with the production process, provide preparatory training in a broad range of skills, and help employees to understand how their jobs fit into the overall framework of production. The plant uses a small number of broadly defined job classifications so that workers gain broad on-the-job skills, and additional formal training is provided in statistical process control.

There are many opportunities for employees to participate in management decisions. Work is organized into small production teams and these teams are self-managed. For example, instead of using time clocks or having supervisors monitor work time, each team tracks its own hours and overtime. Almost all the production workers also participate in quality circles. While quality circles are used primarily to solve problems, the experience that workers gain working in quality circles also allows them to work together more effectively and to train other workers more quickly.

Similarly, suggestions for productivity improvement are routinely solicited by management and are often adopted. Examples of workers' suggestions that have been implemented include 1) revising the employee evaluation form to improve objectivity and fairness and 2) instituting a wage differential for the least pleasant or most difficult jobs as identified by the workforce.

At least one hour of each nine-hour shift is largely dedicated to quality circle meetings, discussions about continuous improvement, and training. The ninth hour was added to the workday and is paid at overtime rates to underscore the importance of employee participation. Through teamwork, intensive training, flexible work organization, and employee involvement, the plant is able to switch easily between products and to quickly meet orders for relatively small batches of product.

Managers in this plant are very attentive to building the loyalty and commitment of their workforce as an element in their high performance strategy. One way of accomplishing this is through acting on workers' suggestions; others include providing substantial job security, paying high wages, and ensuring fairness in pay and promotions. Job security is maintained through work sharing rather than layoffs. During periods of low demand, shifts are cut back to eight hours while still retaining the hour allotted to training and productivity improvement.

The plant pays wages that are at the top of the local wage structure and wage increases are based on performance, seniority, and the skills a worker develops through cross-training. These compensation practices balance management's need for flexibility with employee preferences for pay that is fair, as well as high. Pay increments for cross training, for example, give workers an incentive to acquire the broad skills needed to support flexible staffing practices while seniority payments allow all employees to receive earnings gains, even in the absence of promotions. Performance pay is used to reward both individual merit and collective, plant-wide productivity gains. Fairness in individual performance evaluation is achieved through peer assessments, rather than assessment by management. Front-line workers also assess the performance of workers who are on probation, determine who gets promotions, and participate in the performance evaluations of supervisors.

## A Domestically Owned Electrical Equipment Start-Up

A second example of a start-up that has adopted a large number of high performance management practices is a domestic plant located in Georgia that produces electrical equipment for the automobile industry. This plant is one of the few start-ups that is unionized, and its high performance arrangements have been negotiated with the union.

The plant's parent company has unionized operations across the Midwest. In the late 1970s, it decided to institute innovative labor management practices in its new plants, believing that experimenting with new management practices would fail at its existing plants because of their history of adversarial industrial relations. It had hoped to remain non-union at its Georgia location, but the plant was subsequently incorporated into a larger company-wide bargaining unit that is represented by the United Automobile Workers (UAW). Nevertheless, the high performance management practices remained in effect.

Wage rates and job security reflect the influence of collective bargaining. Wages are at the top of the local wage scale and are 25% to 30% higher than wages at non-union start-ups in our sample in the same industry and region. Workers are subject to layoff under the collective bargaining agreement, but the success of the plant in enhancing productivity and controlling costs has virtually guaranteed job security as a practical matter. As a result, extraordinarily large numbers of workers continue to apply for jobs. In contrast to the example of the Japanese transplant described above, however, selection of employees is based largely on traditional criteria such as education and the quality of prior work experience, and front-line workers are not involved in the hiring process.

The high performance strategy of the plant is based on the principle that "operators are their own managers." Work in the plant is organized into teams that are largely self-managed, so that there is only one supervisor for every 51 production workers. Teams order parts, set overtime, and elect team leaders. Hourly employees are trained to use workstation computers to track costs and profitability and have access to all of the plant's financial data (except for managers' salaries). Teams do their own budgeting for labor, materials, and equipment and justify their own expenditures on everything from new gloves to equipment. Every operator knows how to use the computer system to check productivity and budgets, calculate unit costs, and measure material scrapped.

The plant has simplified job classifications and has almost entirely eliminated work rules. The hierarchy of multiple and detailed job classifications has been replaced with one unskilled job classification and two skilled craft classifications. Wage differentials are based on knowledge as well as skill levels, and pay rises with proficiency at multiple jobs. Flexible work practices have been substituted for strict work rules and promotion procedures. There have been no strikes or other forms of work stoppage, and the plant has had a lower rate of grievances than its sister plants.

Managers credit this system with large savings over traditional plants, and the results in terms of productivity gains are impressive. Production had doubled over the five years prior to our interview without investment in additional equipment or the adoption of a new technology. Instead, productivity gains are the result of many small improvements—decreasing equipment downtime, streamlining material throughput, and improving quality control.

## MID-RANGE START-UPS

Start-ups are arrayed along a continuum in terms of the intensity of their strategies for managing labor productivity. A typical example of a start-up in the middle of this range is a Japanese-owned supplier in southern Kentucky that mass-produces auto parts and faces stiff price competition. The plant has only modest skill requirements, repetitive assembly work, limited career ladders, and low profit margins. Many of its competitors have moved to Mexico, and the parent company has also transferred the least-skilled parts of its production process to newly established plants in Mexico.

In the manager's opinion, further automation is not feasible, and he sees high performance management practices as the only source of productivity improvement that would allow the plant to remain competitive. Workers are given intensive training and are all involved in continuous improvement groups on a systematic basis. While this manager characterizes his plant as a "hybrid" of Japanese and U.S. management practices, several key high performance management practices have not been adopted. Line operators are not entrusted with most of the quality control work; instead specialized inspectors are used. The limited range of production activities constrain opportunities for promotion and job rotation. Low profits are limiting the company's ability to pay high wages, but it's able to offer generous fringe benefits and a firm commitment to avoid layoffs. Although there is a higher rate of turnover and lower morale than management wants, it has successfully implemented problem-solving groups. These groups have brought forward a number of proposals for modest improvement in productivity and these suggestions are credited with substantially reducing the plant's costs. It has successfully gained market share and output, and employment had grown substantially above the levels originally anticipated by the parent corporation.

## LOW-END START-UPS

Although all of the start-ups surveyed use advanced technologies and the vast majority have adopted at least one other high performance management practice, a small number of the plants use relatively few of such practices and do not integrate them systematically with their overall management strategies. Roughly 10% of the start-ups are at this low end of the high performance management spectrum. These plants are modern and professionally managed, but they produce products with relatively low value added. They also provide little training and minimal efficiency incentives, and they rely more heavily on simplifying jobs and using work organization and supervision to control output and costs.

A typical low-end start-up is an assembler of combustion engines located in Georgia. The parent company built this plant in the mid 1980s to move production out of unionized and higher-cost North-Central states where its production had been centered. The plant is located in an area with low high school graduation rates and a low work ethic. There is readily available alternative manufacturing work in nearby textile mills, but at lower pay and with somewhat less attractive working conditions.

The plant competes primarily on price. Because "quality takes care of itself," its customers assume that all suppliers offer equivalent quality and "look only at the price tag." Dedicated machinery is used to produce standardized parts, jobs involve only routine and repetitive motions, production is machine-paced, and quality is managed by "methodizing" jobs so that they are "foolproof." The plant manager's principal hiring criterion is that workers be able to "show up" every day.

This manager described his ideal of the high performance workplace as one in which he could "engineer the operator out," the antithesis of the strategy of most start-ups of basing efficiency on capturing the operators' knowledge, skill, and motivation. Quality circles exist but "in name only," and they are used as one-way communication conduits from management to production workers. More typical quality circles providing input from employees were rejected because "workers are not skilled enough to identify problems, let alone solve them." No attempt has been made to develop problem-solving skills, and there are no alternative avenues of employee participation.

## SUMMARY

This chapter describes the characteristics of our sample of start-up factories. It shows that the vast majority of the plants studied use state-of-the-art technologies, which they combine with high performance management practices. In particular, these high performance start-ups emphasize a set of employment practices that raise labor productivity through intensive training and opportunities for the expression of worker voice to improve productivity. They also pay high wages and offer relatively secure jobs.

However, not all start-ups adopt high performance practices to the same degree, even within the same industry and region. In particular, start-ups that produce relatively low-value-added products often adopt relatively few high performance management practices and tend to rely instead on more traditional management strategies to control productivity and costs.

These differences in adoption patterns are examined in greater detail in the next chapter. By looking at both specific management practices and at clusters of practices, a more refined understanding is developed of complementarities among management practices and of how coherent clusters of practices are formed.

# Notes

1. None of the plants originally calculated refused to participate in the study. However, in two cases, managers could not be available for our scheduled trips and in these cases we substituted alternative firms. In two instances, domestic plants defined as start-ups in business directories turned out to be acquisitions of established facilities by companies outside the region. However, in both cases, employment and investment growth and management reorganization in these facilities was so substantial that these were deemed to be the equivalent of start-up situations.
2. There were four instances in which we were unable to conduct our interviews on site because of last-minute conflicts that developed with our interviewees' schedules. In all cases, however, we acquired comparable information through lengthy telephone interviews with management.
3. These can only be approximate comparisons because the industry composition of our sample is not strictly identical to that of Osterman's establishment survey. Moreover, the high performance practices in our sample are applied to all production workers, whereas the threshold for inclusion in the Osterman data is that they apply to at least 50% of the production workforce.
4. For comparison purposes, we report data from Osterman (1994) for those practices that were applied to at least half of the workforce in each plant. In all of the start-ups in our sample, these practices applied to all production workers

# 4
# Hybrid Systems of Management Practices

The literature on high performance management practices often mentions the importance of the interactions among "bundles" or "clusters" of practices adopted (Holmstrom and Milgrom, 1994; Milgrom and Roberts 1990; Baker, Gibbs, and Holmstrom 1994; Appelbaum and Batt 1994; Ichniowski et al. 2000), and there is some empirical support for such complementarities. For example, Ichniowski, Shaw, and Prennushi (1997, p. 291) concluded that "groups or clusters of complementary human resource management (HRM) practices have large effects on productivity, while changes in individual work practices have little or no effect on productivity" in their study of 36 steel production lines. Similarly, Hwang and Weil (1997) and Abernathy et al. (1999) found evidence of complementarities among high performance management practices in the U.S. apparel industry.

The concept of complementarities among practices is also central to the idea that there are systematic patterns to the adoption of high performance management practices that can be used to define models of "best" management practice. Behavioral theories of labor productivity, for example, posit a general set of performance-enhancing practices that can be widely applied to large business organizations. Economic theories of labor efficiency typically argue that there should be particular clusters of high performance management practices that most effectively offset market failures attached to specific technologies and industries. Power theories often focus on national differences in public policy, trade union strength, and bargaining structures that result in national models of high performance management. At the other extreme, some organizational theorists reject the idea of generalizable best-practice models because organizational arrangements are governed by idiosyncratic combinations of technologies, business cultures, and site-specific labor market environments (Fruin 1999). Nevertheless, all of these theories accept the proposition that management practices adopted at the plant level represent a blending of market and organizational considerations and are designed to increase profits.

The evidence on whether this process results in generic systems of high performance management models is mixed. For example, one broad-based study of U.S. industry, based on both survey data and case studies, found considerable variation in the adoption of high performance management practices (Appelbaum and Batt 1994). However, it concluded that two clusters of practices are emerging that represent unique U.S. adaptations of high performance models pioneered in other countries. One is a modified version of team production that combines the Scandinavian socio-technical systems approach of using autonomous work groups with U.S.-style quality engineering. This approach emphasizes shifting the control of quality and productivity to the shop floor. The other is based on Japanese lean production methods and involves more-centralized management decisions that rely on managerial and technical expertise to eliminate bottlenecks in production and logistics.

Both of these systems share an emphasis on quality engineering and quality management, and both use U.S.-style wage incentives to reward performance. They also rely heavily on careful workforce selection, intensive training, and consultation with workers on production and quality issues. The main distinction is in the extent to which authority and control over production and quality are shifted from management to peer groups of shop-floor workers.

Similarly, a large study of Japanese-owned factories in the United States found that Japanese transplants are adopting "a new model of production organization that mobilizes workers' intelligence as well as physical skill" (Kenney and Florida 1993, p. 9). This "innovation-mediated production" model relies heavily on Japanese-style high performance management practices, especially those involving worker participation and continuous improvement in productivity, and it is argued to be the model that will eventually replace more traditional U.S. management practices. While these studies highlight somewhat different descriptions of high performance management models, both conclude that differences in management strategies are not strongly linked to particular products and technologies.[1]

A second set of studies has suggested that there may indeed be a strong industry dimension to the adoption of innovative practices for improving workplace performance. Studies of Japanese transplants in the electronics industry (Milkman 1991; Kenney and Florida 1993; Kenney 1999), for example, while finding a wide variation in the use of Japanese-style practices, still revealed a tendency for electronics plants to emulate traditional U.S. workplace practices. The conclusion is that relatively simple electronic assembly operations do not require much training and offer little potential for improvement through worker participation in problem solving and quality-control decisions. Thus, the more typical strategy is to minimize production costs.

Conversely, studies of Japanese transplants in the auto industry find that much more of the Japanese high performance management system is transferred intact to the United States (Fucini and Fucini 1990; Kenney and Florida 1993; Abo 1994; Pil and MacDuffie 1999; Adler 2001). Similar findings have been obtained in the steel and tire industries (Kenney and Florida 1993). A common conclusion is that these practices are a source of competitive advantage for the Japanese firms and that U.S. firms will sooner or later have to adopt them.

Looking at U.S. manufacturing more broadly during this period, however, Osterman (1994) found that only 5% of U.S. manufacturing plants adopt two or more innovative practices from a list consisting of teams, job rotation, TQM, and quality circles. Within this small group of firms that adopt multiple practices, there is no indication of a dominant pattern of clustering of practices.[2]

## ONE MODEL OF HIGH PERFORMANCE OR MANY?[3]

Which of these perspectives best characterizes the future direction of high performance management practices in the United States? Will one or two models prevail, or will there be a pluralistic outcome in which different models emerge around specific technologies, products, and even locations? Are high-performance management practices in such a developmental phase that no generalizations can yet be made about which practices can most effectively enhance productivity?

A first cut at answering these questions with data from our sample of start-up factories is to examine the frequency with which various clusters of practices associated with high performance management systems are adopted by start-ups. In order to compare our findings with a national sample of U.S. manufacturing plants, we restrict our analysis initially to those high performance practices that were analyzed by Osterman (1994), i.e., total quality management, teamwork, job rotation, and quality circles.

This exercise shows much more clearly than the comparisons of single practices made in the preceding chapter that start-ups are far more likely to adopt multiple practices than are more-established manufacturing plants (Table 4.1). Our sample adopts at least one of the high performance clusters at over twice the rate of the national sample, a difference that is statistically significant. In particular, the clusters of TQM (defined as the use of daily or weekly meetings or reliance on production workers for quality control) and quality circles combined with teamwork (and sometimes also with job rotation) are adopted by a significantly higher percentage of the start-ups in our sample.

Upon closer inspection of these data, however, an even sharper distinction exists between Japanese transplants and the more general U.S. experience (Table 4.2). While some domestic start-ups are among the leading adopters of high performance practices and some Japanese

**Table 4.1  Case Study Sample and U.S. Clustering of Management Practices (% of total establishments)**

| Cluster | Case study sample | U.S. manufacturing |
|---|---|---|
| 1) TQM/QC/team only | 14.6*** | 4.2 |
| 2) TQM/rotation/team only | 4.2 | 1.6 |
| 3) QC/rotation/team only | 0.0 | 3.4 |
| 4) Rotation/TQM/QC only | 4.2 | 2.9 |
| 5) TQM/QC/team/rotation only | 12.5** | 5.0 |
| % adopting at least one of clusters 1–5 | 35.4*** | 17.1 |
| % adopting TQM/QC/team [1+5] | 27.1*** | 9.2 |

NOTE: Significance test: We employed a significance-of-difference test using Pearson $\chi^2$ with Yates continuity correction. When the expected frequency is too small, Fisher's Exact Test is used. *** = Statistically significant at the 0.01 level; ** = statistically significant at the 0.05 level.
SOURCE: Authors' survey and Osterman (1994).

transplants are among the least frequent adopters of such practices, the average Japanese transplant uses high performance practices far more often than its domestic counterpart.

As this chapter will show, the high ranking of Japanese transplants among our sample of start-ups is not the result of the wholesale adoption of home country management practices, as suggested by previous studies of the automobile industry. Within our sample of Japanese start-ups, we find no instances of the "auto assembly" experience in which Japanese multinationals transfer Japanese practices largely intact to the United States. Conversely, there are only isolated examples of the "electronic assembly" approach in which Japanese transplants largely emulate U.S. employment practices. Instead, we observe Japanese transplants adopting a sophisticated blend of U.S. and Japanese practices in a very systematic way.

**Table 4.2  Clustering of Management Practices: Japanese Transplants, Domestic Start-Ups, and U.S. Manufacturing (% of total establishments)**

| Cluster | Japanese transplants | Domestic start-ups | U.S. manufacturing |
|---|---|---|---|
| 1) TQM/QC/team only | 17.9*** | 10.0 | 4.2 |
| 2) TQM/rotation/team only | 3.6 | 5.0 | 1.6 |
| 3) QC/rotation/team only | 0.0 | 0.0 | 3.4 |
| 4) Rotation/TQM/QC only | 7.1 | 0.0 | 2.9 |
| 5) TQM/QC/team/rotation only | 17.9*** | 5.0 | 5.0 |
| % adopting at least one of clusters  1–5 | 46.4*** | 20.0 | 17.1 |
| % adopting at least TQM/QC/team | 35.7*** | 15.0 | 9.2 |

NOTE: Significance of differences measured between Japanese start-ups and U.S. manufacturing. Differences between Japanese and domestic start-ups and between domestic start-ups and U.S. manufacturing are not significant at the 0.05 level of confidence. The significance test is the same as for Table 4.1. *** = Statistically significant at the 0.01 level.

SOURCE: Japanese and domestic start-ups, authors' survey; U.S. manufacturing, Osterman (1994).

For example, 18% of the Japanese plants in our sample adopt a cluster of high performance management practices consisting of TQM, quality circles, and teamwork, while only 10% of our domestic sample uses this cluster (Table 4.2). More than twice as many of the Japanese transplants adopt one of the high performance practices in the cluster than do their domestic counterparts, and the Japanese transplants adopt all four practices (cluster 5) at over three times the rate of domestic start-ups.

In comparison with the overall experience of U.S. manufacturing firms, the Japanese transplants in our sample adopt clusters of three or four practices at over 2.5 times the corresponding U.S. rate, and all four practices at over three times the U.S. rate (Table 4.2).[4] While national surveys of U.S. manufacturing do not find any specific cluster of practices being favored (Osterman 1994, 2000), our data show that the cluster that includes quality circles, TQM, and work teams is clearly preferred by Japanese start-ups. Among Japanese start-ups in our sample, 35.7% adopt this combination, compared with only 9.2% of U.S. manufacturing establishments. All of these differences are highly significant according to standard statistical tests.

This does not mean that domestic start-ups fail to use leading-edge performance strategies; they do adopt many high performance practices with considerable frequency. Our data also suggest that they do so at a higher rate than established manufacturing plants, although the size of our sample is too small for this finding to be statistically significant. However, the Japanese transplants in our sample show a greater tendency than do domestic start-ups to integrate these practices with their overall management strategies in ways that emphasize complementarities among practices. This can be seen, for example, in the greater frequency with which Japanese transplants combine quality circles with TQM practices (Table 4.2). It is also manifest in greater use of compensation incentives that reinforce other high performance management practices, such as teamwork and training in multiple skills.

The strongest evidence of such complementarities, however, comes from our case study interviews. While both Japanese and domestic firms adopt high performance management practices, they integrate these practices into their overall management strategies in very different ways. We repeatedly received reports of the importance Japanese transplants place on coordinating plant location decisions with their preferences for a workforce with attitudes that support training and cooperative problem solving.  The availability of a labor supply with these attitudes, in turn, contributes to the development of training and employee involvement in ways that foster continuous improvements in quality and productivity.  It is this emphasis on capturing systematic complementarities among high performance management practices, as well as integrating these practices in a larger strategic framework, that defines an innovative "hybrid" model of high performance management practices (Abo 1994; Doeringer, Evans-Klock, and Terkla 1998; Liker, Fruin, and Adler 1999; Westney 1999).

## COMPARING MANAGEMENT PRACTICES IN JAPANESE AND DOMESTIC START-UPS

High performance management strategies begin with the choices of technology and plant location.  These decisions are always made at the corporate level by the parent companies.  However, the choices of specific high performance management practices are made at the plant level by local managers.

In Japanese transplants, the initial responsibility for designing human resources practices is usually assigned to American (rather than Japanese) managers.  These American personnel managers are commonly selected for their commitment to collaborative employment relationships, and they are often sent to Japan for orientation to Japanese employment practices at one or more comparable plants before any production workers are hired.  While this might appear to be the human resources counterpart of using Japanese managers to transfer manufacturing practices to the United States, the interview evidence points to a very different conclusion.

The American personnel managers of Japanese transplants are expressly instructed not to copy Japanese human resources systems. Instead, they are encouraged to develop new workplace organizational practices that will yield comparable levels of efficiency to those of best-practice Japanese factories in Japan, while also being compatible with the norms of the U.S. workforce and with U.S. labor market institutions.  Even those transplants that elected initially to transfer as much as possible of the Japanese system to the United States quickly learned that adaptations were required. A human resources manager of a Japanese transplant in Massachusetts expressed succinctly what many others reported—it was his job "to understand American workers and to translate the Japanese objectives into effective American strategies."

This decentralized process for designing and adapting workplace management policies yields substantial variation among plants in the specific details of management practices. Nevertheless, our interviews confirm that there are substantial rates of adoption of practices that resemble high performance management practices common to large manufacturing plants in Japan. Sometimes these "Japanese-style" practices are identical to those in Japan, such as just-in-time supply procedures. A much larger set, however, includes "closely equivalent" practices such as the use of "no-layoff" policies in place of lifetime employment guarantees, quality circles that have less supervisory input than is typical in Japan, and the use of intensive workplace orientation in place of job rotation as a means of familiarizing employees with the overall production process (Westney 1999; Fruin 1999; Jenkins and Florida 1999).

These Japanese-style practices are then systematically blended with other practices, such as the organization of work into departments and job ladders, which are traditional to the U.S. industrial relations system. This blending often involves systematic experimentation to find the most effective hybrid of Japanese and U.S. practices and to determine how the Japanese practices should be modified to yield equivalent results in the U.S. context (Westney 1999).

While counterpart domestic start-ups also adopt a blend of Japanese and domestic management practices, it is less common for them to systematically design a hybrid model of workplace practices. Instead, they continue to view traditional U.S. human resources practices as the foundation for workplace management. They often adopt innovative high performance practices management as "add-ons" to their traditional management systems and are sometimes skeptical about the potential effectiveness of these add-ons. The result of this approach is that domestic start-ups tend to incorporate fewer high performance management practices than Japanese start-ups in the United States, and they try less often to systematically identify and exploit complementarities among these practices that they do adopt.

We explore these differences in the adoption of high performance management practices under three broad categories: human resources strategy (compensation, recruitment practices, layoff policies, and training), work organization strategy (design of job ladders, job rotation, and the use of teams), and operations management strategy (quality circles, holding frequent meetings with employees, and giving production workers direct control over production and quality). Over two-thirds of the Japanese plants in the sample adopted at least one high-performance feature in each of these categories, while the adoption rates were uniformly lower for the counterpart domestic plants.

The following sections demonstrate the extent of the differences between domestic start-ups and Japanese transplants in terms of both the adoption rates of these specific high performance management practices and the degree to which these practices are integrated with other management strategies.

## COMPENSATION PRACTICES

Japanese transplants in the United States describe their compensation packages as "competitive," which translates into the payment of relatively high efficiency wages. Almost half the sample pay starting wage rates in the top 20% of the local wage distribution (Table 4.3), and most of the remainder pay above the average for comparable workers in their labor market areas.[5]   Wage levels in comparable domestic start-up plants tend to lie in the same ranges but are slightly below those in Japanese plants.  These compensation premiums are further reinforced by relatively generous fringe benefit packages, particularly among Japanese transplants.

Seniority-based wage systems, characteristic of the Japanese *nenko* pay system, are rarely adopted by either Japanese or domestic plants. When they are adopted, they apply only to earnings during the first 12 to 18 months of employment.  Instead, individual merit plays a more important role in wage increases and promotions in Japanese transplants, as well as in the non-union domestically owned start-ups.  For example, 50% of Japanese transplants and 40% of domestic start-ups have some form of individual merit pay.  Merit pay premiums also tend to be greater in Japanese transplants than in domestic start-ups.  The

**Table 4.3  Comparison of Start-Up Human Resources Practices (%)**

| Practice | Japanese | Domestic |
|---|---|---|
| Compensation | | |
| Pay in top 20% of area manufacturing | 46.4 | 45.0 |
| Team/plant-wide bonuses | 29.6 | 15.0 |
| At least one practice | 67.9 | 55.0 |
| Recruitment and selection | | |
| Evidence of being a team player | 46.4** | 15.0 |
| Written exams | 32.1** | 5.0 |
| At least one practice | 53.6** | 20.0 |
| Employment security | | |
| No-layoff policy | 42.9*** | 5.0 |
| Hire temporary workers | 35.7 | 30.0 |
| At least one practice | 71.4** | 35.0 |
| Training | | |
| Substantial job-entry training | 93.0*** | 60.0 |
| Cross-training | 42.9** | 15.0 |
| Teamwork training | 42.9 | 45.0 |
| Technical training | 71.4 | 55.0 |
| At least one practice | 100.0*** | 80.0 |
| N | 28 | 20 |

NOTE: Significance test is the same as for Table 4.1.  *** = Statistically significant at the 0.01 level; ** = statistically significant at the 0.05 level.
SOURCE: Authors' survey.

merit pay scale for Japanese plants can run as high as 5–6% for "meeting" requirements and, in one plant, up to 9% for "far exceeding" requirements. For the domestic plants that used merit pay, most yields averaged under 5%.

Both Japanese and domestic plants base individual merit pay on improvements in skill and knowledge of the work group, quality of work, quantity of output, attendance, and work attitudes. However, the Japanese plants also give substantial weight to social and psychological qualities of workers—the effectiveness of relationships with supervisors and co-workers, communication skills, drive and initiative, and dependability—and to problem-solving skills.

A second important set of wage premiums has to do with group performance incentives. Almost 30% of the Japanese firms in the sample provide performance-based group bonuses based on productivity gains or profit sharing, as does a much smaller share (15%) of the domestic start-ups (Table 4.3). In addition, a small fraction of the Japanese transplants (11%) has "pay-for-knowledge" systems that reward workers for acquiring multiple skills, compared with 5% for the domestic start-ups.

On balance, start-ups provide compensation that is high enough to satisfy a variety of efficiency wage objectives, ranging from matching efficiencies and the reduction in turnover to the motivation of effort through pay premiums and performance incentives. In all cases, the Japanese transplants use high performance compensation practices more intensively than the domestic start-ups.

## RECRUITMENT AND SELECTION

Consistent with relatively high compensation, start-ups draw large pools of job applicants, which allows them considerable latitude in defining high performance employee matches. One Japanese electronics firm in a rural area outside of Atlanta, for example, received between 4,000 and 5,000 applications for 300 jobs. Even before the widely publicized Toyota assembly plant in Georgetown, Kentucky, was opened, a local newspaper article about a Japanese company's visit to a potential plant site in Kentucky generated 3,000 job applications that were filed with the state employment service.

Both Japanese and domestic start-ups use education, personal references, and prior work experience as selection criteria. These are the central selection criteria for domestic start-ups, but the Japanese transplants use them largely as indicators of reliability and attitude and as a means of initially narrowing the applicant pool. After controlling for these threshold-screening criteria, Japanese transplants typically report 20 or more qualified applicants for each vacancy, compared to 10–15 for the counterpart domestic plants.

Japanese firms typically devote more resources to identifying hard-to-observe workforce qualities such as flexibility, teamwork, loyalty, motivation, and problem-solving capacity than do domestic start-ups. Screening of applicants frequently takes as long as three days, during which time a variety of written tests are administered and the ability to work in teams is assessed, often through interviews with front-line workers as well as supervisors. The difference in utilization rates of these selection practices between the Japanese and domestic samples is statistically significant (Table 4.3.)

Japanese plants also use preemployment training programs to evaluate problem-solving skills and personal interaction in team settings (Saltzman 1994).[6] This was most evident in Georgia, where all but one of the transplants in our sample took advantage of a preemployment program that was partly subsidized by the state. One Japanese transplant in Georgia asked applicants to take 15 hours of such "preemployment training" on weekends and evenings without pay. A small assembly plant in Georgia invited 32 applicants, from a pool of 1,000, to an unpaid 40-hour training course to allow management to observe their "work habits" and whether people got along well together on breaks. Only one-fourth of the new domestic plants surveyed in Georgia took advantage of this program.

## Employment Security

Japanese transplants do not offer the lifetime employment commitment that is characteristic of their plants in Japan and that is associated with gift and fairness efficiencies in non-union high performance companies in the United States (Doeringer 1991). Nevertheless, almost half (43%) of the Japanese plants have no-layoff policies that provide substantial job security to their employees. Only 5% of the domestic plants offer similar levels of job security, a difference that is statistically significant (Table 4.3).

Japanese and domestic start-ups make equivalent use of temporary workers, as can be seen from Table 4.3, but the Japanese plants report that they explicitly use temporary workers as an on-going buffer to enhance the employment security of their core workforce. In contrast, U.S. start-ups almost always use temporary labor to meet transitory production or shipping needs and lay off regular employees when there are shortfalls in demand.

For example, several domestic auto parts firms typically laid off employees for periods of one month whenever retooling was required to meet new customer specifications. In contrast, Japanese transplants were more likely to tolerate periods of substantial underemployment of their workforces in order to avoid layoffs during similar periods of reduced production. One illustration is a small machinery producer with close ties to a major Japanese auto assembler that paid its workforce for several months to remain "on-call" until orders were renewed, and there were several cases where Japanese management "donated" their employees to perform community service during temporary slowdowns.

### Training

Both Japanese and domestic start-ups are training-intensive, providing substantial job entry training, technical training (such as statistical process control), and teamwork training (Table 4.3). However, the prevalence of training is significantly greater in Japanese transplants (100% of the Japanese plants adopt some form of high performance training practices, compared with only 80% of the domestic plants), particularly in the areas of job-entry training and cross-training for multiple skills (Table 4.3).

Production workers in both Japanese and domestic plants typically go through orientation training before starting work. The orientation period in Japanese transplants is substantial, involving exposure to the entire range of jobs in the plant. Almost all plants had at least a three-day orientation period, and over one-fourth spent five days on orientation. Much of this training focuses on how to achieve continuous organizational improvement. In contrast, orientation in the domestic plants commonly takes less than a day and deals mostly with bureaucratic personnel matters.

Once orientation is completed, workers in both Japanese and domestic start-ups are assigned to their production departments, where they initially receive on-the-job training in a single skill. Japanese plants, however, subsequently provide significantly more cross-training than do the domestic start-ups (Table 4.3). Most of this cross-training occurs within, rather than between, departments.

These training investments are secured through the payment of efficiency wages that are sufficiently high to reduce labor turnover and by limiting layoffs. However, consistent with slightly lower wages and more frequent reliance on layoffs among domestic start-ups, the domestic plants in the sample tend to accept higher rates of labor turnover than do the Japanese transplants.

## TECHNOLOGY AND THE ORGANIZATION OF WORK

There are many common elements in the technology and internal labor market structures of Japanese transplants and counterpart domestic firms. Both the Japanese and domestic plants adopt advanced technologies and often make substantial use of computer-controlled production processes. Jobs are typically arranged into functional "lines" or departments consisting of roughly 10 to 20 employees, each of whom hold job classifications with relatively well-defined duties. Departments often have skill-based job ladders and are always supervised by a foreman.

Within this common framework, however, Japanese transplants are more likely to use a Japanese-style work organization—job rotation, teams, and daily work-group meetings—and to adopt U.S.-style promotion ladders than their domestic counterparts. Over 85% of our Japanese sample had adopted at least one of these practices, compared with 55% of the domestic sample (Table 4.4). In particular, Japanese transplants are almost four times more likely to use daily work-group meetings than are domestic start-ups.

**Table 4.4  Comparison of Start-Up Work Organization Practices (%)**

| Practice | Japanese | Domestic |
|---|---|---|
| Job rotation | 35.7 | 15.0 |
| Small production teams | 46.4 | 35.0 |
| Daily work-group meetings | 39.3** | 10.0 |
| Job ladders | 46.4 | 35.0 |
| At least one practice | 85.7** | 55.0 |
| N | 28 | 20 |

NOTE: Significance test is the same as for Table 4.1.  ** = Statistically significant at
the 0.05 level.
SOURCE: Authors' survey.

Even where differences in work organization are not great enough
to achieve statistical significance, there are often major qualitative dis-
tinctions in the way work is organized.  For example, the domestic
start-ups that adopt small-team production techniques typically view
them as experiments.  In the vast majority of cases, these experimental
teams are little more than administrative units for managing several
independent work stations where similar types of batch production are
performed.  In contrast, Japanese teams involve considerable collaboration among workers, and employees often participate in daily operations meetings.

## OPERATIONS MANAGEMENT AND
## DYNAMIC EFFICIENCY

Regardless of the particular product and production process,
achieving and surpassing quality and output goals in Japanese plants is
treated as a collective responsibility in which dynamic efficiency practices of peer supervision and self-supervision play a more central role
than in domestic plants.  One American vice president at a Japanese-
owned company explained that each employee is responsible for quality at his or her own work station and that "quality control" is such an

inherent part of operations that formal "zero defect" or TQM programs are not needed.[7]

Whether or not they work in formal teams, workers in Japanese plants are generally encouraged to think of themselves as being collectively engaged in, and responsible for, the quality and level of output. This culture of responsibility for operating efficiency is reinforced by frequent opportunities for employee participation in shop-floor management. Every Japanese plant in our sample used group meetings with managers to discuss guidelines for production levels and procedures for handling problems. Workers are also given considerable latitude in implementing these understandings, as exemplified by the frequency with which production workers are responsible for quality control (Table 4.5).

Long-term as well as short-term issues may also be discussed at these meetings. At one Japanese start-up, the manager discusses work and production schedules with employees and solicits their input before submitting bids for additional work. At another, a proposal by management to change the merit pay system was presented to the workforce, but was then abandoned after workers expressed reservations about the plan. Such meetings may be convened as often as once or twice per shift during the first year or so of operation and can last an hour or more. Once quality and output norms are achieved, the frequency of workforce meetings declines, but the general practice is to continue to meet at least weekly to monitor quality and to identify additional improvements that can be made in manufacturing processes.

Japanese managers closely monitor plant learning curves. Such learning is measured against benchmark cost and productivity·standards set by their company's most efficient branch plants in Japan, and there is pressure to meet or exceed these benchmarks as soon as possible. However, Japanese plants appear willing to tolerate an extended period of low output and slow growth in physical productivity during the start-up phase of operations in order to achieve quality standards.

Managers in the sample of domestic companies often express a similar commitment to both quality and efficiency. They also use a variety of arrangements (ranging from quality circles to one-on-one discussions) for soliciting employee advice on how to improve quality and reduce unit costs. However, only 45% hold weekly or monthly shift meetings (Table 4.5). Those that do hold such meetings are less

**Table 4.5  Comparison of Start-Up Operations Management Practices (%)**

| Practice | Japanese | Domestic |
|---|---|---|
| Quality control | | |
| Quality circles/*kaizen* | 64.3** | 35.0 |
| TQM | | |
| Weekly/monthly shift meetings | 100.0*** | 45.0 |
| Quality control by production workers | 50.0** | 20.0 |
| At least one of these management practices | 100.0*** | 45.0 |
| N | 28 | 20 |

NOTE: Significance test is the same as for Table 4.1.  *** = Statistically significant at the 0.01 level; ** = statistically significant at the 0.05 level.
SOURCE: Authors' survey.

likely than the Japanese plants to work with employees to invest in "consensus" problem solving or to delegate quality-control responsibilities to production workers.

More generally, the domestic plant managers tend to see quality and cost as "control" functions that are rooted more in technology, engineering design, and the direct costs of factors of production than in the commitment of the workforce. They are also more likely to view problem identification and problem solving as management prerogatives, rather than as responsibilities to be shared with employees. A manager at a new affiliate of a U.S. company said his ideal was to "engineer the operator out, rather than base the engineering on the operators' knowledge and skill." He described various technical quality control measures and investments in automation his plant had made. This strategy is in vivid contrast to the worker motivation, training, and human relations approach to quality control prevalent in the Japanese plants.

The tension between authoritarian control and social motivation as a means to achieve efficiency is illustrated by the experience of a domestic plant that manufactures electrical components for the automobile industry. The plant manager had visited a number of Japanese-owned facilities and had decided to adopt a highly participatory approach to meeting the quality standards set by its parent automobile manufacturer. The plant established a bottom-up quality improvement program using quality teams, and it was in the process of adopting employee suggestions for modifying production procedures when a headquarters-based industrial engineering team was dispatched to the local facility to assist with quality control.

The engineering team focused on specific production operations that were not meeting technical production standards. It recommended introducing a series of "best practices," drawn from other plants around the country, that would bring each operation up to established quality standards. The local quality teams complained that these practices were not consistent with their analysis of how to solve the problems and that the top-down involvement of a corporate-level engineering team undermined the participatory quality-improvement procedures that had been initiated at the plant. The corporate engineering team reviewed the local quality improvement plan but continued to insist that its recommendations be adopted, while the local plant manager sided with his employees' recommendations. This impasse was ultimately resolved in favor of the local plant, although only months later after it was elevated to the highest corporate level.

In most Japanese transplants, corporate benchmarking focuses on the desired outcomes to be achieved rather than on the adoption of specific practices. Similarly, efficiency is seen as requiring a coherent system of practices, not a piecemeal assemblage of independent best practices.


## EVALUATION AND REFORM OF
## HIGH PERFORMANCE STRATEGIES

Managers of Japanese transplants regularly evaluate their human resource management systems and often report systemic shortcomings. Common concerns encountered during our field interviews include problems in identifying subtle workforce qualities, limiting turnover sufficiently to justify intensive and costly human capital investments, reducing absenteeism, ensuring commitment to the goals of the firm, and raising labor productivity.[8] These concerns were typically addressed through continuing experimentation with, and the adaptation of, high performance management practices within the framework of hybrid management systems.

For example, a Japanese auto parts manufacturer adopted a provisional set of wage grades based on job content and benchmarked to the top of the wage distribution in the area. This wage structure performed satisfactorily in terms of recruiting labor, rewarding skill differentials, and controlling turnover, but the personnel manager wanted to be sure that the performance incentives were optimal and that the wage structure was perceived as fair and efficient by employees.

After two years of operation, the hourly workforce was invited to evaluate the wage structure. Suggestions for change were solicited, various options were discussed during a series of small group meetings with employees, and a new "consensus" compensation structure was introduced that incorporated seniority-based wage improvements for employees who had exhausted their job ladder promotion opportunities.

Managers of domestic start-ups are less likely to revise their management systems. They do not routinely evaluate their selection, training, and employee involvement practices as long as overall corporate cost targets are being met, and they do not subject these practices to a requirement of continuous improvement.

## HIGH PERFORMANCE MANAGEMENT "SYSTEMS"

The interviews suggest that these differences in the adoption rates of high performance management practices result in distinctly different management systems in Japanese transplants and domestic start-ups. Japanese transplants are likely to adopt a hybrid model in which high performance management practices are integrated into a coherent management system. Quality and cost are approached as part of an overall production system in which efficiency is benchmarked against performance standards in best-practice Japanese plants that are also improving their performance over time.

Human resources development, meaningful employee participation in operations management and quality control, and the active promotion of social and organizational learning are key to achieving efficiency goals. Continuous improvement is secured largely through managing labor productivity: recruiting employees that are compatible with a workplace culture of responsibility and cooperation; developing workforce commitment to the company; using communication and employee involvement to make the workforce responsible for quality and output improvement; and rewarding peer group collaboration and problem solving. The result is a process that is smoothly coordinated and continuously improved by employees who are encouraged to find better and faster ways to operate the production process.

The approach bears a superficial resemblance to the "management-by-stress" approach described by Parker and Slaughter (1988) in their study of Japanese auto assembly plants, in which production speeds are continuously increased to reveal bottlenecks that can then be corrected. However, in the assembly line operations we visited, we did not observe evidence of practices of the kind that have been associated with this type of management, i.e., heavy monitoring by managers, deliberate increases in line speeds to identify weak links in the production process, audiovisual devices to monitor line performance, or high accident rates. Japanese start-ups did try to improve line speeds through learning and problem solving, but there was no unusual pressure for speed. Moreover, Japanese plants gave the safety of production and the cleanliness of the plant equal priority with speed and quality in production.

The systems approach to high performance management practices is less evident among domestic start-ups, which are more likely to follow a piecemeal approach. Like the Japanese transplants, most of the domestic firms articulate a similar set of policies for achieving workplace efficiency. They pay relatively high wages, seek to hire a "quality" workforce, and emphasize high labor productivity. They describe their operating strategies largely in terms of lean management, quality control, frequent communication with employees, intensive human resources development, and the empowerment of employees. Nonetheless, there are major differences in the way Japanese and most of the domestic plants implement their workplace efficiency practices.

For example, domestic start-ups place relatively less emphasis on improving quality and productivity by managing social relationships with workers, among managers, and with suppliers. They tend to emphasize improvements in technology and engineering instead of incorporating social learning and workforce commitment into an integrated set of high performance management practices. These differences are most apparent in the ways that domestic firms define workforce quality, motivate quality production, and involve employees in production decisions. Many domestic plants have TQM programs, but these are typically implemented from the top down and are oriented towards relatively technical management practices. The domestic plants are not as committed to teamwork or other forms of employee input and often have only the half-hearted support of local managers, who regard TQM as simply the latest fad from corporate headquarters.

Overall, domestic start-ups approach efficiency from the perspective of reducing factor payments, supervising labor, and controlling manufacturing processes. They also tend to construct a single "best" employment system by copying best practices drawn from many different organizational settings, while the Japanese plants focus on improving what they see as a unified employment system that must evolve in its own way within the setting of a single plant.


## SUMMARY

Other studies have looked for models of high performance workplaces, either in the context of established manufacturing plants that are being "transformed" or in experimental situations, such as the Saturn and Nummi auto assembly plants, that are designed to test new forms of work organization. The results of these studies, however, are often ambiguous or contradictory.

Our study of a sample of start-up factories yields a different set of conclusions, and it helps to reconcile some of the apparent inconsistencies in the earlier research. We conclude that Japanese transplants are likely to adopt systematic clusters of high performance management practices that are designed to meld Japanese workplace management strategies with organizational practices drawn from the traditions of the

U.S. industrial relations system. Their goal is to create hybrid management systems that are as efficient as those of their parent corporations in Japan.

These hybrid management systems emphasize social and organizational learning, employee participation in problem solving, and worker commitment as the principal means of motivating labor efficiency and productivity. They typically reward their employees with career employment, as well as high wages, and their employees reciprocate with high labor productivity. Firms do draw on centralized corporate assistance for matters related to technology, information systems, and plant location. However, decisions about which high performance management practices to adopt are determined locally, so that many aspects of human resources strategy, work organization, and operations management can be tailored to the circumstances of individual plants.

The result is the adoption of coherent systems of high performance management practices of the kinds identified by theories of efficiency wages, internal labor markets, and various social and psychological theories of labor productivity. The key ingredients of these high performance systems are the recruitment of a collaborative workforce with problem-solving skills, intensive training, high levels of employee involvement in management decisions, and both individual and group performance incentives. However, the particular combinations of efficiency practices that are adopted by each transplant are shaped by the plant-specific production technologies, by the types of products that are being manufactured, and by relationships with customers.

The most common cluster of practices among the sample of Japanese transplants comprises teamwork, quality circles, and TQM, but this cluster is found in only a little over one-third of the transplants. Nevertheless, whatever cluster is selected, the practices are combined in ways that take advantage of complementarities and are systematically integrated into a coherent set of overall management strategies.

Domestic start-ups aspire to similar levels of performance and also perceive themselves as adopting best-practice workplace arrangements that incorporate many of the same techniques as the Japanese transplants. In practice, however, the domestic start-ups differ significantly from their Japanese counterparts. Domestic start-ups define workforce quality in different ways and tend to favor controlling costs over managing productivity through employee participation and motivation.

They take a more limited and piecemeal approach when grafting such practices onto their traditionally managed workplaces, and they do not give the kind of attention to the consistency of practices within an overall system of efficiency management found in Japanese transplants. It is probably this piecemeal model that is being observed by other studies that conclude that the adoption of high performance management practices in the United States is "eclectic" and "experimental" and does not follow a definitive pattern.

## Notes

1. Other studies of Japanese transplants, however, emphasize the importance of location-specific factors and difficulties in generalizing organizational practices (Fruin 1999).
2. This estimate is based upon manufacturing plants in the "high penetration" categories, where these practices must apply to half or more of the workforce.
3. Much of the rest of this chapter parallels material developed in Doeringer, Evans-Klock, and Terkla (1998).
4. The percentages of adoption by manufacturing firms in the United States taken from Osterman (1994) assume these practices involve the participation of at least 50% of core workers. The sample of Japanese firms in this study achieved 100% participation among core production workers.
5. The rare exceptions are low-value-added assembly plants, such as cable assembly, where there is little latitude for employees to affect plant efficiency and where direct competition with low-wage foreign producers is also a consideration.
6. Japanese plants also use the selection latitude afforded by large applicant pools to accomplish objectives other than securing a well-qualified workforce. They often recruit workforces that closely mirror the race and gender demographics of the local labor market, and they try to avoid pirating large numbers of employees from local companies, particularly Japanese-owned.
7. Formal quality checking is also done throughout the production process using statistical process control (SPC) techniques, and individual workers are trained to understand how the quality of the work affects SPC outcomes.
8. This conclusion is further reinforced by a Wyatt survey (Wyatt Company 1990) showing that motivating and retaining personnel were among the four most difficult general human-resource management problems experienced under the Japanese export model in the United States.

# 5

# High Performance Management and the Quality of Jobs

Whether or not one believes fully in the thesis that America is deindustrializing, there is widespread evidence that the kinds of good jobs for high school graduates that were generated in large numbers by the postwar U.S. economy are declining (Borjas, Freeman, and Katz 1997; Mishel, Bernstein, and Schmitt 1999; Kletzer 1998). Because the economy continues to generate good jobs for workers with high levels of skill and education, wage differentials by education are widening (Berman, Bound, and Griliches 1994; Berman, Bound, and Machin 1998).

These trends are particularly apparent in manufacturing, where the combination of global competition, skill-biased technological change, and the decline of unions has eroded jobs and wages of front-line workers. Between 1970 and 1999, the share in employment of front-line production workers in the economy fell from 17.8% to 9.8%, and there was an absolute loss of 1.36 million production-worker jobs. There is also evidence that recent productivity gains are not being as readily transferred into wage gains and job security as they were in the past (Osterman 2000; Mishel, Bernstein, and Schmitt 2001).

The start-up firms in our sample, however, exhibit very different patterns. These plants are adopting the kinds of advanced technologies that are supposed to be biased against workers that only have high school degrees and toward those with higher levels of education and skill. Yet, based on our interviews and plant visits, workers with only a high school education are filling the vast majority of the jobs generated by these start-ups. These workers are operating the new technologies and are often responsible for inspection and quality control as well. Although we did not systematically interview workers during our plant visits, we had ample opportunity to observe shop-floor operations, and there were numerous occasions where we were able to discuss the work environment with front-line employees as well as supervisors. Employees, in general, seem to value working for start-ups, and many had previous experience in manufacturing upon which to base their employment comparisons.[1]

As shown in the previous chapter, start-ups provide high wages and good fringe benefits. Compared with other manufacturing plants we have studied (Doeringer and Piore 1971; Doeringer, Terkla, and Topakian 1987; Doeringer and Terkla 1995; Doeringer and Watson 1999), the pace of work was not unusually fast, quality was often stressed over speed, and rest breaks were frequent. Similarly, workplaces were modern, clean, and well lit, equipment embodied the latest safety features, and workplace injury rates were low relative to industry averages. In addition, there were open communication channels, opportunities for growth and development, employee involvement in decision making, and performance-based pay. Workers did not appear to be closely monitored. Supervisors and technicians were "on-call" in production departments, but workers seemed to be largely self-supervised. Except where the production process was highly automated, production workers appeared to control work speeds. Shop-floor relationships between employees and management, with few exceptions, seemed cordial and collaborative. The overall impression is that start-ups offer the kinds of compensation practices and other job characteristics that are widely believed to make jobs attractive to workers (Cappelli 1999).

## JOB EXCELLENCE IN START-UP FACTORIES

To provide a more detailed portrayal of the jobs offered by start-ups, we examine six categories of job characteristics commonly associated with high-quality jobs: high wages, job security, flexible work organization, intensive training, employee voice, and worker power. In each case, these characteristics are defined very conservatively, and a plant is considered to have them only when they apply to all production workers (Table 5.1). For example, a start-up is defined as offering job security only if there is an explicit no-layoff policy, and the measure of intensive training requires that a start-up provide at least two different types of training.

**Table 5.1  Characteristics of High-Quality Jobs**

| Characteristic | Definition |
| --- | --- |
| High wages | Wages in top 20% of local (within a 100-mile radius) wage structure |
| Job security | Plant has an explicit no-layoff policy |
| Flexible work | One or more of the following practices: small production teams, job rotation, interdepartmental project teams |
| Intensive training | Two or more of the following practices: intensive entry training, cross-training, teamwork training, training in statistical process control |
| Worker voice | One or more of the following practices: daily or weekly group meetings, quality circles, evidence of high worker participation outside formal structures for providing voice |
| Worker power | One or more of the following practices: unionization, production workers have significant responsibility for quality control, substantial evidence of reliance on peer supervision |

The data confirm our impressions from the shop-floor visits. While the number and mix of the specific job characteristics varies among plants, the overall incidence of valued job characteristics is high. It is also clear that Japanese transplants adopt many of these high-quality job characteristics with statistically significant greater frequency than do their domestic counterparts.

## High Wages

As noted in Chapter 4, 46% of the start-ups pay wages in the top quintile of the area wage distribution (Table 5.2), and it was reported during our field interviews that fringe benefits are equal to or more generous than those of the firms with which they compete. Almost as large a fraction (42%) of the start-ups augment base pay with some form of compensation that is contingent upon performance (e.g., profit-sharing, bonuses, or pay for knowledge). The managers we inter-

**Table 5.2   Rate of Adoption of High-Quality Job Characteristics by
Start-Ups (%)**

| Practice | Total | Domestic | Japanese-owned |
|---|---|---|---|
| High wages | 45.8 | 45.0 | 46.4 |
|   Profit sharing | 20.8 | 25.0 | 17.9 |
|   Bonuses | 22.9 | 15.0 | 28.6 |
|   Pay for knowledge | 8.3 | 5.0 | 10.7 |
| Job security | 27.1 | 5.0*** | 42.9 |
| Flexible work organization | 52.1 | 40.0 | 60.7 |
|   Teams | 41.7 | 35.0 | 46.4 |
|   Rotation | 27.1 | 15.0 | 35.7 |
|   Interdepartmental | 14.6 | 10.0 | 17.9 |
| Intensive training (at least two) | 68.8 | 55.0 | 78.6 |
|   Entry | 79.2 | 60.0*** | 92.9 |
|   Cross | 31.3 | 15.0** | 42.9 |
|   Team | 43.8 | 45.0 | 42.9 |
|   Statistical process control | 64.6 | 55.0 | 71.4 |
| Employee voice | 75.0 | 40.0*** | 100.0 |
|   Quality circles | 52.1 | 35.0 | 64.3 |
|   Frequent meetings | 75.0 | 40.0*** | 100.0 |
|   High participation | 20.8 | 10.0 | 28.6 |
| Worker power | 45.8 | 25.0*** | 60.7 |
|   Peer supervision | 12.5 | 10.0 | 14.3 |
|   Workers control quality | 37.5 | 20.0** | 50.0 |
|   Union | 6.3 | 10.0 | 3.6 |

NOTE: We employed a significance-of-difference test using Pearson $\chi^2$ with Yates continuity correction. When the expected frequency was too small, Fisher's Exact Test was used. *** = Statistically significant at the 0.01 level; ** = statistically significant at the 0.05 level.
SOURCE: Authors' survey.

viewed estimate that these pay supplements yield an average of 10% to 20% over base pay.

## Job Security

Start-ups generally offer above-average job security because their advanced technologies and high performance management practices give them a competitive edge with respect to other branch plants within their parent companies, and also over other competing firms that have older technologies. These advantages almost always result in sustained employment growth (discussed in Chapter 8), so that the need for lay-offs rarely arises. However, over one-fourth (27%) of the start-ups have gone a step further by adopting explicit no-layoff policies that offer an even stronger guarantee of employment security (Table 5.2). These job security policies cover almost all of the workforce and are typically reinforced either by deferring training and non-essential plant maintenance to periods of slack demand or by the use of temporary employees to absorb large fluctuations in labor demand. Such no-lay-off policies are found much more often among Japanese transplants than among domestic start-ups, and this difference is statistically significant.

## Flexible Work Organization

Half of the start-ups use some form of flexible work organization (Table 5.2). The specific form of work organization adopted varies considerably with the character of the underlying technology. Teamwork is the most common type of work flexibility (used by 42% of the start-ups), followed by job rotation (27%) and interdepartmental project teams (15%).

## Intensive Training

Start-ups are almost always very training-intensive. About 70% provide two or more types of training including substantial job entry training (79%), instruction in statistical process control (65%), and team training (44%). In general, new Japanese plants do more training than new domestic plants.

### Employee Voice

In previous chapters, we showed that start-ups offer many different avenues through which employees can exercise voice, ranging from quality circles to informal opportunities for employees to participate in management decisions. In order to illustrate the relative importance of voice, we only count active opportunities for voice through frequent formal meetings with management to discuss production or quality decisions, or through informal mechanisms that result in a similar frequency of consultation. Three-quarters of the start-ups (and all of the Japanese-owned start-ups) in the sample provide employees with such active forms of voice. The most common forms are daily and weekly meetings (75%) and quality circles (52%).

### Worker Power

Since only three of the start-ups in the sample are unionized, we expected to see relatively little opportunity for workers to exercise power. However, we found from our interviews that there were a number of instances where employees articulate voice in ways that also allow them to exercise power through their decision-making autonomy. These include the ability to control production and quality and to supervise co-workers. By this broad definition, employees in almost half of the start-ups exercise some form of power, and this is much more often the case in the Japanese plants. The most common type of employee power is final control over product quality (38%), and the least common is collective bargaining (6%).

### Clustering of Job Characteristics

The vast majority of the start-ups offer clusters of these six attractive job characteristics, but again, Japanese start-ups tend to provide larger clusters of these job characteristics than do the domestic start-ups. Four-fifths of all start-ups offer two or more of the job traits described in Table 5.1, and almost half offer four or more of these job traits (Table 5.3). Only four plants in the sample fail to offer any of these elements of valued job characteristics. Among the more common pairs of characteristics are job security and flexible work, and worker voice and intensive training. There are also relatively high correlations

**Table 5.3  Distribution of High-Quality Job Characteristics (%)**

| Sample group | Number of characteristics offered | | | | | | |
|---|---|---|---|---|---|---|---|
| | 0 | 1 | 2 | 3 | 4 | 5 | 6 |
| Japanese | 0 | 0 | 18 | 21 | 25 | 25 | 11 |
| Domestic | 20 | 25 | 15 | 15 | 15 | 10 | 0 |
| Total sample | 8 | 10 | 17 | 19 | 21 | 19 | 6 |

**Table 5.4  Correlations among High-Quality Job Characteristics**

| | High wages | Job security | Flexible work | Worker voice | Worker power | Intensive training |
|---|---|---|---|---|---|---|
| High wages | 1 | | | | | |
| Job security | 0.10 | 1 | | | | |
| Flexible work | −0.12 | 0.30** | 1 | | | |
| Worker voice | 0.05 | 0.35** | 0.51*** | 1 | | |
| Worker power | 0.16 | 0.10 | 0.38*** | 0.34** | 1 | |
| Intensive training | −0.01 | 0.31** | 0.34** | 0.44*** | 0.17 | 1 |

NOTE: *** = Statistically significant at the 0.01 level; ** = statistically significant at the 0.05 level;

among intensive training, flexible work organization, worker power, and worker voice (Table 5.4).

**The Best Start-Ups**

To further illustrate the excellent quality of jobs in start-ups, we identified the dozen start-ups in our sample that have clusters of at least five of the six traits described above (Table 5.5). Flexible work organization and widespread opportunity for worker voice are universal. Almost all (92%) offer intensive training; 75% pay very high wages and a similar fraction offer high job security; and over 80% adopt practices that empower employees at the workplace.

**Table 5.5  Job Quality Characteristics of the Best Start-Ups**

| Firm | High wages | Job security | Flexible work | Worker voice | Worker power | Intensive training |
|------|-----------|--------------|---------------|--------------|--------------|--------------------|
| B1   | no  | yes | yes | yes | yes | yes |
| B2   | yes | no  | yes | yes | yes | yes |
| B3   | no  | yes | yes | yes | yes | yes |
| B4   | yes | yes | yes | yes | no  | yes |
| B5   | yes | no  | yes | yes | yes | yes |
| B6   | yes | no  | yes | yes | yes | yes |
| B7   | no  | yes | yes | yes | yes | yes |
| B8   | yes | yes | yes | yes | no  | yes |
| B9   | yes | yes | yes | yes | yes | yes |
| B10  | yes | yes | yes | yes | yes | no  |
| B11  | yes | yes | yes | yes | yes | yes |
| B12  | yes | yes | yes | yes | yes | yes |
| % with trait | 75 | 75 | 100 | 100 | 83 | 92 |

## Why Are Jobs in Start-Ups So Good?

There are a number of reasons why the quality of the jobs found in start-up factories might be so high.  One possibility is that workers incidentally value the management practices adopted by start-ups to improve business performance.  Flexible job assignments and opportunities for voice, for example, are high performance management practices that can raise productivity and may also be perceived as beneficial by workers.  If this were the whole story, however, we would expect to find start-ups being able to compensate for the presence of attractive nonpecuniary job characteristics by paying lower wages.  Since compensation in start-ups is unusually high and working conditions are very good, there must also be other factors that contribute to high job quality.

A more likely hypothesis, derived from theories of efficiency wages discussed in Chapter 2, is that offering good jobs is a device adopted by employers to offset various market failures associated with new technologies and advanced management practices. For example, high wages and other beneficial job traits may be used to retain employees in whom employers have invested heavily in training. Alternatively, high-quality jobs and performance-based pay may help to secure employee cooperation with various high performance practices that might otherwise be undermined by worker resistance and shirking. In both cases, we would expect to find a causal relationship between the use of high performance management practices and good jobs.

Another hypothesis is that good jobs are related to the balance of bargaining power between workers and employers. Unionization and collective bargaining are one obvious source of worker power that often contributes to higher wages, better job security, and greater employee voice than profit-maximizing employers would otherwise choose to provide. Since only three plants in our sample are unionized, however, it is unlikely that collective bargaining power can explain much of the job quality in start-ups.

It is also well established that workers in non-union establishments can exercise power through noncooperative behavior such as shirking, slowdowns, and "working to rule" (Mathewson 1931). For example, giving workers decision-making authority can increase their ability to slow production and can increase the degree to which workers can exclusively control knowledge of the production process. Similarly, teamwork and other group activities can build collective solidarity among employees. Employers may, therefore, see providing good jobs as a way of forestalling solidarity and reducing the likelihood of workers disrupting production. Another possibility is that employers use high wages and job security to reduce employee power by encouraging the workforce to be committed to the goals of the firm so that various high performance management practices will work most effectively. Whether good jobs are the result of the exercise of worker power or are an instrument for controlling worker power, power theories predict that there will be a positive relationship between various measures of worker empowerment and high performance management practices, as well as between empowerment measures and job quality (Goldberg 1980; Pfeffer 1982; Jacoby 1985).

Our interviews with managers are consistent with all three explanations. Chapter 4 provides ample evidence that high labor productivity is a major goal of the managers of start-ups. These employers also recognize that many of these practices contribute to the overall quality of the employment package being offered. However, they reject the idea that good job benefits can justify lowering wages. Instead, employers report that keeping turnover very low and getting employees to focus on problem solving are critical to gaining the full efficiency benefits of high performance management practices, and they regard good jobs as the instruments for achieving this goal. Finally, employers in start-ups are acutely aware of (and often seek to avoid) union power, and they routinely attempt to develop a sense of cooperative employment relationships.

In order to test for the relative importance of these efficiency and power theories of job quality in start-up factories, we classify good job characteristics into three categories: job quality, high performance management, or employee power. While any such classification scheme is somewhat arbitrary, the data will show that our findings are robust with respect to small changes in how we define the categories.

### Job Quality Measures

Our initial definition of what job characteristics most clearly represent job quality for workers consists of four components: high wages (HIWAGE), high job security (SECURITY), worker power (POWER), and a workplace culture that emphasizes employee voice (HIPARTICIP). High job security and strong employee power come closest to capturing job characteristics that are more beneficial to workers than to employers. While more debatable, high wages and a culture of participation are also placed in this category (Table 5.6). Because start-ups will not necessarily select the same mix of job quality characteristics to achieve their goals, a binary variable, JOBQUALITY, is used to indicate start-ups that offer at least two of these job quality characteristics. When the relationship between power and job quality is analyzed, this variable is modified (MODQUALITY) to exclude the measure of worker power.

### Efficiency Practices

Four management practices are chosen to represent the types of organizational arrangements that are most clearly related to efficiency

**Table 5.6  Definitions of Variables in Factor Analysis Models**

| Variable | Definition |
|---|---|
| BONUS | Team or plant-wide bonuses |
| CONTINGENT | One or more of the following practices: BONUS, KNOWPAY, PROFIT |
| EMPGRO | Average annual compound growth rate of employment from year of start-up to the time of the interview |
| FLEX | One or more of the following practices: small production teams, job rotation, interdepartmental project teams |
| HIPARTICIP | Employees have high levels of informal participation in management decisions outside of formal structures designed to facilitate participation |
| HIWAGE | Wages in top 20% of local (within a 100-mile radius) wage structure |
| JAPAN | Start-up is a Japanese transplant |
| JOBQUALITY | Two or more of the following: HIPARTICIP, HIWAGE, POWER, SECURE |
| KNOWPAY | Pay for knowledge |
| MEET | Daily or weekly work group meetings |
| MODQUALITY | Two or more of the following: HIPARTICIP, HIWAGE, SECURE |
| PEER | Peer supervision |
| POWER | One or more of the following: PEER, QUALCONTROL, UNION |
| PROFIT | Profit sharing |
| QC | Start-up uses quality circles |
| QUALCONTROL | Production workers have significant responsibility for quality control |
| SECURITY | Explicit no-layoff policy |
| SIZE | Number of production workers |
| TRAIN | Two or more of the following practices: intensive entry training, cross-training, teamwork training, technical training |
| UNION | Unionized start-up |

and productivity growth, even though they may also offer incidental benefits to workers. Quality circles (QC) and frequent meetings with employees (MEET) are elements of employee voice that are directed primarily towards solving production and quality problems; intensive training (TRAIN) directly raises worker productivity, and the use of small production teams, job rotation, or interdepartmental project teams (FLEX) are ways of efficiently organizing work (Table 5.6). These are the kinds of practices that other studies regularly find are related to improved efficiency (Black and Lynch 1996, 1997, 1999; Cappelli and Neumark 1999; Freeman and Kleiner 2000; Osterman 2000; MacDuffie 1995; Ichniowski, Shaw, and Prennushi 1997).

Apart from the high performance management practices, over 40% of the start-ups in the sample use some type of compensation that is contingent upon performance. Because such direct performance incentives differ conceptually from organizational efficiency practices, we also examine performance bonuses, profit sharing, pay-for-knowledge, and a binary variable (CONTINGENT) for plants that use one or more of these contingent pay practices.

In addition to the management and compensation practices that represent inputs into the production function, a variable to capture output effects is also introduced. Because such direct measures of productivity and unit costs are not available for the firms in the sample, the rate of employment growth (EMPGRO) is introduced as an outcome measure of improved efficiency in production. In Chapter 8, we demonstrate that employment growth rates in start-ups are in fact an excellent approximation of changes in productivity.

### Employee Power

We define employee power using three measures: unionization (UNION), peer supervision and evaluation by workers (PEER), and employee authority to control production quality (QUALCONTROL). While these variables may indirectly contribute to efficiency, our interviews suggest the power component dominates. A binary variable (POWER) is also created to indicate if a start-up offers one or more of these components of power.

## TESTING THE THEORIES

Testing the causal relationships implied by these two theories of job quality—efficiency and power—is problematic, because start-ups simultaneously optimize their efficiency practices and responses to worker power. Given the limits of these data and the relatively small sample size, it is not possible to estimate precisely the simultaneous relationships among job quality, high performance efficiency practices, performance incentives, and employee power.[2] However, factor analysis procedures provide an alternative method for analyzing the relative strength of the simultaneous relationships among these variables.

Factor analysis identifies different clusters of variables that share common underlying relationships. This technique does not identify causal mechanisms among variables, but the factor loadings on different variables can be used to show the key relationships among variables and to define composite factors that explain a substantial amount of the variance in the data. The relative importance of each factor can then be determined by the amount of variance that it explains (Harman 1976; Jackson 1991; Rencher 1998).

### Workplace Efficiency and Job Quality

The first hypothesis we examine is that good job characteristics are used to strengthen high performance management strategies. This efficiency theory of job equality predicts, for example, that high wages could reflect the intensive training provided by start-ups and that job security is a necessary condition for getting workers to contribute to productivity improvement (through quality circles and group meetings) without fear of losing their jobs.

The efficiency thesis is the one most commonly mentioned in our interviews with plant managers, who claim that high labor productivity is one of their major goals. These managers report that the successful implementation of high performance strategies depends in part upon having a workforce that is motivated and cooperative with respect to training and teamwork, flexible, and that contributes to improving production efficiency and quality control. Because these are also productive qualities over which individual workers can exercise considerable control, high job quality may be necessary to secure employee collaboration.

Our first test is a factor analysis of the relationships among the measures of job quality, efficient organizational practices, and growth of employment (Table 5.7). We also introduce controls for size of establishment (SIZE), because size often influences compensation levels (Katz and Summers 1989), and for Japanese ownership (JAPAN), because Japanese-owned start-ups have a higher incidence of good job characteristics than domestic start-ups.[3]

The first and most important factor identified by this procedure reveals a strong relationship between job quality and efficiency practices. This "efficiency" factor explains 61% of the total variance among the variables being analyzed. No other variables are sufficiently related to one another to constitute a second underlying explanatory factor.[4] The factor loadings within this efficiency factor are relatively high for JOBQUALITY and for almost all of our measures of efficiency (FLEX, MEET, QC, and TRAIN). Three of the four separate components of JOBQUALITY—employee participation, worker power, and job secu-

**Table 5.7   Factor Analysis of Job Quality and Efficiency Practices**

| Variable | Factor loadings |
|---|---|
| JOBQUALITY | 0.73 |
|    POWER | 0.63 |
|    HIPARTICIP | 0.61 |
|    SECURITY | 0.46 |
|    HIWAGE | 0.17 |
| QC | 0.76 |
| MEET | 0.74 |
| FLEX | 0.62 |
| TRAIN | 0.56 |
| EMPGRO | 0.49 |
| JAPAN | 0.61 |
| SIZE | 0.38 |
| Variance explained (%) | 61 |

rity—also have high factor loadings (0.61, 0.63 and 0.46, respectively). These findings show that high-quality jobs are associated with the adoption of high performance practices. Moreover, the relatively high factor loading on EMPGRO (0.49) indicates that firms that both adopt high performance practices and offer high quality jobs experience faster employment growth. The high factor loading on worker power implies that firms that use large numbers of high performance practices are also likely to empower their employees and that employee power is not a deterrent to growth.

In contrast, HIWAGE has a very low factor loading (0.17), meaning that high wages are not an important component of the efficiency factor. This indicates that high wages are not being used as part of high performance management strategies in ways that correspond to the various standard theories of efficiency wages discussed in Chapter 2.[5] The small value of the factor loading on HIWAGE is also inconsistent with high wages being the result of a compensating differential for some unobserved adverse working conditions associated with high performance management practices.

The variable measuring Japanese ownership (JAPAN) has a loading of 0.61, indicating a strong association with the other key variables in this factor. Previous chapters have shown that Japanese transplants are more intensive and systematic adopters of high performance management practices than their domestic counterparts. Both the descriptive data (see Table 5.2) and the factor analysis indicate that Japanese transplants seem to hold an edge in the quality of jobs offered by start-ups.[6] The loading on SIZE (0.38) indicates only a weak tendency for the adoption of high performance practices and the presence of high job quality characteristics to be higher in large firms.

While the evidence so far points to a strong relationship among job quality, efficiency, and business success, compensation incentives contingent upon either business performance or the acquisition of skill may also be important contributors to the firm's success. These incentives may even be partial substitutes for the efficiency effects of high wages and other job quality characteristics. We test for these two effects by adding several contingent pay variables to the efficiency model reported in Table 5.7: profit sharing (PROFIT), pay premiums for acquiring additional skills (KNOWPAY), pay that rewards group performance through bonuses (BONUS), and a binary variable (CONTINGENT) for firms that use any of these three types of contingent pay.

This expanded test of the efficiency–job quality relationship confirms the initial efficiency findings (Table 5.8). The first factor (which we label "efficiency") continues to reflect the strong relationship between job quality and organizational efficiency practices, and the factor loadings on the measures of performance incentives are very low.[7]  This efficiency factor explains 43% of the variance among the variables and a second factor now accounts for another 22% of the variance in the data.[8]  We label this second factor "incentives,"

**Table 5.8  Factor Analysis of Job Quality, Efficiency Practices, and Performance Incentives**

| Variable | Efficiency factor loadings | Incentives factor loadings |
|---|---|---|
| JOBQUALITY | 0.66 | –0.53 |
| POWER | 0.59 | –0.31 |
| HIPARTICIP | 0.59 | –0.20 |
| SECURITY | 0.47 | –0.03 |
| HIWAGE | 0.10 | –0.49 |
| CONTINGENT | 0.37 | 0.82 |
| BONUS | 0.23 | 0.64 |
| KNOWPAY | 0.23 | 0.31 |
| PROFIT | 0.10 | 0.48 |
| QC | 0.75 | 0.11 |
| MEET | 0.78 | –0.09 |
| FLEX | 0.64 | 0.11 |
| TRAIN | 0.58 | 0.10 |
| EMPGRO | 0.50 | 0.11 |
| JAPAN | 0.62 | –0.02 |
| SIZE | 0.34 | –0.28 |
| Variance explained (%) | 43 | 22 |

because measures of contingent pay are prominent (i.e., have high factor loadings).

A key result shown by this incentives factor is that none of the performance-based compensation incentives is related to either the input measures of efficiency practices or to the output measure of business growth (the factor loadings on all of these variables are extremely low in the second factor). However, these performance-based incentives are strongly and inversely related to job quality, as reflected by the high negative factor loading on JOBQUALITY (–0.53). Moreover, among the job quality measures, HIWAGE (with a factor loading of –0.49) has the strongest negative relationship with incentive pay. What appears to be happening among the start-up firms in the sample is that various pay-for-performance incentives are being used as substitutes for paying high wages.

### Power and Job Quality

The second hypothesis to be examined is the relationship between employee power and job quality. The analysis of the efficiency factor has already demonstrated a relationship between JOBQUALITY and POWER in firms that adopt high performance management practices when POWER was included as an element of job quality (see Table 5.7). In order to conduct a more refined test of the power hypothesis, we test for a relationship between measures of power and measures of job quality (MODQUALITY) that exclude power.

According to this analysis, there is again only one significant factor, which explains 52% of the variance among the variables (Table 5.9).[9] We label this the "power" factor because POWER has the highest loading, with MODQUALITY being a close second. This confirms that there is a strong relationship between the empowerment of workers and the quality of jobs and that this relationship is robust to different definitions of job quality.

Looking at the separate components of POWER provides additional insights into how employee power shapes job quality. The loadings on these components show that the ability of employees to exercise voice through various kinds of participation in workplace decisions is significantly greater than is power exercised through unionization. Given the very few plants that are unionized in our sample, it is not surprising

**Table 5.9  Factor Analysis of Job Quality and Employee Power**

| Variable | Power factor loadings |
| --- | --- |
| MODQUALITY | 0.74 |
| HIPARTICIP | 0.70 |
| SECURITY | 0.44 |
| HIWAGE | 0.24 |
| POWER | 0.79 |
| QUALCONTROL | 0.67 |
| PEER | 0.58 |
| UNION | 0.10 |
| EMPGRO | 0.38 |
| JAPAN | 0.49 |
| SIZE | 0.20 |
| Variance explained (%) | 52 |

that the voice components of employee power are most directly associated with the quality of jobs in start-ups. Interestingly, these elements of employee power are more closely associated with improvements in job security and voice than with very high wages.

A further finding is that the factor loading on EMPGRO is positive but relatively low (0.38). This shows that worker power is more strongly related to job quality than to business performance, which is not surprising. What is also interesting is that the positive sign on the factor loading for the employment growth variable reaffirms that worker empowerment, as well as higher job quality, is positively associated with business growth. Japanese ownership remains moderately associated with job quality and power, showing that Japanese-owned start-ups offer better jobs and provide more worker empowerment.

## SUMMARY

While there is considerable evidence that the quality of jobs held by high school graduates in manufacturing has been declining in recent decades, the start-ups in our sample reveal a very different experience. These plants are generating new jobs for high school graduates that pay relatively high wages, provide considerable training, flexible work organization, substantial job security, opportunities for employee participation, and worker empowerment. If the sample of start-ups is representative of the types of technology, management strategies, and job quality among new branch manufacturing plants more generally, the newest generation of manufacturing plants may reverse the trend of declining job quality.

We pose three possible reasons why jobs in start-ups are of such high quality: 1) job quality is an incidental by-product of high performance management practices, 2) high quality jobs complement the efficiency effects of high performance management practices, and 3) job quality is rooted in the exercise of power by employees. The first reason may partly explain job quality, but the evidence for this interpretation is not fully consistent with the case study findings or with the economic theory of compensating wage differentials.

The explanation that high job quality contributes to efficiency is strongly supported by the factor analysis and by our interviews with start-ups. Start-ups that frequently use high performance management practices typically offer jobs of high quality and experience higher rates of growth. When we examine the role of high wages in contributing to high performance management practices and business growth, we find only marginal support for efficiency wage theories and for an efficiency effect of direct compensation incentives. However, the data reveal that performance-based wage incentives and high wages are substitutes for one another in the compensation strategies of start-ups.

While it is reassuring to find that high efficiency practices and business growth are linked to high job quality, the most surprising evidence is the importance of employee power in these new workplaces. Although our field research finds that start-ups often try to avoid unions and that managers have difficulty in ceding power to workers, employee power makes an important direct contribution to job quality.

Furthermore, employee power goes hand in hand with the adoption of high performance management practices, so that power also has an indirect influence on job quality, and these relationships are also associated with higher rates of employment growth.

Having established that start-ups are relatively intensive adopters of high performance management practices, that they provide very good jobs for high school graduates, and that they exhibit high rates of job growth, the next two chapters turn to the question of what regional characteristics attract the location of such high-performing start-ups. This analysis will show how the distinctive hybrid management systems adopted by Japanese transplants translate into different regional location preferences when compared with the location choices of domestic branch plants.

## Notes

1. Forty-four percent of the firms in our sample indicated an applicant's previous manufacturing experience was important in hiring decisions.
2. In technical terms, our data on workplace practices adopted by start-ups are affected by simultaneity biases, and we lack the exogenous variables needed to identify a structural model.
3. We also tested for industry differences, using both factor analysis and logit models. Industry differences were never found to be significant in any of the analyses, and thus we have dropped type of industry as a control.
4. The eigenvalue for the first factor is 4.10, and the difference between the second and third factors' eigenvalues is only 0.40, compared with a difference between the first and second factor eigenvalues of 2.92. A sudden drop in this difference implies that the subsequent eigenvalues are merely sampling noise (Jackson 1991). Moreover, even under the more liberal rules for retaining more factors (retain any factor with an eigenvalue greater than 1.0), there is only a marginal case for retaining two factors, because the second factor's eigenvalue is only 1.18.
5. We examine the efficiency wage thesis further in Chapter 8 and there we also find no evidence that high wages contribute to productivity growth.
6. Some authors have suggested that these advantages might be reduced by debilitating production speeds and high stress associated with Japanese-style management practices (Parker and Slaughter 1988), but our field research did not reveal any obvious examples of such adverse working conditions.
7. There is also a strong relationship between Japanese ownership and firms that use high performance practices, while the control variable for size has a low factor loading.
8. The eigenvalue for the first factor reported is 4.30, and the difference between the second and third factors' eigenvalues is only 1.18, compared with a difference

between the first and second factor eigenvalues of 2.09. This difference falls to 0.08 between the second and third factor eigenvalues, supporting the retention of two factors.

9. The eigenvalue for the factor reported is 3.14, and the difference between the second and third factors' eigenvalues is only 0.23, compared with a difference between the first and second factor eigenvalues of 1.91. Again, the second eigenvalue is only marginally greater than 1.0.

# Part III
# Defining Regional Advantage for
# High Performance Start-Ups

# 6
# High Performance
# and Regional Advantage

Many of the high performance management practices examined in Chapters 4 and 5 are affected by the local economic environment in which the firm operates. This is especially true for practices designed to raise labor productivity. Efficiency wages, for example, will have stronger effects when local unemployment rates and the costs of job loss are high; employee commitment will depend on the attitudes of the local workforce; and the choice of procedures for workforce participation in management decisions may be affected by whether or not unionization is likely. Because of these links between geography and the use and effectiveness of high performance practices, the location decisions of start-ups were explored thoroughly during the field research.

Location decisions turned out to rank among the most carefully analyzed of the strategic choices made by our sample of start-up plants. While all start-ups use a similar set of criteria in determining their location choices, the discussion of the case studies in Chapter 4 reveals dramatic differences between start-ups that adopt the hybrid model of workplace performance (primarily Japanese transplants) and those that rely on more eclectic piecemeal models (primarily domestic start-ups). Start-ups using hybrid models of high performance practices assign greater weight to some location factors than start-ups that follow more traditional management strategies, and in some cases, both groups valued similar factors, but for different reasons.

In this chapter, the location criteria used by Japanese transplants and domestic start-ups are examined to determine the extent to which they are linked to the adoption of the hybrid model or the more traditional piecemeal models of workplace management. The chapter begins with a review of the literature on plant location in order to identify the set of core factors that is typically found to be most important to firm location decisions. This is followed by a discussion of whether the findings from the case studies confirm the importance of these core location factors to start-ups in the sample or suggest alternative factors of equal or greater importance to their location decisions. In the following chapter, the importance of both the core location factors and the additional factors identified in the case studies are tested against actual location decisions of domestic and Japanese-owned start-ups.

## DEFINING "CORE" BUSINESS LOCATION FACTORS

There is a vast literature on business location decisions, including a number of comprehensive literature reviews (Herzog and Schlottmann 1991; Bartik 1991; Newman and Sullivan 1988; Wasylenko 1997; Evans-Klock, in preparation). Many different methodologies are used to study what matters in plant location. Some studies use opinion surveys that enumerate the reasons for location choices, while others rely on multivariate econometric techniques to test formal location models. Some of the latter studies explain differences in the growth of regional economies using state-level data (Doeringer, Terkla, and Topakian 1987), others look at employment changes in particular locations (Wasylenko and McGuire 1985; Quan and Beck 1987; McGuire and Wasylenko 1987; Carroll and Wasylenko 1994), and still others focus on the location decisions of new plants (Bartik 1985, 1989; Levinson 1996; Papke 1991). Location decisions are analyzed by regional, state, or local areas, and some studies characterize location decisions as being made in two stages, in which a state or region is selected first, followed by the choice of a specific locality (Schmenner, Huber, and Cook 1987).

This mix of methodologies notwithstanding, most studies are based on the standard economic theory of business location, which assumes that locations are chosen so as to maximize profits, subject to the constraints of location-specific costs. According to this theory, business location choices should primarily reflect considerations such as proximity to markets, costs of local factor inputs, business climate factors (such as state and local taxes), and access to transportation networks.

Standard location theory is consistent with firm-specific managerial strategies having an influence on location decisions. For example, a firm may evaluate a location in terms of its ability to enhance the implementation of efficient employment practices or maintain cost-reducing relationships with customers or suppliers. Firms that adopt high performance workplace strategies may seek different labor market environments from those that rely on financial incentives and managerial authority to control productivity.

The effects of different management strategies, however, are rarely explored in either the theoretical or empirical location literatures. Most studies implicitly assume that management practices are uniform across firms or relatively unimportant to the location decision process, and they focus instead on the differential effects of various cost factors (Chapman and Walker 1987; Schmenner 1982).

In general, these studies incorporate a set of "core" location factors that typically include measures of taxes, wages, education levels, proximity to markets, accessibility of transportation networks, unionization, and agglomeration economies. Some findings, such as the positive effect of proximity to markets and the negative effect of unions, are almost universal across studies. Other findings, including the effects of taxes and wage costs, vary according to what other factors are included in the location model, how the variables are defined, what statistical procedures are adopted, what database is used, and what period of time is covered by the data. While these differences among studies often make meaningful comparisons difficult, the following section summarizes the factors that commonly and consistently matter most to business location (Bartik 1991; Wasylenko 1997).

## Labor Market Factors

Labor market factors are widely perceived as central to understanding business location decisions. The most common labor market factors examined in the location literature are wages, labor force quality, and unionization.

### Wages

The importance of wages to business location is often reported by business surveys, which typically find that wages matter most in "first cut" decisions such as the choice of geographic region or of a rural or urban locale. Other labor market factors may then exert a stronger influence on the "second cut" choice of a specific location (Herzog and Schlottmann 1991). Bartik's (1991) survey of the econometric evidence confirmed that the influence of wage differentials on business location is well established. However, the magnitude of wage effects is far smaller than might be expected, and studies often have found that wages have no significant effect on location (Schmenner, Huber, and Cook 1987; Levinson 1996). Typical explanations for these anomalies involve inadequate measures of wages actually paid by new firms (Wasylenko 1997) and the inability to adjust wages for labor quality.

### Labor Force Quality

A second widely held view is that workforce quality and labor productivity are major concerns for business location decisions (Herzog and Schlottmann 1991). As Newman and Sullivan (1988) noted, "It is inappropriate to say that labor-cost oriented firms will locate where wages are low, but rather where they are low relative to productivity." Despite the consensus that labor quality is important, there is considerable debate over how workforce quality and productivity are best measured.[1]

Professional location consultants, for example, report that start-ups will often request detailed information on the fiscal resources devoted to education, the types of skill training programs that are available, and measures of student performance (Ady 1997). The availability of post-secondary education and the quality of local collaborations between business and education may also be important. Econometric location studies typically attempt to capture these influences through various measures of education attainment and education expenditures, but such measures rarely appear to be significant to location choices. For example, Bartik (1985) and Levinson (1996) found no effect of median years of education on location choice, while Schmenner, Huber, and Cook (1987) found that higher high school graduation rates are negatively associated with business location.[2]

### Unions

A third dimension of labor quality is the adversarial characteristics and future wage pressures that are associated with a unionized workforce. Most studies in the last two decades have found that firms avoid locating in areas where unions are powerful (Bartik 1985; Plaut and

Pluta 1983; Schmenner, Huber, and Cook 1987),[3] and this union effect may be quite strong   Bartik, for example, concluded that a 10% reduction in the rate of unionization in a state is expected to lead to a 30–40% increase in the location rates of new branch plants.[4]

## State and Local Taxes

Taxes are a second prominent element addressed by research on business location decisions.  While most studies focus on corporate income taxes, some have also examined the influence of personal income and sales taxes.  The case study and survey evidence, however, usually find that taxes are relatively unimportant relative to other factors (Herzog and Schlottmann 1991; Kieschnick 1981; Crandall 1993).  Econometric evidence has traditionally supported similar conclusions, but more recent studies reopen this question.

Bartik (1991), for example, concluded that there is "some evidence of significant negative effects of state and local taxes on regional business growth" (p. 38), and a more recent review by Wasylenko (1997) reported that 24 of 34 studies surveyed find a statistically significant effect of taxes on business location.  However, Wasylenko also reported that the estimated size of these tax effects varies considerably.  Roughly equal numbers of well-designed studies using similar methodologies find very small or statistically insignificant tax effects (Carroll and Wasylenko 1994; Schmenner 1982; McGuire and Wasylenko 1987) as find large tax effects (Bartik 1989; McConnell and Schwab 1990; Papke 1991; Wasylenko and McGuire 1985).

Wasylenko also found some evidence that the influence of taxes on location declined between the 1970s and the 1980s as effective rates of taxation among states converged (Carroll and Wasylenko 1994).  Bartik (1985) reported that property taxes have a small impact on business location decisions, but Schmenner, Huber, and Cook (1987) found no significant effect of property taxes on the choice of the state in which to locate branch plants.  Some authors have also argued that the negative impact of taxes depends on whether revenues raised are matched by government expenditures on infrastructure or other areas that enhance business profitability (Bartik 1991), but statistical studies that include both tax and spending levels have yielded a wide range of ambiguous and contradictory findings (Fisher 1997; Bartik 1985; Ondrich and Wasylenko 1993).[5]

Other government-imposed costs on business, such as unemployment insurance or workers compensation, have generally not been found to be important (Bartik 1985; Schmenner, Huber, and Cook 1987). Similarly, environmental regulations have been considered to be an implicit tax on business, but their effects on location are found to be relatively unimportant because they are small in proportion to other business costs and are often countered by higher environmental quality (Bartik 1991; McConnell and Schwab 1990; Levinson 1996).

### Market Size and Access

There is a clear consensus that proximity and access to large markets are important determinants of business location. Herzog and Schlottmann (1991), for example, concluded that the size of regional markets and the availability of a good transportation infrastructure are two of the three most important influences on location (the third being labor quality).

Market size is typically measured by the amount of personal income in a state or region. The most reliable measure of proximity to large markets used in the literature is personal income that is then "gravity weighted" by the distances among these states. This variable is correlated with both business location in general (Plaut and Pluta 1983) and with foreign-owned plant location (Friedman, Gerlowski, and Silberman 1992; Woodward 1992). Population, average personal income, and population growth are also used as proxies for market size, but the estimated effects of such variables are often inconsistent (Bartik 1985; Schmenner, Huber, and Cook 1987).

Case studies of business location find that highway access is the most commonly reported indicator used to measure access to markets. Its importance is confirmed by econometric studies, which regularly conclude that the number of interstate highway connections influences the likelihood of branch plants locating in a region (Bartik 1985; Levinson 1996.)[6]

## Agglomeration Externalities

Locating in areas with a critical mass of manufacturing firms may provide firms with valuable pools of trained labor, proximity to potential suppliers or customers, and just-in-time supply opportunities that can lower their production costs. There is a general consensus, among both econometric and field research studies, that such agglomerations of manufacturing plants are a significant determinant of business location (Wasylenko 1997; Bartik 1985; Levinson 1996).[7] Typically, the extent of general manufacturing activity in a region (as measured by manufacturing hours or the number of production workers per square mile) is used as a measure of agglomeration economies. This agglomeration measure, however, is typically so highly correlated with market size that most studies include only one of these measures.

## Other Location Factors

Labor markets, taxes, transportation, proximity to markets, and agglomeration economies are the factors that most frequently appear in the literature on business location. However, numerous other variables are sometimes incorporated into location analyses to augment these core factors.

Bartik (1985), for example, argued that the total number of potentially attractive location sites is a function of the geographic size of the state. Other things being equal, the larger the state, the higher the probability of the state being selected by a firm. Bartik finds evidence in support of this "dartboard" theory of business location by showing that a 10% increase in state land area, other things being equal, results in a proportionate increase in the number of new plants. Variables measuring the land area of states are becoming a standard component of the core location model.

Another obvious candidate for inclusion as a core location factor is state and local economic development incentives. However, one of the most comprehensive studies of this issue (Luger 1987) concluded that location incentives have only a marginal effect on business location.[8] A more recent study of business taxes and incentives (Fisher and Peters 1998) found that location rankings by tax burden in the early 1990s did not change materially after taking a broad range of non-tax incentives for business recruitment or expansion into account, even though such incentives may be substantial.[9]

Energy costs are a third possibility. After the OPEC crises of the 1970s, the role of regional differences in energy costs also received considerable attention. Common measures of energy costs include direct measures of electricity prices and usage estimates based on temperature or climate (Doeringer, Terkla, and Topakian, 1987). Energy costs and climate, however, are highly correlated. Meteorological measures of climate are often preferred to energy because climate also captures the effects of inclement weather on transportation, and it can also serve as an indicator of the quality of life. Many econometric models find that climate variables are significant (Bartik 1985; Schmenner, Huber, and Cook 1987), but climate is not usually ranked as a crucial location factor in business surveys.

A few studies augment the core location factors with various industry and firm characteristics, such as size of firm, capital intensity, type of production process (mass production, continuous process, batch production, custom production), and the skill makeup of the workforce. One study, for example, concluded that large plants are more likely to be concerned about the effects of unionization and high wages than are small plants, but that high wages are positively correlated with the location of capital-intensive plants (Schmenner, Huber, and Cook 1987).[10] Similarly, high education levels matter to start-ups with R&D facilities, but not to plants that use assembly line technologies.

Other studies approximate firm-specific characteristics by examining location preferences of plants grouped by industry. Papke (1991), for example, found that there are industry differences in the sensitivity of the location decisions to wages and taxes from a comparison of five 3-digit industries.[11] Similarly, Markusen, Hall, and Glasmeier (1986) found that plants in three-digit high technology industries place more emphasis on climate and on education opportunities in making location decisions than they do on the traditional labor market characteristics that are important to other industries.

Despite these widespread tests of more complex location models, the only variable that comes close to qualifying as an addition to the core location model is a measure of the geographic size of states based on Bartik's dartboard theory. However, these more complex models do raise the possibility of there being numerous other factors that could collectively have a substantial impact on business location. One device often used to control for the combined effects of the miscellaneous regional factors that are omitted from location models is the inclusion of regional dummy variables. Such variables are often significant, but they do not explain what important elements of the location decision are missing.[12]

## CORE LOCATION CRITERIA
## FOR JAPANESE TRANSPLANTS

Most of the findings on business location in the United States represent the location decisions of domestic companies because of their overwhelming numerical dominance compared to foreign-owned businesses. There is, however, a small literature on the location of Japanese transplants that could hold clues for whether there are significant differences in the location criteria of manufacturing plants that use different management strategies from those of the typical domestic start-up.

The dearth of these studies and the widely different methodologies employed, however, make it difficult to draw general conclusions about the location decisions of Japanese transplants. Nevertheless, this literature suggests that there are likely to be some differences between the location criteria used by Japanese transplants and domestic start-ups, as well as a number of elements that both types of plants share in common.

A recent survey comparing the location decisions of Japanese and domestic firms, for example, found that Japanese firms place a greater weight on the general community environment and market logistics (transportation services, proximity to suppliers), and less weight on taxes and development incentives, than do domestic firms (Ulgado 1996).[13] This finding about the importance of development incentives, however, contradicts Kujawa (1986), who reported that a state government's industrial recruitment effort is the most important location factor considered by Japanese transplants.

The general impression from this literature is that Japanese transplants value many of the same core location criteria used by domestic businesses. Kujawa (1986), for example, reported that Japanese transplants consider workforce quality second only to recruitment efforts by government agencies as the most important location consideration, followed by proximity to suppliers and amenities for Japanese expatriate personnel. These themes of workforce quality and product market logistics are further confirmed by Yoshida (1987) in his study of high-tech greenfield plants. Yoshida found that managers rank quality of labor, proximity to markets, and low unionization as the most important location factors.

## Labor Market Factors

Almost without exception, studies indicate that Japanese firms weigh labor market factors heavily in their location choices. Case studies of Japanese transplants (Kujawa 1986; Yoshida 1987) routinely report that labor quality is of the highest priority to Japanese firms when choosing plant locations, and Woodward (1992) provided econometric support for location probabilities being positively associated with productivity levels. However, as in the literature on the location decisions of domestic plants, there is no consistent view of how workforce "quality" should be measured.

The most frequently reported complaints about labor quality involve the ability of U.S. workers to adapt to Japanese workplace practices (Haitani and Marquis 1990). Similarly, Milkman (1991) reported that Japanese electronics firms place high priority on tractable labor. This "labor quality" thesis may explain why Japanese transplants often seek to locate in medium-sized towns and less-unionized rural areas that they believe offer an ample quantity of workers with a "good work ethic" (Abo 1994; Reid 1989; Mair, Florida, and Kenney 1988).

Econometric studies of the location of Japanese transplants typically use education levels as their measure of workforce quality, and the results often confirm the relevance of the availability of a pool of educated workers. Smith and Florida (1994) found a positive effect of high school graduation rates across U.S. counties, and Woodward (1992) found that higher median years of education is associated with the choice of county within a group of "auto alley" states, but not elsewhere.

Econometric studies often differ in their conclusions about the importance of wages. Friedman, Gerlowski, and Silberman (1992) found a substantial negative effect of wages in their state location model (but the specification of their model is somewhat suspect because it also shows unionization rates have a positive effect on location). Woodward (1992) reported that neither state nor county wage rates matter to the location of Japanese transplants, and Smith and Florida (1994) reported that Japanese firms prefer counties with higher wages, after controlling for education.[14]

Case studies that compare the locations of Japanese and domestic start-ups often conclude that Japanese and domestic firms have very similar preferences for avoiding unionization (Freed 1990; Milkman 1991). Milkman also reported that both Japanese and domestic firms in California consider relatively weak levels of unionization to be a prime location asset.[15] Econometric studies regularly find that higher unionization rates are associated with lower selection probabilities at the state level (Woodward 1992; Friedman, Gerlowski, and Silberman 1992). However, Smith and Florida (1994) found tentative evidence of a significant correlation between unionization and location at the county level.

## State and Local Taxes

Standard corporate taxes are not found to be a significant factor in the location of Japanese transplants (Yoshida 1987; Kujawa 1986; Haigh 1990; Chernotsky 1983.)[16] However, branch plants of foreign multinationals in some states are also affected by special "unitary" taxes that apply to all profits, regardless of where they are earned. Friedman, Gerlowski, and Silberman (1992) found no unitary tax effect on the location of Japanese transplants, while Woodward (1992) found that unitary taxation reduces location probabilities. The evidence on other types of taxes is also mixed. Friedman, Gerlowski, and Silberman (1992) and Smith and Florida (1994) found a large negative effect of personal tax burdens, while Woodward (1992) found that neither property taxes nor unemployment taxes matter in the location of Japanese transplants.

## Market Size and Access

Both survey data and statistical evidence show that market size and access are positively associated with the location of Japanese transplants. Based on evidence gathered in her plant questionnaire and factory interviews, Milkman (1991) reported that serving the large California market is the principal drawing factor for both Japanese and U.S. firms choosing California. Surveys of Japanese plants in the southeastern United States also found that the rapidly growing regional market and good transportation networks are the largest contributors to those states' success in recruiting Japanese investors (Haigh 1990; Chernotsky 1983). A "gravity-adjusted" market size variable is significant and positive in the state level econometric studies of Woodward (1992) and Friedman, Gerlowski, and Silberman (1992), although the estimated effect is large only in the Woodward model. There is also evidence that transportation infrastructure is important, although different measures are often used (Smith and Florida 1994; Woodward 1992; Friedman, Gerlowski, and Silberman 1992).

## Agglomeration Economies

There is evidence that agglomeration economies also matter to location. Woodward (1992), for example, found a strong relationship between overall manufacturing activity at the county level and the location of Japanese transplants. A second study (Head, Ries, and Swenson 1995) concluded that both U.S. and Japanese manufacturing activity attract Japanese factory location in the same industry.

## Agglomeration Externalities

One thread that also runs through many of these studies is that special location considerations may affect Japanese transplants in particular industries. Japanese auto supplier transplants are most frequently singled out as having unique location concerns related to auto assembly plants. Japanese auto supplier transplants, for example, often follow Japanese auto assembly investments in the United States and may choose locations that will facilitate the scheduling and delivery requirements of just-in-time (JIT) supply relationships (Head, Ries, and Swenson 1995).[17] A number of studies confirm that linkages to Japanese auto assemblers are important (Smith and Florida 1994; Abo 1994; Reid 1989; Mair, Florida, and Kenney 1988; MacDuffie and Helper 1999).

However, these studies also find that proximity to the U.S. auto assemblers and parts suppliers is important, and our interviews show that JIT-based location strategies do not require immediate proximity to customers. JIT requirements can be met within a radius of up to 250 miles, provided good transportation networks are available. Conversely, there are reports of auto parts plants deliberately distancing themselves from other Japanese firms to avoid driving up wages for high-quality workers or creating a too-visible Japanese presence (Reid 1989).

The high technology industry is also sometimes cited as having distinctive location concerns (Kenney and Florida 1993). One hypothesis is that high technology firms favor areas with a high concentration of technical workers. Another is that they locate near major high technology research centers to gain access to state-of-the-art research.

**Other Factors**

Case studies frequently document the importance of intangible location assets, such as good working relationships with government. Industrial recruitment efforts by states, for example, are valued by Japanese executives because they signal that state and local government can be counted on to resolve problems that might arise during the start-up or later operation of the plant (Milward and Newman 1989), rather than because of their explicit economic value.[18] The statistical evidence, however, is divided on whether state industrial recruitment matters. Friedman, Gerlowski, and Silberman (1992) found a large positive effect of state spending on efforts to attract foreign investors, while Woodward (1992) found no effect.[19]

Other intangible factors mentioned in the literature include amenities for employees such as education opportunities for their children and low crime rates (Nakabayashi 1987; Kujawa 1986; Yoshida 1987; Haigh 1990). Some studies also suggest that proximity to Japan may matter, as evidenced by the high concentration of Japanese transplants in California (Milkman 1991; Woodward 1992; Friedman, Gerlowski, and Silberman 1992).[20]

Regional dummy variables provide a partial test of the importance of intangible factors that cannot be explicitly incorporated into location models. Woodward (1992), for example, found that the East North-Central and East South-Central regions comprising the auto alley also have a demonstrable attraction for Japanese firms after controlling for other location attributes.[21]

## EVIDENCE FROM THE CASE STUDIES

The preceding review of survey and econometric studies of business location identifies a set of criteria—labor market factors, market access, agglomeration economies, and land area—that are thought to be central to business location decisions. While there are a few studies that point to factors (such as unitary taxes or proximity to an international airport) that uniquely affect the location of Japanese transplants, these transplants generally appear to value many of the same core location criteria as their domestic counterparts.

Our field research provides an opportunity to probe further the location decisions of start-up factories, particularly with respect to the relationship between business location and high performance management strategies. During our interviews with managers of start-ups, we explored why specific location factors matter and whether there are differences between Japanese transplants and domestic start-ups.

In general, the case studies corroborate much of the literature on business location decisions.[22] Both the Japanese transplants and domestic start-ups typically follow a two-stage location search process: firms select a state or region based primarily on a set of factors that includes many of the standard location criteria, and then they select a specific site within the region that meets additional secondary location criteria. Proximity to customers, highway access, unionization, wages, and labor supply ranked among the location factors that were most frequently mentioned as important by both groups of start-ups, and both ranked taxes considerably less often (Table 6.1).

The role of the labor market environment in location decisions is particularly striking. Among factors that were mentioned as important by 30% or more of the Japanese transplants and domestic start-ups, about half are related to labor market considerations (Tables 6.1 and 6.2).

The size of regional markets, unitary taxes, and agglomeration economies are in the second tier of location factors (factors that are considered important by 16% to 30% of the plants surveyed) among Japanese transplants, while regional market size, site availability, and development incentives are second-tier considerations for domestic start-ups (Tables 6.1 and 6.2). Both groups also place "warm climate" in this category. Both Japanese transplants and domestic start-ups rank energy costs, land prices, and low urbanization among the least important location considerations (those ranked as important by 15% or less of the firms interviewed).

While the frequency and ranking of the importance of different location factors varies somewhat between Japanese transplants and domestic start-ups, the overall pattern is quite similar. Among the 24 location factors identified in the field research, the differences between Japanese and domestic start-ups are statistically significant for only five factors (Table 6.2). Among these five factors, unitary taxes and the presence of a Japanese population are irrelevant to domestic start-ups, and it is not surprising that access to international airports is more highly valued by Japanese transplants.

In contrast, the other two distinctive factors involve decisions about business strategy. The business climate, as measured by the hospitable attitudes of state governments, is particularly important to Japanese transplants, as are labor force quality indicators such as the availability of workers with high school degrees.[23] As the following sections will show, there is a more complex explanation of the location decisions of each group of new factories that focuses on labor market influences and which departs in several respects from the standard location literature.

### The Location Choices of Domestic Start-Ups

Labor supply and freedom from unionization were the location criteria most frequently mentioned by managers of domestic start-ups, and there was widespread agreement that labor costs mattered to location decisions. However, there was far less agreement on how labor costs should be defined. Only one-third of the domestic start-ups, for

**Table 6.1  Ranking of Location Criteria ( % of managers identifying location attributes as important)**

| Japanese transplants | | | Domestic start-ups | | |
|---|---|---|---|---|---|
| Rank | % | Attribute | Rank | % | Attribute |
| 1 | 61 | Highway access, unionization | 1 | 55 | Labor supply |
| 2 | 43 | Airport access, local government relations | 2 | 50 | Unionization |
| 3 | 39 | Proximity to main customer(s), state welcoming efforts | 3 | 45 | Highway access |
| 4 | 36 | Labor supply, state training programs, work ethic | 4 | 35 | Amenities, wages, proximity to main customer(s) |
| 5 | 32 | Wages, Japanese population | 5 | 30 | Agglomeration, supply of professionals/ technicians |
| 6 | 29 | Education | 6 | 25 | Work ethic, warm climate |
| 7 | 25 | Agglomeration, amenities, no unitary tax, regional market size, warm climate | 7 | 20 | Financial incentives, site/ building availability, regional market size |
| 8 | 21 | Supply of professionals/ technicians | 8 | 15 | Corporate tax rate, local govt. relations |
| 9 | 18 | Site/building availability | 9 | 10 | State training programs, land prices |
| 10 | 14 | Financial incentives Land prices | 10 | 5 | Airport access, state welcoming efforts, energy costs, education, low urbanization |
| 11 | 11 | Low urbanization | 11 | 0 | No unitary tax, Japanese population |
| 12 | 7 | Corporate tax rate | | | |
| 13 | 4 | Energy costs | | | |

**Table 6.2  Important Location Criteria by Category (% of managers identifying location attributes as important)**

| Attribute | % of Japanese transplants | % of domestic start-ups |
|---|---|---|
| Labor factors | | |
| Low unionization | 61 | 50 |
| Labor supply | 36 | 55 |
| Work ethic | 36 | 25 |
| Wages | 32 | 35 |
| Education | 29** | 5 |
| Supply of professionals/technicians | 21 | 30 |
| Business climate factors | | |
| Local government relations | 43 | 15 |
| State welcoming efforts | 39*** | 5 |
| State training programs | 36 | 10 |
| No unitary tax | 25** | 0 |
| Financial incentives | 14 | 20 |
| Corporate tax rate | 7 | 15 |
| Market size and access factors | | |
| Highway access | 61 | 45 |
| Airport access | 43*** | 5 |
| Proximity to main customer(s) | 39 | 35 |
| Regional market size | 25 | 20 |
| Agglomeration | 25 | 30 |
| Other factors | | |
| Japanese population | 32*** | 0 |
| Amenities | 25 | 35 |
| Warm climate | 18 | 20 |
| Land prices | 14 | 10 |
| Low urbanization | 11 | 5 |
| Energy costs | 4 | 5 |

NOTE: Chi-square test, with Yate's continuity correction and Fisher's Exact Test when expected frequency is less than five in any cell of the $2 \times 2$ table, comparing the share of interviewed managers in each national group that considered the attribute to be important.  *** = Statistically significant at the 0.01 level; ** = statistically significant at the 0.05 level.

SOURCE: Authors' survey.

example, reported that average wage rates in manufacturing were an important consideration in selecting the locations. Even among the start-ups that were the most cost-conscious (those that were explicitly avoiding what they described as "high-cost" states), this fraction only rises to 43%.

The availability of an adequate labor supply was the most frequently mentioned labor market factor. However, upon closer examination, most of the start-ups that are concerned with labor availability use it as an indicator of the *future* labor force at different locations. Their intention was to locate where the pool of available workers was large enough to meet the long-term labor needs of a new plant that might expand in the future, without driving up wages.

The second most influential labor factor was the likelihood of unionization, reported as an important location consideration by half of the domestic start-ups. Domestic start-ups in Georgia were particularly attracted by Georgia's low unionization rate (13.6% of production workers in manufacturing, compared with the national average of 20.5%), and they often cited Georgia's right-to-work and employment-at-will policies as indicating a low probability of unionization in their new plants. Most of the domestic start-ups sought to avoid the constraints on management prerogatives and the potential for work stoppages that they associated with unions, as well as the effect that unions might have on wages. The preference for avoiding unions was most pronounced among the most cost-conscious domestic plants, where 70% mentioned unionization rates as being important to location.

Automotive suppliers were particularly sensitive to the possibility of unionization. Sixty-two percent of the domestic automotive suppliers mentioned unionization as important to their location decisions. They considered themselves to be at risk of being targeted for an organization campaign because of the high unionization rate in the auto industry and because of their relatively large size and visibility.

Somewhat surprisingly, the education levels of the workforce were considered important by only 5% of the domestic start-ups. This lack of interest in education was typically explained by the expectation that the high wages and good working conditions of start-ups would be sufficient to attract adequate numbers of workers with high school degrees to meet staffing needs.

A larger fraction (25%) mentioned the importance of the local work ethic when selecting new plant locations. However, there was no consistent definition of what the term *work ethic* meant. It was variously defined as a low probability of quitting, a long-standing attachment to the area, familiarity with factory work, and the absence of pro-union sympathies.

Among location factors other than those related to labor concerns, the most frequently mentioned was proximity to markets, as measured both by good access to interstate highways (45%) and proximity to major customers (35%). In addition, one in five domestic start-ups identified the size of the regional market as being important (see Table 6.1).

Access to agglomeration economies, as reflected by the presence of other manufacturing companies, appears to be moderately important for location. About one-third of the sample preferred to locate in areas with a critical mass of manufacturing activity. Fiscal concerns are at the low end of the range; only 15% of the domestic start-ups cited corporate tax rate differentials as an important influence on location selection.[24]

Non-economic factors, such as local amenities that make transfers attractive for corporate personnel, are taken into account by about one-third of all domestic start-ups. In addition, opinions about the importance of climate, which are often interpreted as a proxy for the quality of the living and recreational environment, varied by region. Most managers in Georgia said climate was a positive factor, while most of those in the Northeast said it did not matter. Two of the domestic start-up manufacturing plants also had R&D responsibilities for developing new technologies and products and placed a high priority on locations close to scientific or industrial research centers with large supplies of professional workers.

## Comparisons with the Location Choices of Japanese Transplants

Despite the many similarities among the location criteria reported as important by both Japanese transplants and domestic start-ups, the case study interviews show that factors such as proximity to key customers and workforce cost and quality take on a very different meaning for Japanese transplants. These and other differences between Japanese transplants and domestic start-ups strongly suggest that those factories that are most likely to adopt the hybrid model of high performance practices (i.e., the Japanese transplants in the sample) define regional advantage differently from those start-ups that are managed more traditionally.

### Labor market factors

Japanese transplants mentioned the importance of some labor market factors (unionization, work ethic, and education) with slightly greater frequency than did domestic start-ups (see Table 6.2). However, the distinctive role that labor market factors play in the location of Japanese transplants comes through even more strongly in the interviews.

The case studies make it abundantly clear that labor market factors are the most prominent considerations in the location decisions of Japanese transplants, and these are the factors where the sharpest contrasts with domestic start-ups are found. Unlike domestic start-ups that see labor market influences primarily in terms of wage costs, work stoppages, and limitations on management prerogatives, Japanese transplants are most concerned with how labor market factors affect productivity and labor efficiency.

A low rate of unionization is the location factor most frequently mentioned by Japanese transplants and was considered important by three out of five of the managers interviewed. Unionization was mentioned twice as often as wages, which were reported as important by only one-third of the Japanese transplants. Managers at the Japanese transplants emphasized more strongly than did those at domestic plants the widespread effect that they felt unions would have on their ability to implement high performance management strategies.

They were concerned, for example, that collective representation of their employees by unions would inhibit individual workers from making suggestions or providing assistance in solving production and quality control problems. They felt that union work rules would decrease flexibility in organizing work, that formalized layoff procedures in union contracts would interfere with more creative alternatives to layoffs, and that strikes could disrupt just-in-time delivery schedules.[25] More broadly, the managers of Japanese transplants reported that unions would interfere with their employees' loyalty to the objectives of the firm and their trust in management to share fairly the benefits of strong business performance.

Avoidance of unions was also the reason that some managers of Japanese transplants gave for favoring rural locations, where they felt it was less likely that workers would have worked in union settings or harbor pro-union sentiments. Others chose medium-sized cities or counties neighboring larger cities in order to minimize the risk of attracting union organizing efforts by not being the largest company in the area.

Low wages were rated as important by less than one-third of the Japanese transplants, substantially below the concern with unionization. The importance of unionization relative to wages was even more dramatic among the Japanese transplants that supplied the automobile industry. Among the Japanese auto-industry transplants, only 11% considered wage rates to be an important location factor, compared with 66% who cited unionization.

About one-third of the Japanese transplants identified the availability of labor supply (36%), good work ethic (36%), and education levels (29%) as important to location.[26] Unlike domestic start-ups that often equate these criteria with labor costs and productive skills, the interviews show that Japanese transplants consider large pools of high-quality labor to be central to their workplace performance strategies. As documented in Chapter 4, Japanese transplants are typically interested in hiring workers with the ability to learn, an aptitude for teamwork, and a strong work ethic. Workplace training is intensive, and Japanese transplants seek to secure the returns to such investments by hiring workers who will be loyal and committed to the company. Attracting and keeping the "right" workers, rather than minimizing wage costs, is their preeminent concern in both their location decisions and their workplace management practices.

One such quality measure, a high school education or its equivalent, was universally required of job applicants and was rated as important much more frequently by Japanese transplants than by domestic start-ups. Education, however, is seen as reflecting qualities such as basic literacy, work attitudes, and the ability to learn on the job, rather than as a source of productive knowledge.[27] Even government-sponsored skill training programs, which were identified as important to location three times as often by Japanese transplants as by domestic start-ups, are valued for the opportunity for companies to screen workers for preferred attitudes rather than for the skills that they provide.

A good work ethic is important to Japanese transplants more frequently than the level of education. When asked to define what they mean by *work ethic*, managers of the Japanese transplants typically report qualities such as flexibility, ability to learn, motivation, loyalty, and capacity to work in teams. These are the same qualities for which they use education as a screening criterion and to which they attach importance in implementing their high performance management strategies. One manager described his preferences for hiring workers who were flexible about work assignments, able to accept training for a variety of tasks, and willing to take responsibility for the quality of their work.

These worker qualities provide an essential foundation for the intensive training investments provided by Japanese transplants. Because of their greater investment in worker training, managers of Japanese plants expressed a greater interest in locating in areas (such as those that are rural) where workers are thought to be less prone to turnover than did their domestic counterparts.[28] For example, one manager of a domestic plant in Georgia considered an annual turnover rate of 18% acceptable, while managers of Japanese transplants in Georgia complained if their turnover rate was as high as 5%.

The importance of work attitudes and aptitudes as a basis for intensive training by Japanese transplants can also be seen in the role of work experience as a criterion for plant location. Japanese transplants had little interest in locating in areas with a concentration of industries that used similar skills, and such work experience was even considered a disadvantage, because old workplace habits might interfere with learning. One manager summed it up by explaining that they were looking for "good," as opposed to "skilled," workers.

While managers of domestic start-ups typically valued many of these same characteristics, they did so primarily from the perspective of minimizing direct labor costs rather than improving productivity. They spent less time in screening job applicants and gave more weight to skills that workers had learned in school and through prior work experience than did Japanese transplants. Managers at domestic start-ups were also much more likely to view previous work experience in the same industry or with similar technologies as an indicator of ability to perform well in their own plant. The presence of other firms in the area in similar lines of work was often taken as an indicator of a high probability of finding applicants with preferred characteristics.

### Nonlabor location factors

Despite the qualitative importance of labor practices to the high performance strategies of Japanese transplants, four of the top five most frequently mentioned location concerns involve nonlabor factors (see Table 6.2). These are good access to highways (61%), the availability of a large international airport (43%), relationships with local governments (43%) and state governments (39%), and proximity to customers (39%). Highway and airport access are mentioned with substantially greater frequency than by domestic start-ups, with the presence of a major international airport being important for executive travel between the transplants and their parent companies in Japan.[29]

The combination of good highway networks and proximity to customers is indicative of the importance of just-in-time production and supply strategies among Japanese transplants, particularly among suppliers of Japanese auto assembly plants in Tennessee, Kentucky, Ohio, or Indiana.[30] Japanese transplants typically seek to keep shipping times to eight hours or less to ensure the ability to meet quality control standards by maintaining close cooperation with their customers.

These auto parts suppliers were four times as likely as start-ups in other industries to consider proximity to a main customer an important factor in location selection.[31] While domestic start-ups also favor good transportation networks that facilitate delivery of supplies and shipments to customers, they do not report the same intensity of commitment to just-in-time logistics.

Among the nonlabor factors that influence location, the sharpest contrast between Japanese transplants and domestic start-ups is in the criteria for the quality of local governmental relations (43% vs. 15%), and efforts by state governments to welcome Japanese transplants (39% vs. 5%). Japanese transplants looked for indications that the state and local government and the business community would be cooperative and helpful in setting up operations, as signaled by the welcome extended to corporate executives in site visits, facilitation of

Japanese investments by a state government office located in Japan, and state assistance for training new workers.[32]

Quality of life factors (climate, recreation facilities, proximity to a sizeable Japanese community with Japanese-language schools and social organizations, and good schools for the children of American managers) were taken into account by between one-fourth and one-third of the Japanese transplants. Warm climate was also mentioned by some plants as conferring a production advantage in terms of the transferability of technology and equipment from Japan to locations in the United States with similar temperature and humidity conditions.

As with the domestic start-ups, factors such as taxes, location subsidies, land prices, and energy costs were much less frequently ranked as important by Japanese transplants.[33] Only one-fourth of the managers considered freedom from unitary taxes (which particularly affect foreign-owned plants) as an important element in choosing states in which to locate, and corporate tax rates were mentioned by only 10% of the Japanese transplants.

There were also a few Japanese transplants whose location preferences were strongly influenced by special factors that were rarely, if ever, mentioned by their domestic counterparts in our sample. One group was high-technology transplants that were heavily involved in R&D activities and whose location decisions were shaped by proximity to research institutions and to the availability of scientific and technical labor.[34] For example, a computer equipment manufacturer had established facilities in Massachusetts in order to develop ties to the Massachusetts Institute of Technology, conduct research on the U.S. market, and provide technical and market advice to its parent plant in Japan. A second group consisted of transplants that located in the New York City area to be close to their U.S. corporate headquarters.

## REGIONAL ADVANTAGE FOR START-UP FACTORIES

The literature on business location highlights a set of core factors that are likely to be important to location choices. Tabulations of those location factors used most frequently by the start-ups in our case studies largely confirm the relevance of these core factors for both Japanese transplants and domestic start-ups. Of the 24 location factors identified in the field research, three-fourths are reported with similar frequency for both groups of new plants.

However, even for this modest-sized sample of plants, the differences in location strategies of Japanese transplants and domestic start-ups are quite apparent and reveal substantial divergence in the way that these two groups of new factories define regional advantage. Labor force quality indicators, such as education levels and the availability of training programs, are significantly more important to Japanese transplants than to domestic start-ups, and these labor quality differences are even more sharply revealed in the interview findings. The second distinctive feature of regional advantage for Japanese transplants is the business climate, as measured by the hospitable attitudes of state and local governments.

In comparison, regional advantages for the domestic start-ups that adopt relatively more traditional management strategies tend to be the standard ones identified in the plant location literature: an adequate supply of workers for factory work and in professional occupations, and amenities for management personnel moved into the area from the company's other locations. Wage rates and agglomeration appear to be considered of equal importance by both domestic and Japanese plants.

For the group of start-ups that adopts high-performance practices most frequently (Japanese transplants), regional advantages are more subtle. Proximity to markets and transportation networks tends to be defined in terms of specific customers rather than general markets. Clearly, a cooperative labor-management environment and accommodating local governmental organizations are much more important to high performance than to traditionally managed firms. On balance, for firms adopting high performance practices, wage costs and the abundance of the available labor pool in a location are less critical than how productive labor can become through training, motivation, and cooperative problem-solving efforts.

## Notes

1. Measures of average productivity, such as value added per manufacturing worker, are rarely included in location models because productivity is substantially influ-

enced by firm-specific practices, such as work organization, capital intensity, and pay incentives.

2.  There are several explanations for the lack of evidence supporting the belief that labor quality (as measured by education) affects location selection: difficulty in measuring education quality, time lags between the education paid for with current taxes and the quality of education provided in the past to workers currently in the labor market, and nonfinancial inputs that affect education quality, such as socioeconomic conditions and effectiveness of using public education resources (Bartik 1997; Fisher 1997).

3.  Measures of unionization include work stoppages due to strikes and the presence of state right-to-work laws, but the consensus favors average unionization rates of manufacturing workers.

4.  This evidence is based on models which also control for regional differences in climate and market growth that are often correlated with unionization.

5.  Often neglected in taxation discussions are the benefits that tax revenues can provide in terms of public expenditures that lower business costs. A survey of these benefits by Fisher (1997) found positive and statistically significant effects in 8 out of the 15 studies that included highways, 4 out of 9 that included public safety services, and 6 out of 19 that included measures of education levels. Because expenditures on highways may reflect the poor quality of infrastructure, public safety expenditure may reflect the incidence of crime, and education expenditures may be remedial, these results are difficult to interpret (Helms 1985; Bartik 1985) and there may be long time lags between expenditures and the increased attractiveness of a business location (Herzog and Schlottmann 1991, p. 270).

6.  Urbanization is also sometimes included in location models as an indicator of both market and business activity size and concentration. Alternatively, it is associated with large labor pools and markets, educational and recreational amenities, and transportation facilities that may be attractive to business location. However, urbanization can also be a proxy for higher land prices, more crime, poverty, and other social problems, which may negatively affect location.

7.  In addition to capturing agglomeration economies, a measure of general manufacturing activity existing in the area prior to a new arrival's location decision captures the effects of omitted variables that are constant over time and that may affect profitability, and therefore location choice (Bartik 1985).

8.  Luger included measures of land and building subsidies, debt and equity capital assistance, tax incentives, postsecondary education support, job training, labor and environmental regulation, industrial recruitment, and R&D assistance. He omitted support for primary and secondary education and investment in transportation and public utilities infrastructure because their benefits cannot be directly connected to businesses (well-trained graduates may leave the area; benefits of infrastructure investments extend beyond employer and potential employees).

9.  This study compares taxes, tax incentives, and non-tax incentives on business location or expansion across the largest cities in the 24 most industrialized states, calculating after-tax returns for typical hypothetical manufacturers in each loca-

tion. The range of incentives included jobs credit, exemptions from property or sales taxes, grants, loans and loan guarantees, and job training and infrastructure subsidies.

10. This study also concludes that location decisions may be made in two stages, whereby a subset of likely states is identified before a final selection of a single state is made. It surveys new plants established by large enterprises (mostly Fortune 500 firms) between 1970 and 1980 to obtain subjective data on the set of finalist states. Only responses from the 114 companies that seriously considered more than one state are included in the models. These companies listed the states which they had "seriously considered" for the new plant's location. The first-stage choice model attempts to explain the selection of 3 states for consideration out of 48 possible, and the second-stage models the decision to select the eventual state of choice.

11. Papke (1991) explained that her choice of independent firms as a proxy for branch start-ups was determined by her inability to identify start year for establishments in the Dun and Bradstreet data set. However, due to this limitation, her model is more about how location factors affect entrepreneurship than interstate location.

12. It can also be argued that controlling for regional effects helps to reduce simultaneity biases that are inherent in standard econometric specifications of location models (Bartik 1985; Levinson 1996). As further explained in Chapter 7, the conditional logit technique for state location models is potentially problematic because of the assumption that neighboring alternatives are no more like each other than are alternatives on opposite coasts of the United States. Bartik (1985) showed that using regional dummy variables is essentially equivalent to a "nested logit" technique for which the condition of "independence of irrelevant alternatives" is not required. This approach to accounting for the likelihood that unmeasured attributes of states that affect location probability are correlated within regions is computationally simpler than the nested logit technique.

13. Ulgado (1996) reported survey findings from 69 Japanese and 77 domestic manufacturers, based on a nationwide survey mailed to new, acquired, joint ventures and wholly owned plants. The respondents ranked the importance of 58 location attributes. Ulgado reported similarities and differences in location attribute preferences between the two groups based on a significance test of the differences of the means.

14. These ambiguous findings may be explained by regional differences in industrial composition of the three econometric studies of Japanese plant location, in particular whether they exclude auto-part manufacturers (Friedman, Gerlowski, and Silberman 1992) or include only plants connected to the auto industry (Smith and Florida 1994). For example, Haitani and Marquis (1990) reported that Midwestern Japanese companies put far less weight on wages and unionization than on labor quality of productivity in their location decisions, while Milkman (1991) found that electronics firms in southern California sought low-wage and anti-union locations. There is also the possibility that local wages do not matter much because Japanese transplants tend to pay higher wages than either domestic firms

or affiliates of other foreign-owned firms (Graham and Krugman 1989). Also see Evans-Klock (in preparation) for more detailed comparisons of research methods used in the discrete choice models of Japanese transplant locations.

15. Milkman (1991) also documented that the counties with the most Japanese plants tended to be those with lower unionization rates. Yoshida (1987) reported that larger plants tend to consider unionization an important factor while smaller-sized plants do not. Kujawa (1986), however, reported a low priority being placed on either unionization rates or right-to-work laws in location decisions in his case studies, but noted that his sample of transplants implemented specific workplace practices to deter union organizing or to reduce the risk of a pro-union vote.

16. Woodward (1992) found no effect of state corporate tax rates, while Friedman, Gerlowski, and Silberman (1992) found an unexpected and unexplained positive effect. However, credence is higher in Woodward's findings because he used the standard measure, average effective tax rate on corporate income, while Friedman and his colleagues used a dummy variable indicating whether a state has a corporate income tax, which captures very little of the variation in business taxation among states. (Only four states had no corporate income tax in 1980; see Table 7A.3, pp. 221–222.)

17. Head, Ries, and Swenson (1995) used a set of state dummy variables to capture the pattern of U.S. establishment agglomeration instead of specifying factor cost and other location attributes. They criticized the latter approach because of the inherent danger of omitting important variables whose effect is absorbed in the variables that are included. They concluded that a state that experiences a 10% increase in either U.S. or Japanese or *keiretsu* agglomeration increases its probability of future selection by 5–7%, and that this effect is robust when controlling for state effects, time trends, and industry-level stocks and flows of U.S. investment. The results for *keiretsu* agglomeration, however, hold only for auto-related plants. Latecomers report that they try to avoid locating in areas already dominated by Japanese firms (Reid 1989).

18. Direct financial incentives may actually be disdained because of the perceived expectation of reciprocal obligations (Nakabayashi 1987). Kujawa (1986) and Yoshida (1987) reached similar conclusions about the relative unimportance of direct financial incentives, but Kujawa attributed it to low variance among states and localities in the availability of location subsidies for Japanese transplants.

19. Woodward's model uses Luger's (1987) index of state industrial recruitment programs as a measure of recruitment effect. It also includes a dummy variable indicating whether the state had a development office in Japan in the early 1980s, which is likely to be correlated with the use of other industrial development policies.

20. Workforce demographics may also be of special significance to Japanese transplants. Cole and Deskins (1988), for example, concluded that "by siting their plants in areas with very low Black populations, [Japanese firms], in effect, exclude Blacks from potential employment" (p. 13). However, they do not take into account any other differences among locations, some of which may be corre-

lated with race. Nakabayashi (1987) documented that Japanese firms tend not to locate in areas with low education levels or that suffer problems typically associated with inner cities, such as high poverty and crime rates, and Woodward (1992) confirmed that urbanization and poverty, rather than race, are generally the more important considerations.

21. Given the huge investment and thousands of jobs at stake, state location subsidies also influenced the location decisions by Japanese automakers (Milward and Newman 1989; Yanarella and Green 1990). Milward and Newman pointed out that the importance placed on worker productivity and transportation access is apparent in the types of recruitment incentive packages sought by Japanese auto assembly transplants. Training funds accounted for between 33% and 43% of the incentive packages, and improving highway access was the single feature common to each of the five cases in their study.

22. Chapter 3 provides a more detailed description of the process for eliciting this information and the precautions that were taken to ensure that the same set of location factors was mentioned in each interview.

23. Differences by nationality of ownership in other location attributes may well be substantial but fail to meet the statistical threshold for significant difference, a criterion that is acknowledged to be particularly difficult to meet in $\chi^2$ tests on samples of this size. For example, positive relationships with local government were almost three times as important to Japanese transplants, and there is a 19 percentage point spread between the share of domestic and the share of Japanese plants that labeled labor supply as an important location attribute (55% compared with 36%, but this differential is not statistically significant).

24. This finding corresponds to that of some studies (Carroll and Wasylenko 1994; Schmenner 1982; Schmenner, Huber, and Cook 1987; Doeringer, Terkla, and Topakian 1987), but contradicts the more general view that taxes are an important location factor (Bartik 1991; Papke 1991). The relatively low weight given to tax factors, however, is consistent with the small fraction (20%) of the managers citing location subsidies and incentives as important. Similarly, only 10% rated land costs as important, and even the availability of sites or a building was considered important by only 20% of the sample.

25. Typical union strategies for job protection, creating workforce divisions by skill and department and narrowly defining jobs, would explicitly rule out job rotation and flexibility in assigning workers to different tasks as changes in demand warranted. These traditional means of protecting workers' interests have been developed within the U.S. system of firing-at-will. They are inconsistent with those of Japanese corporations, where employment has traditionally been protected during downturns by rotating workers to different operations or to satellite companies, sending workers for additional training, and assigning workers temporarily to nonproduction work in plant maintenance or community service.

26. Milkman's (1991) description of desired worker characteristics in the electronics assembly plants in southern California concluded that the Japanese companies seek tractable labor at low wages. Skill requirements are low because of the rou-

tinized nature of most of the production processes. None of the plants she visited had specific education requirements for its production workers and only one conducted preemployment aptitude tests. This description does not match the human resource preferences or practices of any of the Japanese transplants visited in the present study in Georgia, Kentucky, or the Northeast.

27. Several Japanese-national managers admitted that a high school diploma had turned out to be a poor indicator of literacy, "numeracy," and ability to learn on the job. Several transplants had instituted remedial math training for high school graduates as a precursor to training in statistical process control.

28. Other examples of the efficiency benefits of rural location come from the diminished competition from other high-wage employers. Managers of transplants in Georgia and Kentucky (the states in our sample with substantial rural populations) often reported that locations in rural communities or small cities were chosen because workers would have fewer well-paying alternative employment opportunities, as well as for reducing the likelihood of being a target for unionization. Similarly, half of the managers of Japanese transplants in Georgia expressed reluctance to locate too near other Japanese-owned manufacturing plants out of a concern for the adverse consequences of too much competition for preferred workers among high-wage firms.

29. Transportation infrastructure to facilitate importing materials from Japan was less commonly regarded as important than was access to transportation networks for receiving supplies and shipping products within the United States. However, managers in New Jersey typically mentioned the New York port facilities as an important attraction to the area. Managers in Georgia and Kentucky expressed satisfaction with cross-country transport of imported supplies from the West Coast.

30. These findings corroborate earlier studies of the location patterns between Japanese auto assembly plants and their parts or sub-components manufacturers in the United States (Smith and Florida 1994; Reid 1989; Mair, Florida, and Kenney 1988). The exceptions were auto parts plants that had been established in the late 1970s or early 1980s to sell to U.S. automakers before the arrival of the Japanese auto assembly plants.

31. Seven of the 9 auto parts manufacturers in the field sample consider proximity an important location attribute, compared with 3 of the 10 components or parts suppliers to the electronic consumer industry.

32. Informally, many managers also mentioned poverty measures as being inversely related to good governance and community harmony. They discussed this aspect of location alternatives in terms of likelihood of social problems (property crime, incidence of substance abuse among potential workers) and the greater claims that might be made on them to participate in community-improvement programs or local charity activities.

33. Some Japanese managers also suggested that infrastructure improvements, such as access roads and interstate interchanges, did not figure prominently in comparing locations because they were so commonly available for new plants.

34. One Japanese president of a non-electrical equipment manufacturer in New Jersey explained that, as a relatively small company in Japan, it had difficulty attracting first-class engineers from good schools because these graduates preferred to work for larger, more prestigious corporations. Once employed there, engineers "never change companies"; in effect there is a very limited labor market for experienced engineers. In the United States, "excellent, experienced" engineers are available for half the salary that would be required in Japan. This company was starting up a new product for the U.S. and export markets, and the company president believed that the availability of engineers in the United States would cut the time of moving the product into production. In turn, this had led them to look for areas with a good supply of engineers, using the presence of other machine tool manufacturers and specialized curricula at vocational schools as the main indicators.

# 7
# What Attracts High Performance Factories?

Both the literature on location decisions and our case studies suggest that there is a set of core cost factors that influence the location of start-up factories, regardless of their particular managerial strategies and organizational structures. The case studies, however, show that there are important linkages between the extent to which high performance management practices are adopted by start-ups and how start-ups define regional location advantages. Specifically, Japanese transplants that frequently adopt high performance management strategies appear to value different location factors more than traditionally managed domestic start-ups. However, business location decisions are sufficiently complex to make it difficult to draw complete and reliable conclusions about location differences in the perception of regional advantage from a small sample of case studies conducted in a few states.

In this chapter, information from the case studies provides a basis for challenging hypotheses about how start-ups with different management strategies perceive the advantages of different locations. For example, are high performance workplace practices most effective in locations where there is an abundant pool of workers who can be quickly trained, accommodate easily to teamwork, and participate in consultative relationships with management? Or, do start-ups that depend on more traditional management methods place a higher value on core cost variables such as wages and taxes? Hypotheses such as these are tested using formal models of business location decisions combined with a unique national database of start-up firms specially compiled for this study. This modeling framework allows us to control for a wide range of standard location factors in order to isolate the independent effects of management practices on location choices.

First, a "core" location model is developed based upon those variables (such as rates of unionization, wages, taxes, and education) that are most commonly found to explain the plant location decisions of domestic manufacturing start-ups. This core model provides a baseline against which the results of more elaborate models can be compared.

A second set of models is then presented, which we characterize as "field research" models, that incorporate additional location considerations that managers of start-ups in the case studies identified as important. These field models include variables that capture the effects of labor force quality, the perceived helpfulness of state and local government officials, and various plant characteristics associated with high performance workplace factors. Adding these variables both improves upon the explanatory power of the core model and helps to identify the specific factors that differentiate the location preferences of Japanese transplants from those of domestic start-ups.

These field research models largely confirm the interview findings reported in the previous chapter. Japanese transplants, with their high performance management practices, define regional advantage in somewhat different ways than do domestic start-ups. After controlling for other location factors, Japanese transplants are attracted to regions having workforce characteristics that are consistent with their high performance workplace strategies. In contrast, the location decisions of domestic start-ups largely reflect the predominant importance of traditional location factors.

## THE LOCATION DATABASE

We constructed a unique national database that combines information on the location of start-up factories with that on various state-level location factors. These data on location characteristics—wages, education, unionization, taxation, transportation access, market size, and possibilities for agglomeration economies—represent the core variables identified in the business location literature. Additional variables (such as population demographics, educational expenditures, and climate) were then added to reflect location considerations that the case studies indicate are important.

Data on domestically owned manufacturing start-ups were derived from the U.S. Establishment and Enterprise Microdata Files (USEEM), a panel database prepared by the Small Business Administration (SBA) from biannual company reports submitted to Dun and Bradstreet.[1] Data on the location, size, type of ownership, and industry was extracted from the USEEM files for nearly 150,000 individual manufacturing plants established between 1978 and 1988 (the latest year for which data are available). This universe of start-ups was then narrowed to 33,541 new branch establishments of multiplant companies by excluding independent establishments (i.e., "entrepreneurial" plants), small establishments (with fewer than 20 employees), and establishments that moved from one state to another or changed their industry during the period. To facilitate econometric estimation, a random sample of approximately 1,000 establishments was drawn from this universe of new domestic branch plants.[2]

A counterpart universe of new manufacturing plants established by Japanese multinational enterprises was drawn from detailed directories of U.S. manufacturing affiliates of Japanese firms, *Japan's Expanding U.S. Manufacturing Presence,* published annually by the Japan Economic Institute (JEI). These annual directories are the best available micro-data on Japanese-owned manufacturing plants in operation in the United States. They provide plant-specific information on location, corporate ownership, type of investment (acquisition or a start-up), date of start-up, approximate number of employees, and the type of products. The JEI directory for 1991 provides information on 498 Japanese-owned manufacturing transplants established in the continental United States between 1978 and 1988.[3]

These data on start-ups were then merged with information on state characteristics collected from a variety of government sources and other studies (Table 7.1; also, Appendix A Tables 7A.1 to 7A.4 on pp. 217–224). In each instance, the data on start-ups and state characteristics cover approximately the same time period.

## REGIONAL AND STATE LOCATION PATTERNS

The data on plant location show quite clearly that domestic start-ups and Japanese transplants tend to locate in different states and regions (Figure 7.1). Japanese transplants are concentrated on the East

**Table 7.1  Variable Definitions and Data Sources for the National Database Models**

| Location factors | Variable | | Data | |
|---|---|---|---|---|
| | Name | Definition | Year | Source |
| Labor | HSGRAD | % population over age 25 w/4 yr. high school only | avg. 1980, 90 | U.S. Dept. of Education, *Digest of Education Statistics* |
| | UNION | % production workers unionized | avg. 1984, 86 | Grant Thornton (1989) |
| | WAGE | ln(avg. hourly wage of production workers) | 1985 | Grant Thornton (1989) |
| Market size and transportation | AIRPORT | ln(no. enplaned passengers, state's principal hub) | avg. 1983, 87 | U.S. Department of Commerce (1987, 1991) |
| | HIGHWAY | ln(interstate miles per sq. mi. of land area) | avg. 1983, 87 | U.S. Department of Commerce (1983) |
| | MARKET | ln(gravity-adjusted state personal income) | 1985 | Income: *U.S. Statistical Abstract* Distance: *Rand McNally Road Atlas* |
| Fiscal policy | CORPTAX | ln(1 – avg. effective tax rate on corporate income) | avg. 1983, 88 | U.S. Department of Commerce (1985, 1990) and ACIR (1986, 1991) |
| | EXPEDUC | ln(state + local expend. on education per pupil/median salary of B.A. occupations) | avg. 1983, 87 | *U.S. Statistical Abstract* |

**Table 7.1 (continued)**

| Location factors | Variable Name | Definition | Data Year | Source |
|---|---|---|---|---|
| | JOF | binary for state economic development office in Japan before 1985 | 1985 | National Association of State Development Agencies |
| | UNITARY | binary for unitary tax base | 1978–84 | Tannenwald (1984) |
| Miscellaneous | AGGLOM | ln(manufact. production hours/ 1,000 acres nonfederally owned land) | avg. 1983, 87 | U.S. Census of Manufactures |
| | JTEMP | ln(avg. Jan. temperature) | 30-yr. avg. | *U.S. Statistical Abstract* (1986) |
| | NYC | binary variable for New York City area, N.Y., N.J., and Conn. | (1951–08) | |
| Controls | LAND | ln(nonfederally owned acres) | | *U.S. Statistical Abstract* (1986) |

Regions:[a]

| | | |
|---|---|---|
| PAC | Pacific | Calif., Ore., Wash. |
| ENC | East North-Central | Ohio, Mich., Ind., Ill., Wisc. |
| WNC | West North-Central | Minn., Iowa, Mo., N.Dak., S.Dak., Nev., Kan. |
| ESC | East South-Central | Ky., Tenn., Ala., Miss. |
| WSC | West South-Central | Ark., La., Okla., Tex. |
| SAT | South Atlantic | Va., N.C., S.C., Ga., Fla. |
| MAT | Middle Atlantic | N.Y., N.J., Pa., Del., W.Va., Md. |
| NEW | New England | Mass., Conn., R.I., Vt., N.H., Me. |

[a] Mountain region (Mont., Idaho, Wyo., Colo., N.M., Ariz., Utah, Nev.) omitted.

and West coasts, while domestic start-ups are more highly concentrated in the Midwest and New England. These differences in distribution are statistically significant as revealed by a $\chi^2$ test of the differences in regional proportions of Japanese and domestic plants (Table 7.2).

The differences in location patterns are even more apparent when regions are disaggregated into their component states (Table 7.2 and Figure 7.2). California accounts for the largest share of both domestic and Japanese plants, but the share of Japanese plants is over 50% larger (18.3% of Japanese plants, compared with 11.8% of the domestic plants). Of the 15 states that rank among the top 12 on either list, 4 had twice the proportion of Japanese transplants as domestic start-ups (Ohio, Georgia, Kentucky, and Tennessee), while 4 others captured nearly twice the share of domestic as Japanese plants (Texas, Pennsylvania, Florida, and New York; Figure 7.2). Altogether, these 15 states account for a much larger portion of the Japanese plants (87.5%) than of the domestic plants (67.7%).

Regional disparities in location patterns do not appear to be explained by differences in the industry mix of domestic and Japanese firms. For example, in the case of the automotive industry (which accounts for 25% of the Japanese plants), statistical tests confirm locational differences by nationality.[4]

## MODELING LOCATION DECISIONS

The starting point for determining the particular characteristics that define regional advantage for domestic start-ups and Japanese transplants is a model of the location choice decision. The most widely accepted approach for studying such location decisions is the conditional logit model (McFadden 1981; Maddala 1983). In this model, start-ups make discrete, either/or choices of whether or not to locate in each state, based upon a set of state attributes that determines the profitability of location (Schmenner, Huber, and Cook 1987; Bartik 1985; Friedman, Gerlowski, and Silberman 1992). Each of the 48 contiguous United States represents a different combination of costs and attractions to the plant. The model assumes that the plant will select the

**Figure 7.1  Distribution of Start-Ups by Region, 1978–88**

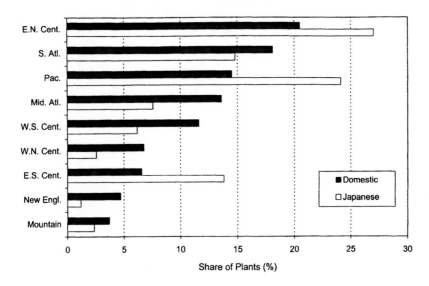

**Figure 7.2  States' Shares of Domestic and Japanese Start-Ups, 1978–88
(top dozen states in either category)**

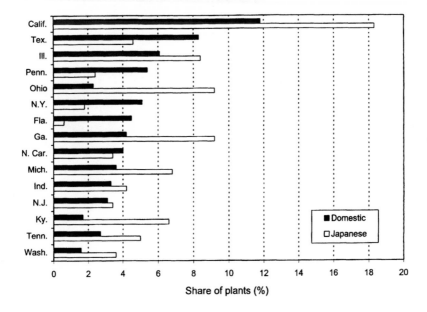

**Table 7.2  Distribution of Domestic and Japanese Start-Ups, 1978–88**

| Region/state | Japanese start-ups (%) | Domestic start-ups (%) |
|---|---|---|
| ENC | 27.0*** | 20.5 |
| Ill. | 6.6 | 6.1 |
| Ind. | 4.2 | 3.3 |
| Mich. | 6.8 | 3.6 |
| Ohio | 9.2 | 5.3 |
| Wisc. | 0.2 | 2.2 |
| PAC | 24.1*** | 14.5 |
| Calif. | 18.3 | 11.8 |
| Ore. | 2.2 | 1.1 |
| Wash. | 3.6 | 1.6 |
| SAT | 14.8 | 18.1 |
| Fla. | 0.6 | 4.5 |
| Ga. | 8.4 | 4.2 |
| N.C. | 3.4 | 4.0 |
| S.C. | 0.8 | 1.8 |
| Va. | 1.4 | 2.1 |
| Del. | 0.0 | 0.1 |
| Md. | 0.0 | 1.1 |
| W.Va. | 0.2 | 0.3 |
| ESC | 13.8*** | 6.6 |
| Ala. | 1.8 | 1.1 |
| Ky. | 6.6 | 1.7 |
| Miss. | 0.4 | 1.1 |
| Tenn. | 5.0 | 2.7 |
| MAT | 7.6*** | 13.6 |
| N.J. | 3.4 | 3.1 |
| N.Y. | 1.8 | 5.1 |
| Pa. | 2.4 | 5.4 |
| WSC | 6.2*** | 11.6 |
| Ariz. | 0.6 | 0.9 |
| La. | 0.0 | 0.8 |
| Okla. | 1.0 | 1.6 |
| Tex. | 4.6 | 8.3 |

**Table 7.2 (continued)**

| Region/state | Japanese start-ups (%) | Domestic start-ups (%) |
|---|---|---|
| WNC | 2.6*** | 6.8 |
| Iowa | 0.6 | 1.3 |
| Kan. | 0.0 | 0.8 |
| Minn. | 0.2 | 1.9 |
| Mo. | 1.4 | 1.9 |
| Nev. | 0.4 | 0.6 |
| N.Dak. | 0.0 | 0.2 |
| S.Dak. | 0.0 | 0.1 |
| MTN | 2.4 | 3.7 |
| Ariz. | 0.4 | 1.2 |
| Colo. | 0.4 | 0.9 |
| Idaho | 0.0 | 0.4 |
| Mont. | 0.0 | 0.4 |
| Nev. | 1.4 | 0.3 |
| N.M. | 0.0 | 0.1 |
| Utah | 0.2 | 0.3 |
| Wyo. | 0.0 | 0.1 |
| NEW | 1.2*** | 4.7 |
| Conn. | 0.6 | 1.1 |
| Me. | 0.2 | 0.2 |
| Mass. | 0.4 | 2.6 |
| N.H. | 0.0 | 0.3 |
| R.I. | 0.0 | 0.4 |
| Vt. | 0.0 | 0.1 |

NOTE: Across all regions, $\chi^2$ test: $H_0$ that nationality and location are independent is rejected at the 0.01 significance level.  *** = Statistically significant at the 0.01 level.
SOURCE: Authors' data from JEI and USEEM.

location that maximizes its profits, given its production function and where its markets are located.

The profitability of a firm locating plant $i$ in state $j$ can be formally expressed as:

**(7.1)**  $\pi_{ij} = \beta'X_j + \varepsilon$

where $\pi_{ij}$ is the profits to be obtained by plant $i$ being located in each state $j$; $X$ is a vector of relevant characteristics of state $j$; $\beta'$ is a vector of coefficients indicating the relative weight of each of these characteristics; and $\varepsilon$ is a term representing any unobserved (to the researcher) location factors and random errors. Choosing state $j$ results in the maximum achievable profits relative to alternative locations. The probability that state $j$ is selected follows the rule

**(7.2)**  Prob $(\pi_{ij} > \pi_{ik})$ for all $k \neq j$.

Assuming the error term $\varepsilon$ is distributed Weibull, a simple probability model of plant $i$ being located in state $j$ that meets this rules is

**(7.3)**  $\text{Prob}_{ij} = \dfrac{e^{\beta'X_j}}{\sum_k e^{\beta'X_k}}$

where $k = 1 \ldots 48$ states.[5] Equation 7.3 can then be estimated using maximum likelihood procedures incorporated into what is commonly referred to as McFadden's conditional logit model, in which the factory location decision is "conditioned" on the cost attributes of all 48 alternative state locations (Maddala 1983).

The state attributes ($X$) in this model can also be modified to reflect how the attractiveness of state attributes may vary according to plant and industry characteristics (Schmenner, Huber, and Cook 1987). For example, the influence of unionization may depend on whether the plant is connected to the auto industry or the apparel industry, or the importance of the quality of education institutions may depend on the type of technology and skills used in the production function. These types of interactions moderate the weights in the $\beta$ vector of coefficients in Equation 7.3 and can be incorporated into the discrete choice model, as shown in Equation 7.4,

(7.4) $\pi_{ij} = \beta' X_j + \Sigma_n \beta'_n X_j Z_{in}$

where $X$ is the vector of state attributes, $\beta'$ reflects the weight of each state attribute, $Z_{in}$ is a vector of plant characteristics $1 \ldots N$, and the $\beta'_n$ account for the moderating impact of the plant characteristics $(Z)$ on the influence of state attributes $(X)$.

A two-stage approach is adopted for analyzing how start-up factories define regional advantage. In Equation 7.5, location factors are divided into those that are identified as core cost factors $(X_{core})$, such as wages, taxes, and proximity to markets, which are featured prominently in the location literature reviewed in Chapter 6, and those that incorporate the findings of the field research $(X_{field})$.

(7.5) $X = X_{core} + X_{field}$

The $X_{field}$ variables include the availability of a supply of workers whose characteristics are most compatible with the use of high performance management practices, the quality of education institutions, and access to international airports that were identified as important to the start-ups in the sample.

The analysis of core factors provides a benchmark for comparing the results of our location analysis with those of similar studies. The field research factors allow us to determine the extent to which the information obtained during the field research improves upon our ability to define characteristics that give regions an advantage in attracting high performance firms.

In addition, a set of regional control variables is included in the model. As McFadden (1974) noted, the assumption of independent error terms in the conditional logit model is problematic in the case of location selection because there are likely to be unmeasured attributes of states, such as workforce attitudes or cultural and social mores, that are correlated within regions.[6] To control for the possibility of unmeasured regional effects, a set of regional dummy variables is included in the model. These variables also provide a test, at the regional level, of whether important location factors have been omitted from either the core or field sets of variables.[7]

## DEFINING THE CORE MODEL

The core model, which serves as the starting point for analyzing the location decisions of start-up factories, is a conditional logit model in which the dependent variable is the state selection probability for a start-up establishment. This model contains seven explanatory variables measuring the types of state economic attributes most commonly identified as important in the location literature.[8]  These variables are grouped into four categories: labor markets, market size and transportation costs, fiscal policy, and miscellaneous. In addition, a set of control variables is included for the size of each state and the region in which it is located (see Table 7.1 for the definitions and data sources for the explanatory variables).

The purpose of the core model is to determine how closely the location decisions of start-ups reflect the kinds of standard economic factors identified by previous research. This allows us to check for any unusual location behavior in our national sample of start-ups and to take a first cut at seeing if there are any substantial differences between start-ups that are likely to adopt high performance workplace practices intensively (Japanese transplants) and those that are less likely to do so (domestic start-ups).

### Labor Market Factors

Average wages, the strength of unions, and the probability of the workforce being unionized are the standard measures of labor costs in the location literature. The WAGE variable used in the analysis is the average hourly wage of production workers, which captures variations among states in the average cost of the largest category of labor employed by start-ups in the case study sample. The share of manufacturing production workers that are unionized, UNION, is used to measure the strength of unions in each state and the probability of a plant being organized by a union.[9]

Workforce quality and availability are usually approximated in the location literature by some indicator of education levels, such as median years of education or the fraction of the population with a high school diploma. High school graduates over 25 were the most common type of labor recruited by the start-ups in the case study sample, and we therefore selected an education measure, HSGRAD, which is the share of the population over 25 having a high school education but no postsecondary education.

## Market Size and Transportation Costs

The size of the regional market for a firm's products and the transportation costs for inputs and products make up a second common category of location factors. Following Woodward (1992) and others, a gravity-adjusted MARKET variable is included, defined as the amount of personal income in a selected state plus the personal income of all other states weighted by their distance from the selected state to indicate relative proximity to product markets.[10]   States with similar total income are weighted differently under this measure depending on the income of, and distance to, all other states.[11]

Managers in the case study sample frequently identified access to the interstate highway network as important for receiving shipments and delivering their products, and new access roads or interchanges are the most frequently provided recruitment incentive offered by host states.   Therefore, the variable HIGHWAY—the number of miles of interstate highway per square mile of state land area—is included to capture this significant influence on the costs of transportation to customers and from input markets.

## Fiscal Policy

Tax rates are commonly included in location models, although the importance of taxes for business location decisions is hotly debated. Therefore, CORPTAX, a measure of the percentage share of income retained by the firm after taxes, is included in the model (Moore, Steece, and Swenson 1987; Bartik 1985). This measure provides a more accurate estimate of potential tax costs than nominal tax rates, which often involve state-by-state differences in exemptions and definitions of taxable income.

## Agglomeration Economies

The presence of other manufacturing companies, particularly supplier firms or those that contribute to the pool of trained labor in the state, may provide a positive location externality for start-up firms. A typical measure of such agglomeration externalities, AGGLOM, defined as manufacturing production hours per 1,000 acres of nonfederally owned land, is used in the model (Wasylenko 1997; Bartik 1985).

**Control Variables**

In order to control for omitted variables that may have a systematic influence on a plant's choice of states, without overidentifying the location model, a vector of regional dummy variables is included. In addition, LAND, a variable which is defined as the total number of acres of nonfederally owned land in each state, is used to control for the "dartboard theory" of industrial location (Bartik 1985). (This theory asserts that the larger the size of the state, the higher the probability of businesses finding suitable sites in the state.)

**FINDINGS FROM THE CORE MODEL**

The model is estimated separately for Japanese and domestic start-ups established between 1978 and 1988, the period for which we have comparable location data for both groups of plants. The results for the sample of domestic start-ups are largely consistent with those in the literature and are also generally in accord with the findings of the field research for the sample of domestic start-ups (Table 7.3).[12] Domestic start-ups are most likely to locate in states that have low levels of unionization and good access to interstate highways. Proximity to product markets and to agglomerations of other manufacturing plants also have positive effects on location. The significance of the LAND variable supports the dartboard theory of business location.

**Table 7.3  Core Location Model for Domestic and Japanese
Start-Ups, 1978–88**

| State attribute | Domestic start-ups coeff. | Japanese transplants coeff. |
|---|---|---|
| UNION | −1.28** | −1.75 |
| WAGE | −0.03 | 5.34*** |
| HSGRAD | 0.02 | −0.01 |
| CORPTAX | −0.16 | 3.14 |
| MARKET | 0.48*** | −0.35 |
| AGGLOM | 0.45*** | 1.47*** |
| HIGHWAY | 0.44*** | 0.28 |
| LAND | 0.79*** | 1.58*** |
| | | |
| PAC region | 0.23 | 0.25 |
| WSC region | 0.00 | −0.86** |
| ESC region | 0.02 | 0.90 |
| SAT region | 0.02 | 0.30 |
| WNC region | −0.09 | −0.86 |
| ENC region | 0.06 | −0.63 |
| MAT region | −0.13 | −0.72 |
| NEW region | −0.39 | −1.61** |
| | | |
| No. of plants | 1,055 | 481 |
| No. of variables | 16 | 16 |
| −2(ln L) | 21,808.51 | 8,941.73 |

NOTE:  *** = Statistically significant at the 0.01 level; ** = statistically significant at
the 0.05 level.

Three variables (education, wages, and corporate taxation) fail to achieve statistical significance when the core model is applied to domestic start-ups. As noted in the previous chapter, the finding that neither education, corporate tax rates, or wages matter to plant location is not uncommon in the location literature (Schmenner, Huber, and Cook 1987; Levinson 1996). In addition, none of the regional control variables is significant. This result makes us relatively confident that important location variables for domestic start-ups have not been omitted from the core model.

The core model, however, provides a much less satisfactory explanation for the location decisions of Japanese transplants (Table 7.3). The opportunity for agglomeration economies and the dartboard effect of large states seem to influence the location of Japanese transplants. The core model fails to corroborate the importance of access to interstate highways, the preference for non-union environments, and the importance of the labor pool of high school graduates, all of which were noted frequently by managers of Japanese start-ups in the case studies.

What is particularly problematic about using the core model to understand the location decisions of Japanese transplants, however, is that high wages seem to be an attraction for Japanese-owned start-ups. The Japanese transplants in the case studies seemed largely indifferent to local labor market competition, because they paid wages that were almost always at the upper end of the local wage distribution.

One obvious explanation for the failure of the core model to yield as sensible results for Japanese transplants as it did for domestic start-ups is that location factors that are important for Japanese transplants have been omitted from the model. This possibility is further supported by the finding that two of the regional variables are significant in the core model for Japanese transplants. Therefore, the core model is likely incorrectly specified in the case of Japanese transplants.

## REDEFINING REGIONAL ADVANTAGE: LESSONS FROM THE FIELD RESEARCH

In order to develop better insights into the regional location advantages valued by Japanese transplants, two "field" models are developed that include variables mentioned during the field research as being important to the location decision of Japanese transplants. These field models are intended to sharpen our understanding of what motivates the location of start-up plants, particularly of Japanese transplants, for which the core model appears to omit some important variables. They also allow for more fine-grained comparisons between the location criteria used by Japanese transplants and domestic start-ups.

The first field model incorporates a number of additional state attributes of importance to Japanese transplants, while a second adds several plant-level characteristics that modify the effects of state attributes in ways suggested by the case study findings. Each model is tested using national data on both Japanese transplants and domestic start-ups.

### The Field Model with Additional State Attributes

We are somewhat constrained by available data in adding the state attributes identified in our case studies as important to high performance workplaces. However, we are able to substantially enrich the core model by incorporating two additional labor quality variables, a second transportation cost variable, a climate variable, and two variables reflecting state policies that only affect Japanese transplants. A control variable was included to test for the effects of Japanese transplants that wish to locate near the New York City area for its Japanese social and cultural amenities.

Both Japanese transplants and domestic start-ups often report placing a high value on the quality of the labor force. Quality is partly defined by having a high school degree, but it also includes a good work ethic, strong ties to local communities that might deter turnover, and the absence of adversarial attitudes towards the employment relationship that are often associated with unions.

One way of approximating the educational dimension of labor quality is by how much states spend on public education. While both types of start-ups generally expressed little interest in educational expenditures per se as a location criterion, location consultants often mention factors such as expenditures on teachers and classroom size, which measure the quality and intensity of educational investments, as being important to firms (Ady 1997). In addition, the Japanese transplants often mentioned skills training and vocational education as important location attractions.[13] To measure these effects, state and local expenditures per pupil on education (standardized for differences in cost of living among states) is used as a proxy for public investment in education.[14] This EXPEDUC variable may also be interpreted more broadly as a proxy for the benefits to business from public services that are financed by state taxes.

Strong work ethic and community ties, according to our case study interviews, are more likely to be found in small communities outside of urban areas, as well as in states with low rates of unionization. To capture these qualities with readily available data, the variable RURAL (defined as the percentage of the state population living in non-urban areas) is added to our field model.

Access to a large international airport is often mentioned by Japanese transplants as a location advantage that facilitates commuting by executives between the branch plant and the company headquarters in Japan. Therefore, the variable AIRPORT, which is calculated as the number of enplaned passengers per year in the state's principal airport hub, is included in the field model.[15]

Climate variables are often used as indicators of weather conditions that facilitate delivery schedules and as proxies for lower heating costs. Climate was also mentioned during our interviews as a quality-of-life variable that makes certain states attractive to managers. This was particularly true of managers of Japanese plants in Georgia and Kentucky. In addition, managers of a few Japanese plants said that they looked for a climate similar to that of their plant locations in Japan in order to avoid potential problems of bringing equipment from Japan to areas with substantially different temperature and humidity. Consequently, JTEMP, the 30-year average January temperature, is used to capture these effects.[16]

State and local economic development incentives were also a candidate for inclusion in the field models because they are commonly used to recruit new companies. Not one of the start-ups in our sample, however, mentioned economic development incentives as being an important factor in its location decision. Even those few start-ups in our sample that took advantage of such incentives said that they made no difference to their choice of location. Nevertheless, we decided to test for the effect of development incentives in our field models by using a broad measure of financial incentives available to recruit industry in each state (Luger 1987). These incentives proved to be so far below the threshold of statistical significance in all cases that we excluded them from further analysis.

There are three other state attributes—unitary taxes on profits, the presence of state-run industrial recruitment offices in Japan, and proximity to corporate headquarters in the New York City area—that the field interviews showed to be of interest to Japanese transplants. While corporate tax rates can affect the location of both Japanese transplants and domestic start-ups, foreign-owned companies may be particularly concerned about states with unitary taxation.[17] The location choices of the Japanese transplants in our sample are also reported to be influenced by the promotional activities of a state's industrial recruiting office in Japan. These firms typically view such offices as an indicator that a state is more likely to continue to be helpful at later stages of setting up and operating a plant, rather than just for the potential location incentives that might be offered. Finally, the field research shows that many East Coast Japanese transplants mentioned the importance of locating near New York City for the quality-of-life amenities that the city offers to Japanese managers and their families.

To test for these effects, three additional variables are included in our field model: one to indicate whether states had a unitary tax law between 1978 and 1985 (UNITARY), another indicating whether the state had an economic development office or representative in Japan prior to 1985 (JOF), and a third variable to indicate whether the plant is located in the New York City area (NYC).

## The Field Model with Additional Plant Characteristics

The second field model adds establishment-level characteristics that the field research suggests might modify the location influences of several state attributes. The key establishment characteristics identified in both the field research and the location literature on Japanese transplants are the size of the plant and whether it is in a high-technology industry or is a supplier to the automobile industry. The case studies point to all three of these factors as being more influential for Japanese transplants than for domestic start-ups.

The most prominent of these plant characteristics is having a supply relationship within the automobile industry. Japanese auto parts transplants reported that they often followed their Japanese automobile assembly customers who had located in the Midwest, despite its relatively high rate of unionization and the corollary risk of being organized. Auto parts suppliers are often required to participate in just-in-time supply and delivery arrangements with specific customers, and therefore highway networks also matter to these auto supplier plants, because they often seek to locate within a day's drive of their assembly plant customers. They also place less emphasis on their proximity to large consumer markets because they produce intermediate products for auto assemblers.

To evaluate the importance of these auto industry effects, the binary variable AUTO is used to indicate whether the plant's principal product is in the automotive sector, and this variable is interacted with three state attributes, i.e., unionization, proximity to markets, and access to interstate highways. The UNION × AUTO interaction is a test for the net result of the concern among auto supplier transplants that they are a particularly likely target of union organizing and the preference for being located near their customers, who are likely to be unionized. Both the MARKET × AUTO and HIGHWAY × AUTO interactions are ways of examining the choices between proximity to consumer markets and being within short travel times to their auto assembly customers.

The field research also suggests that start-up plants in high-technology industries value the availability of technical education more than do plants in other industries. Therefore, the size of the pool of high school graduates and state support for education might have a different effect on the location of high-tech industries. A large pool of workers having only a high school education, for example, could be a deterrent to the location of high-tech plants because (other things being equal) it means a smaller pool of workers with postsecondary technical education. Similarly, high-tech plants are likely to disproportionately favor states that make relatively higher expenditures on education, as these states are likely to have larger pools of workers with the required technical skills.

To test for these location effects, a dummy variable (HTECH) for an establishment being in a high-technology industry is interacted with both HSGRAD and EXPEDUC.[18]   HTECH is also interacted with WAGE to allow for the possibility that the cost of production workers may be less relevant to the location of high-technology plants (with their emphasis on technical skills) than to plant location in other industries.

Finally, the larger plants in the field interviews often mentioned that their size and visibility make them a target for union organizing campaigns.   There is also a substantial literature showing that large establishments tend to pay higher wages, provide more generous fringe benefits, and adopt efficiency-wage incentives more often than small firms (Brown, Hamilton, and Medoff 1990; Yoshida 1987; Katz and Summers 1989).   Since such compensation premiums may reduce the importance of interstate differences in average wages as a location factor for large firms, we interact SIZE (as measured by employment) with unionization and wages in the field location model containing plant characteristics.

## FINDINGS FROM THE FIELD MODELS

As expected from our interviews, including these variables that were omitted from the core model substantially increases the model's ability to explain the location decisions of Japanese start-ups. The increase in the explanatory power of the Japanese field model when compared with the core model is significant at the 1% level (Table 7.4).[19] Although the field model for the domestic start-ups does not have a statistically significant increase in explanatory power over the core model, it does provide a more refined understanding of the differences between Japanese transplants and domestic start-ups in the way in which they define regional advantage.[20]

**Table 7.4  Field Location Models for Domestic and Japanese Start-Ups, 1978–88**

| State attribute | Field model 1 (w/out plant modifiers) | | Field model 2 (including plant modifiers) | |
|---|---|---|---|---|
| | Domestic start-ups coeff. | Japanese transplants coeff. | Domestic start-ups coeff. | Japanese transplants coeff. |
| UNION | −1.75** | −4.64*** | −2.41*** | −4.53** |
| × AUTO | | | 1.33 | 7.87*** |
| × SIZE | | | 0.14 | −0.65** |
| WAGE | −0.11 | 6.50 | −0.42 | 6.06*** |
| × HTECH | | | 1.42*** | 1.60*** |
| × SIZE | | | −0.02 | 0.08 |
| HSGRAD | 0.04** | 0.13*** | 0.06*** | 0.16*** |
| × HTECH | | | −0.07*** | −0.08*** |
| RURAL | 1.09 | 6.29*** | 1.10 | 6.55*** |
| CORPTAX | −0.49 | −0.62 | −0.52 | −0.09 |
| EXPEDUC | 0.01 | 0.09 | −0.16 | −0.14 |
| × HTECH | | | 0.63*** | 0.72** |
| JOF | 0.05 | 0.51** | 0.06 | 0.52** |
| UNITARY | −0.11 | −0.33 | −0.12 | −0.25 |
| MARKET | 0.65*** | 0.23 | 0.65*** | 0.35 |
| × AUTO | | | 0.04 | −0.36*** |
| AGGLOM | 0.35** | 1.13*** | 0.34** | 1.06*** |
| HIGHWAY | 0.52** | 0.33 | 0.52** | 0.36 |
| × AUTO | | | 0.14 | 0.18 |
| AIRPORT | 0.15*** | 0.88*** | 0.15*** | 0.91*** |
| NYC | 0.05 | 1.23*** | 0.04 | 1.18** |
| JTEMP | −0.22 | 0.92** | −0.22 | 0.94** |
| LAND | 0.61*** | 0.94** | 0.61*** | 0.86** |
| PAC region | 0.41 | 0.91 | 0.41 | 1.15 |
| WSC region | 0.05 | −0.56 | 0.06 | −0.42 |
| ESC region | 0.05 | 1.20 | 0.06 | 1.45** |
| SAT region | −0.11 | −0.50 | −0.11 | −0.38 |

(continued)

**Table 7.4 (continued)**

| State attribute | Field model 1 (w/out plant modifiers) | | Field model 2 (including plant modifiers) | |
|---|---|---|---|---|
| | Domestic start-ups coeff. | Japanese transplants coeff. | Domestic start-ups coeff. | Japanese transplants coeff. |
| WNC region | –0.34 | –1.15 | –0.33 | –0.92 |
| ENC region | –0.10 | –0.55 | –0.09 | –0.36 |
| MAT region | –0.32 | –1.37 | –0.32 | –1.09 |
| NEW region | –0.58 | –1.61 | –0.58 | –1.43 |
| No. of plants | 1,055 | 481 | 1,055 | 481 |
| No. of variables | 23 | 23 | 31 | 31 |
| –2(ln L) | 21,798.8 | 8,853.5 | 21,777.4 | 8,763.3 |

NOTE: *** = Statistically significant at the 0.01 level; ** = statistically significant at the 0.05 level.

## The Effects of Additional State Attributes

The presence of an international airport (AIRPORT) influences the location choices of both Japanese and domestic plants, but the estimated magnitude of the effect is over five times higher for the Japanese transplants. The importance of highway networks remains largely unchanged, further confirming the greater role of air transportation networks in influencing the location of Japanese transplants.

The first field model continues to show that corporate taxes have no significant effect on the choice of location for either Japanese transplants or domestic start-ups, and the addition of unitary taxes has no statistically significant effect either. Higher spending on public education does not matter to either type of start-up. However, the fraction of the population that is rural, which is the measure of positive work attitudes, is a relevant location factor only for Japanese transplants. A one-percentage-point increase in the share of rural population in a state increases the probability that it will be selected by over 6%.

The climate variable (JTEMP) is also only statistically significant for the Japanese transplants. While this variable could be capturing the effects of energy costs, the field research suggests that it is much more likely to be representing quality-of-life influences and possibly those associated with technology and equipment transfer from Japan to U.S states having comparable climates.

The field model also enhances the effects of many of the variables included in the core location model. For example, the negative effects of unionization are increased for both types of start-ups, and unionization now appears to exert a much larger negative influence on Japanese location decisions. A one-percentage-point increase in a state's average unionization rate decreases the selection probability of Japanese transplants by almost 5%, compared with a less than 2% decrease in selection probability by domestic plants. The supply of workers with a high school education (HSGRAD) now has a statistically significant positive effect on the location of Japanese, as well as domestic, start-ups. Again, the size of this effect on Japanese plants is larger than for domestic plants, in this instance by a factor of three.[21]

As expected, two of the variables measuring location factors that are specific to Japanese transplants (i.e., the presence of an industrial recruitment office in Japan [JOF] and location in the New York City area) are only statistically significant for Japanese-owned start-ups. However, the puzzling fact still remains that relatively high wages paid to production workers has a positive effect on the location of Japanese transplants, and this effect is even stronger than in the core location model.

A final consequence of improving upon the core location model by incorporating additional state characteristics is that none of the regional control variables remain significant for Japanese transplants. This indicates that the first field model includes at least some of the variables that are important for the location of Japanese transplants that were omitted from the core model.

### Interactions with Plant and Industry Variables

The second field location model involves interacting plant and industry variables with selected core location factors. This modification is a significant improvement over the core model for domestic start-ups and over the simpler field model for Japanese transplants.[22] One important result is that this model confirms that Japanese transplants which supply the automobile industry or assemble vehicles have different location strategies from domestic auto industry start-ups and from Japanese transplants in other industries. This can be seen through the statistically significant interactions between automotive start-ups and both unionization and proximity to major markets.

For example, the overall effect of unionization on plant location for both domestic start-ups and Japanese transplants is strongly negative. However, unionization is positively correlated with the location of Japanese transplants in the automobile industry (see the UNION × AUTO interaction in Table 7.4). A one-percentage-point increase in the unionization rate evaluated at the mean is associated with both a positive and negative union effect, so that there is a 3.3% net increase in selection probability by the average Japanese auto plant.[23] This shows that the attractions of proximity to auto assembly plants outweigh the negative effects of unionization on location.

The distinctive relationship between Japanese transplants in the auto industry and location near major markets supports the importance of proximity for just-in-time supply relationships between parts suppliers and assembly plants. The estimated effect of the MARKET × AUTO interaction is insignificant for domestic start-ups, but it is significant and negative for Japanese auto suppliers. This shows that the predisposition to locate near markets is negated for Japanese transplants by their ties to specific customers.[24] Similarly, general interstate highway networks in a state do not influence the location of either Japanese or domestic auto parts suppliers, because it is the highway links and travel times to their specific customers that are likely to be most important.[25]

Second, the field model with industry and establishment variables shows that high-technology start-ups exhibit a distinctive location pattern. As the field research indicated, both Japanese transplants and domestic start-ups in high-tech industries are attracted to states with relatively higher levels of educational spending (Table 7.4, EXPEDUC × HTECH variable). The negative sign of the variable measuring the size of the pool of workers with only a high school education shows both types of high-tech start-ups steering away from states that have large supplies of workers with only high school degrees. Taken together, these two findings point to the conclusion that high-tech start-ups are more interested in the quality and availability of a well-educated work-force than are start-ups in other industries.  Both high-tech Japanese transplants and high-tech domestic start-ups, however, also exhibit the same puzzling location behavior with respect to wages as do Japanese transplants generally: both tend to prefer states where production workers are relatively highly paid.

Third, the interaction of plant size and unionization only affects the location decisions of large Japanese transplants.  This is again consistent with the case study findings showing that both Japanese and domestic start-ups seek to avoid unionization, that Japanese transplants are more sensitive to unionization than are domestic start-ups, and that large and visible Japanese transplants are more concerned with the possibility of unionization than are domestic start-ups.

The overall results of adding industry and plant variables to the field illuminate further how different types of start-ups define regional location advantages.  However, two of the regional control variables (ESC and PAC) reemerge as significant in the case of Japanese transplants.  This is not wholly surprising, given the disproportionately high shares of Japanese transplants in California (in the PAC region) and Kentucky (in the ESC region) when compared with domestic start-ups. One likely possibility is that the historical preference of Japanese transplants for locating in California (because of its large Japanese population, cultural amenities, and proximity to Japan [Milkman 1991]) continues to be a factor in the location of Japanese transplants.  As for the preference of Japanese transplants for locating in Kentucky, the interviews reveal that labor quality characteristics such as loyalty to firms and strong work ethic is a particularly important factor.  These labor quality factors may well be incompletely captured by the RURAL variable.

### Alternative Tests of the Field Models

The econometric results from the field models mirror quite closely the expectations from the case studies of the differences among the factors that govern the location of domestic start-ups and Japanese transplants.  This correspondence between the field research and the econometric analyses provides independent confirmation of our findings. However, we conducted two additional cross-checks on our field models to evaluate further the robustness of these findings.

One test added the industry and plant variables (SIZE, AUTO, and HTECH) to the first field model. This test would show if the results from interacting plant-specific factors with state attributes are an artifact of more pervasive differences in the location behavior of either automotive or high-technology plants. None of these variables, however, achieves statistical significance in either the Japanese transplant or domestic start-up estimations, and the underlying patterns of the parameter estimates for the state attributes are not affected.

A second test was to estimate a "counterfactual" version of the second field model, which tests for interactions between industry and plant and state characteristics but has no basis in our field research. In this counterfactual model, the three industry and plant characteristics are interacted with the key state attributes UNION, WAGE, HSGRAD, EXPEDUC, MARKET, and HIGHWAY. The results of this test are largely nonsense. Many of the variables that we know from the location literature and our field research should be significant are not, or they have the wrong sign.

Given these results, we conclude that the field model containing the relevant plant modifiers identified by the case studies is a robust and accurate depiction of the decision process made by start-ups in determining where to locate their plants. Also, this model highlights the differences between domestic and Japanese-owned start-ups that can be traced to different visions of what constitutes regional location advantages.

## REGIONAL ADVANTAGE FOR HIGH PERFORMANCE WORKPLACES

The core model accurately characterizes the broad outlines of the location decisions of domestic start-up factories. Production costs, proximity to markets, and other location factors are important determinants of location for domestic start-ups, the plants that are our proxy for the adoption of the piecemeal model of high performance management practices. However, this core model is not a good predictor of location decisions of Japanese transplants that adopt hybrid models of management practices. Transplants are less likely to be concerned with traditional factor costs and more inclined to rely on high performance practices to raise factor productivity.

The findings from the field research enable us to enrich the traditional core location model by adding variables that better explain the location decisions of both Japanese transplants and domestic start-ups. The additional state attribute variables help to clarify other factors that belong in the core model for both types of plants. The presence of a major international airport, for example, is important for the location of domestic start-ups as well as Japanese transplants (Table 7.4). However, the influence of international airports on the location of Japanese transplants remains far larger than for domestic start-ups.[26] Similarly, the field models show that both groups of high-technology start-ups have distinctive location preferences for factors such as high state expenditures on education and larger goals of workers with postsecondary education.

The field models also reveal that Japanese transplants take many of the same core cost factors into account as domestic start-ups, but only after the effects of key omitted factors are controlled for. However, these findings do not change the basic conclusion that new domestic factories rely more heavily than their Japanese counterparts on traditional cost and market criteria when making location choices.

The field models show that Japanese transplants are much more strongly affected by measures of labor quality such as education, stability, cooperativeness, and commitment than are the domestic start-ups. For example, the availability of a rural workforce is an important location consideration for Japanese transplants, although its estimated effect is statistically insignificant for domestic firms. Similarly, the size of the high school labor pool and the low probability of unionization influence the location of Japanese transplants more strongly than they influence domestic start-ups.[27]

The plant modifier terms identified in our field research are also much more important for understanding the location of Japanese transplants than of domestic start-ups. Only three of the eight plant modifier terms were significant for domestic start-ups, compared with six for the Japanese transplants. Similarly, the location of Japanese transplants is sensitive to factors that uniquely affect Japanese transplants, such as the presence of industrial recruitment offices in Japan.

The one persistent result from this analysis that appears anomalous from the perspective of the traditional location literature is the positive effect of wages on location for Japanese transplants and for both Japanese and domestic high-technology start-ups. Many studies have found that wages have a minimal effect on plant location, but only a handful have found a positive effect of wages on location and this has never been satisfactorily explained. The positive effect of high wages on location is all the more surprising because our location models also control for factors such as education, region, and unionization, the variables that typically explain the wages of production workers in manufacturing.

An explanation for this anomaly that is consistent with the overall tenor of our discussions with the managers of the start-ups is that some intangible labor quality factors that influence location choice are positively correlated with average wage rates. One possibility is that states that pay high wages—after controlling for other dimensions of labor quality such as education and unionization—have workers with hard-to-observe abilities that are highly valued by employers.

However, an even stronger candidate for explaining the importance of locating in high-wage states is that labor productivity in these states is high because of efficiency-wage payments. Our discussions in Chapters 2 and 3 both point to the possibility that the states that pay relatively high wages to manufacturing workers are those that are relatively well-endowed with firms that pay efficiency wages and use other performance incentives to motivate high labor productivity (Lang, Leonard, and Lilien 1987; Katz and Summers 1989). The start-ups that most intensively adopt organizational practices for raising labor productivity locate in high-wage states because the labor pools in these states are likely to contain a high proportion of workers who have previously been employed at workplaces where such efficiency-wage incentives are being used. In effect, the workforce "quality" that is attractive to these start-ups is derived from prior work experience in such efficiency wage firms. Our field research shows that the labor force qualities engendered by efficiency-wage incentives are identical to those that high performance workplaces seek to recruit and develop. In this way, high wages can be seen in a similar light as the preferences for rural and nonunion locations. They act as signals of the presence of workers with the kinds of work attitudes that support the hybrid model of high performance management.

These findings on the location decisions of start-ups represent a further link in the chain of evidence about the complementarities among high performance management strategies. Start-ups that adopt the most high performance management practices tend to integrate these practices with larger management strategies, as shown by the importance of differences in the nationality of corporate ownership. These same high performance start-ups tend to reinforce high performance management practices with performance incentives and jobs of unusually high quality. They further reinforce these practices by choosing plant locations having labor pools that are most compatible with the effectiveness of high performance management practices.

The final proof of this thesis, however, lies in "bottom line" measures of business performance. The following chapter provides evidence of the relationships between high performance management practices and growth in output and productivity.

## Notes

1. It is not possible to identify establishments owned by non-Japanese foreign corporations, so to be more exact, the "domestic" database is the non-Japanese set of manufacturing plants. Plants owned by Japanese firms were identified by cross-referencing JEI and Dun and Bradstreet data sets. The Dun and Bradstreet identifier numbers were found for the establishments listed in the JEI directory by consulting the D&B published lists of companies. Records in the USEEM database with these identifier numbers were then verified as the Japanese transplants, by comparing location, industry, and start-up year with the JEI directory, and these transplants were deleted from the domestic database.

2. The Dun and Bradstreet data have a well-known limitation concerning underrepresentation of small and nonmanufacturing plants due to relatively less interest in their creditworthiness. However, this does not present a serious concern in the present context because the smallest plants and all nonmanufacturing establishments were excluded from the database. Due to the large size of the initial database, remaining omissions and errors are not likely to be systematic across states, industries, or size classes.

3. The JEI report is more accurate than the alternative listing by the Japanese Export and Trade Organization (JETRO) because the latter includes Japanese investments in nonmanufacturing activities. Information provided by managers interviewed at

Japanese transplants does not differ materially from establishment data published by JEI.

4. Chi-square tests show that these differences are significant at the 1% level. Only one out of four of the Japanese auto-related plants produce automotive parts (SIC 3714) or assemble vehicles (SIC 3711). The large majority is classified in other industries (primarily electronics, rubber and plastic products, and instruments), but their principal production is components for vehicles. Auto parts producers were identified at the four-digit SIC level. Domestic plants in these same four-digit SIC industries in the USEEM database were likewise labeled auto-related producers.

The relatively low number of Japanese start-ups makes probing the similarity or differences of location patterns in other subsectors of manufacturing difficult. The state rankings were compared for domestic and Japanese plants in the 17 three-digit industries that had at least 10 Japanese transplants. The correlation of domestic and Japanese state rankings was statistically significantly in only 10 of the 17 industrial sectors. Of these 10 industries where location patterns appeared similar, several are associated with auto parts and 2 with food processing (where proximity to assembly plants and agricultural products is likely to be a factor). In no industrial branch was the rank correlation coefficient higher than 0.55.

5. In order to estimate the probability of a start-up factory being located in state $j$, a distribution for the disturbance term ($\varepsilon$ in Equation 7.1) must be defined (Greene 1993). If it is assumed that the $\varepsilon_{ij}$ terms are independent and that they follow the Weibull distribution, it can be shown (McFadden 1974) that $F(\varepsilon) = \exp(e^{-\varepsilon})$.

Thirteen states received no Japanese plants during the study period (1978–1988): Delaware, Idaho, Kansas, Louisiana, Maryland, Montana, New Hampshire, New Mexico, North Dakota, Rhode Island, South Dakota, Vermont, and Wyoming. However, the influence of the attributes of these states on state choice is accounted for in the denominator of Equation 7.3.

6. The assumption of the "independence of irrelevant alternatives" is made for computational convenience in the conditional logit model (McFadden 1974). McFadden assumed that the error terms are distributed Weibull, meaning that they are independent of the other alternatives. In location models, this assumption implies that if a company's profits are higher in North Carolina than they would be in a state in another region, such as Iowa, there is no reason to expect that they would also be higher if the firm were instead located in South Carolina than they would be in Iowa. However, there may be unmeasured factors within regions that make South Carolina more likely to be profitable than Iowa. Bartik (1985) proposed including regional dummy variables to control for this problem as a computationally easier solution to the independence problem in conditional logit than the nested logit model used by McFadden (1981).

7. State dummy variables cannot be used to test for omitted variables because the model would be overspecified.

8. The functional form of the estimated model is based on the logarithm of the profit function, so most variables are measured in their natural logarithms. The excep-

tions are variables measured as percentages, indices, and dummy variables. The values for most of the location attributes are taken from the mid 1980s.

9. States with lower rates of unionization among manufacturing production workers would offer more locales free of unionized plants and a relatively higher proportion of workers whose work experience is less likely to be in unionized plants. Thus, the average unionization rate is a more precise measurement of potential difficulty of finding plant sites with non-unionized workers than the alternative measurement of whether states have right-to-work laws.

10. The gravity-adjusted potential market size is the sum of the state's personal income and personal income of all other states, weighted by distance: $MARKET_j = \Sigma_k(PI_k/d^2_{jk})$, where $PI_k$ is total personal income in state $k$ and $d_{jk}$ is the distance in highway miles from the population center in the selected state $j$ to the population center of state $k$ (Woodward 1992). The distance to states with two principal metropolitan areas, such as California and Pennsylvania, is calculated as the average of the two distances. The distance value used for each state's own market is 1.

11. Many managers of Japanese plants also cite proximity to their main customer(s), usually other Japanese transplants, as a principal location determinant. This suggests that the MARKET variable in the core and field models, which measures proximity to general consumer markets, should be replaced by a variable that captures Japanese-specific markets. However, including such a variable reflecting the proximity of other Japanese transplants introduces too much endogeneity into the model.

12. Interpretation of the magnitude of the coefficient depends on the definition of the variable. Where the independent variables are expressed in natural log form, the coefficients are close approximations to elasticities. The logit specification for location selection, following Bartik (1985), implies

$$(\partial \ln p)/(\partial \ln x) = \beta(1 - p)$$

where $\beta$ is the estimated coefficient, $p$ is the probability of locating in that state, $x$ is the variable, and $\partial \ln p$ is the percentage of change in the probability of locating in a state. Assuming equal probability among states would be 1/48, or 0.0208; thus, $(1 - p)$ is very close to 1. The coefficients estimate the percentage change in new selection probability for a percentage change in the independent variable. For the variables expressed in percentages, such as unionization and high school education, the estimated coefficient can be roughly interpreted as the percentage change in selection probability for a one-percentage-point change in the independent variable. In any given state, the expected effect of a change in the independent variable depends on the deviation from the average value of that variable across the 48 states and the estimated elasticity ($\beta$), holding constant all other variables at their mean value.

13. A measure of vocational and technical training was considered, but the only available information across all states is vocational school enrollment. This variable

includes beautician, childhood education, and other training unrelated to industrial employment and was thus rejected as an explanatory variable.

14. State and local expenditures on education per pupil are normalized for differences in teachers' salaries by dividing these expenditures by the average salary for occupations requiring a college education. With this adjustment, variation in EXPEDUC better reflects real differences among states in spending on education rather than differences in average costs. Because differences among states in teacher salaries would reflect differences in value placed on quality education as well as differences in cost of living, average salary for an occupation requiring similar four-year university training is used instead.

15. An average was taken in states with two or more major international airports. The variable is not normalized by state population because the probability of direct flights and convenient transfers increases with the actual number of passengers.

16. Alternative measures (such as energy costs and energy costs weighted by mean average temperature) were included in other specifications of the model, but they were not significant individually and did not improve the explanatory power of the model.

17. Tannenwald (1984) provided a detailed explanation of unitary taxes, including distinguishing "worldwide" from "domestic" unitary tax bases. The former includes corporate income from operations anywhere in the world, while "domestic" counts only income from affiliates located within the United States. A dozen states had a worldwide or domestic unitary tax base in the early 1980s. Woodward (1992) found that Japanese firms considered either type of unitary tax to be a significant disadvantage, and states with either type are counted here.

18. Start-ups are identified as "high technology" according to the definition devised by Markusen, Hall, and Glasmeier (1986). "High technology" industries are those in which the proportion of engineers, technicians, computer scientists, and other physical and life scientists exceeds the manufacturing average. Twenty-three 3-digit industry sectors, the least aggregated industrial grouping for which occupational data are available, are thus classified as high tech.

19. The difference in the log likelihood statistics between the "unrestricted" Japanese transplant field model (under Field Model 1 in Table 7.4) and the "restricted" core model ("Japanese transplants" column in Table 7.3), $-2(L_R - L_U)$, is distributed $\chi^2$, with degrees of freedom equal to the number of restrictions in the reduced model, i.e., the seven additional parameters estimated for the field model:

$$(8,941.73 - 8,853.5) = 88.23 > \chi^2{}_{0.01,\,7} = 18.48 \text{ (1\% significance level)}.$$

20. $-2(L_R - L_U)$ for the domestic start-ups is distributed $\chi^2$ with seven degrees of freedom:

$$(21,808.51 - 21,798.8) = 9.71 < \chi^2{}_{0.1,\,7} = 12.02 \text{ (10\% significance level)}.$$

21. To test whether the results on labor quality were sensitive to the specific measure of education adopted, alternative measures—including median years of education, percentage of the population with a high school education or higher, value added

per production worker, and the number of engineers measured as the proportion of the total number of employed persons in the state—were substituted for HSGRAD.

In the models of Japanese location, the estimated coefficient on median years of education and proportion of high school graduates consistently had a negative coefficient and high level of significance. Value added was never positive and significant regardless of whether high school education was included in the specification. The estimated coefficient on engineers was negative and had no effect on the coefficient on HSGRAD. Nor was this measure of worker skill a significant location attribute for Japanese transplants in high-tech industries, as evidenced by the high $P$ value of the coefficient on the state measure for engineers when modified by a dummy variable designating Japanese transplants in high tech-industries.

Substituting these variables into the domestic model gave similarly unhelpful results: median years of education was insignificant; value added was negative regardless of whether HSGRAD was also in the model; and engineers as a proportion of total employment was not significant. Because median education loses the distinction between production and professional workers and because value added measures an output rather than quality of labor input, HSGRAD remains the preferable control variable for labor quality.

22. For both Japanese and domestic plants, the models with the plant modifiers are superior to those restricted to state attribute characteristics at the 1% significance level.

23. If the influence of the plant characteristic is to intensify the importance of the location attribute, then the estimated coefficient would have the same sign as the state attribute variable it modifies. If the plant characteristic tempers its influence, then it would carry the opposite sign. The estimated effect of unionization rates on selection probability by auto industry transplants is the sum of the coefficients on UNION and on UNION × AUTO (7.87 − 4.53 = 3.34 for Japanese transplants).

24. Less significance to auto industry plants is shown by the negative sign on the MARKET × AUTO variable and its high significance level ($p = 0.003$), indicating that the difference between the estimated coefficients for MARKET across all the Japanese transplants versus for auto-related plants is statistically significant.

25. Access to interstate highways and proximity to markets are alternative ways of measuring market access. To illustrate this point for the case of auto suppliers, MARKET × AUTO was dropped from the field model with plant characteristics. The result was that HIGHWAY × AUTO interaction became significant for both Japanese transplants and domestic start-ups.

26. A 10% increase in the number of persons using the largest state airport is associated with an 8.8% increase in selection probability by Japanese firms, compared with a 1.5% increase in selection probability by domestic firms.

27. The literature also reports that race may be a factor in the location of Japanese transplants (Cole and Deskins 1988; Woodward 1992), along with concerns with the incidence of poverty and urban social problems. The race composition of the workforce was not mentioned as a location concern in the field research, and

many Japanese transplants had ethnically diverse workforces. However, poverty and urbanization did come up in the context of crime and workplace conflict.

We explored the influence of these variables in a further set of field models by explicitly introducing a series of narrowly defined variables intended to separate the influences of race, urbanization, and poverty. Race was measured as the share of African Americans in the non-urban population with incomes above the poverty line, and the poverty measure was defined as the percentage of population living below the poverty line outside of urban areas. Race had a marginally significant influence on the location of Japanese transplants, but poverty did not, and neither factor mattered to domestic start-ups. However, these factors are also correlated with the HSGRAD and RURAL variables, and our methodology may not be able to capture the underlying relationships among these factors and location decisions.

# Part IV
# Evaluating High Performance Management Strategies

# 8
# The Bottom Line
## Productivity and Jobs

The previous chapters have shown a widespread commitment among start-up firms to adopt high performance workplace practices and to provide high-quality jobs. However, there is a significant difference between Japanese transplants and domestic start-ups in the frequency of adoption and implementation of these practices. On average, Japanese transplants use more high performance workplace practices than do domestic start-ups and adopt them in a more systematic way. These differences also lead to different preferences for employee characteristics and other aspects of the local environment. In short, both the interviews and the quantitative evidence on management strategies from the case studies point to the likelihood of complementarities among workplace employment practices and a series of other business policies, ranging from quality control and plant location to investment in additional plant and equipment.

The discussion of theories of high performance practices in Chapter 2 points to the potential contribution to productivity and efficiency of both individual organizational practices and combinations, or systems, of complementary practices. Tests of these efficiency effects typically employ a standard production function framework that includes various measures of high performance management practices.[1] Some studies use national surveys of establishments (Ichniowski 1990; Black and Lynch 1996, 1997, 1999; Cappelli and Neumark 1999; Freeman and Kleiner 2000; Osterman 2000), while others use detailed small-scale surveys that focus on a single technology, such as automobile assembly, steel finishing, or apparel (MacDuffie 1995; Ichniowski, Shaw, and Prennushi 1997; Abernathy et al. 1999; Ichniowski et al. 2000). The general conclusion is that high performance management practices make at least a modest contribution to business performance, but none of these studies were able to examine the overall organizational regimes within which such practices are embedded.

In this chapter, we examine the extent to which both high performance management practices and the larger Japanese-style hybrid organizational systems influence business performance. We utilize a new "ramp-up production function" based on the relationship among employment growth, output growth, and the growth in productivity among the start-ups in our case study sample. The "ramp-up" rates of employment growth and productivity changes in the case study firms are positively correlated with the use of high performance management practices, particularly in the broader context of Japanese-style hybrid organizational systems. Because the small size of the case study sample limits our ability to control for influences on performance that may vary over time, we also test a variant of this ramp-up model using national panel data on new manufacturing plants. The national data confirm the case study findings that the effects of differences in overall organizational regimes are large and robust across alternative specifications of the empirical models.

## RAMP-UP CYCLES AND THE RAMP-UP PRODUCTION FUNCTION

A key characteristic of the start-up process for all of the firms in our sample is that the growth in both output and employment is largely a function of increases in the number of shifts being operated and of investment in new capacity. The speed of this "ramp-up" process to full three-shift capacity is governed by the rate at which productivity growth causes unit production costs to fall. The initial corporate decision to invest in new plant and equipment for a start-up is based on the expectation that "full-capacity" unit costs will be lower than those elsewhere in the parent company. However, start-ups in the sample industries invariably began operations at much less than full capacity by starting with a single shift, and they initially experienced unit costs that were higher than those elsewhere in the company. Output is then increased to full capacity in stages by adding a second, and then a third shift as warranted by reductions in unit costs.

The pattern of output in the case study sample of firms typically involves gradual growth within each shift as production and quality problems are solved and as workers learn to operate more efficiently. Growth in output within shifts, however, is overshadowed by increases in output as the firm moves through the ramp-up cycle from one to two shifts, and then to three-shift operation.

Employment follows a similar pattern, in that there are large changes whenever a new shift is added or when new investments are made in plant and equipment and a new ramp-up cycle is triggered. These periodic employment increases involve equal numbers of workers, because each shift uses the same capital equipment and approximately the same complement of production workers, technicians, and direct supervisors. Productivity improvements within a single shift, however, do not affect employment because staffing levels are fixed on each shift.

The rate at which a start-up passes through the stages of this ramp-up cycle is conditional upon achieving corporate efficiency benchmarks that are defined in terms of measures such as "output per employee" and "unit cost." In order to be authorized to add a shift, a start-up must equal or exceed the productivity benchmark levels set by the most efficient counterpart plants in the company. Once target productivity standards are achieved in round-the-clock operations, it is often common for the parent corporation to expand capacity further through additional investments in plant and equipment at the same location. Start-ups that do not meet corporate efficiency standards are not allowed to add shifts or otherwise expand capacity. Failure to achieve these standards can eventually lead to a decrease in employment as production is reallocated to more efficient branch plants.

The productivity improvements that govern the speed of the ramp-up cycle come almost exclusively from improvement of workforce skills, greater employee effort, and employee involvement in solving production problems. There was remarkably little technological change in this sample of start-ups for periods of up to a decade or more. The very few instances of technology change occurred when new product lines were introduced after three-shift capacity had been reached in the initial product lines.

The managers of the Japanese transplants often attribute the speed of the ramp-up cycle to the way in which they fostered problem solving, skill acquisition, and organizational learning. For example, Japanese transplants initially seem to spend more time achieving productivity benchmarks on the first shift because they intentionally use high performance management practices that emphasize learning to perfect production techniques, achieving high standards of quality, and developing procedures for continually improving productivity. As a result, they tend to complete the full ramp-up cycle more rapidly and receive additional investment in new plant and equipment from their parent companies sooner than do the domestic start-ups.

Managers of domestic start-ups also associate ramp-up speeds with high performance management practices. However, in comparison with Japanese start-ups, they use fewer of these practices and tend to subordinate organizational learning and quality goals to achieving gains in physical output and technical economies of scale as quickly as possible. They also tend to emphasize technology as the source of enhanced productivity and managerial control as a means of lowering unit costs. These differences result initially in a faster ramp-up rate than in Japanese transplants, but they appear to slow the long-term progress through the ramp-up cycle and delay investment in new capacity.

## RAMP-UP PRODUCTION FUNCTIONS

The ramp-up cycle described above implies a somewhat different production function from those with continuously variable inputs, which are typically assumed in other studies of high performance management practices. Stable technology and fixed-coefficient inputs of capital and labor on each shift characterize the ramp-up production function for long periods of time, while increases in productivity are closely related to the adoption of high performance management practices and efficient organizational regimes. This information on production in start-ups provided by the case studies can be expressed in terms of the following "ramp-up" production function in which new factories have an initial fixed endowment of plant and equipment:

$$Q_t = f[S_t L, e(P, J), E_t(P, J)]$$

In this function, $Q_t$ is plant output at time $t$. The labor input $(S_tL)$ is the product of the number of shifts operating at time $t$ $(S_t)$ and the fixed labor coefficient per shift $(L)$. The functions $e(P, J)$ and $E_t(P, J)$ represent factors that contribute to improving static and dynamic efficiency. The function $e(P, J)$ captures the static improvement in output per worker resulting from the adoption of high performance management practices (P) and Japanese-style organizational regimes (J). The function $E_t(P, J)$ reflects the additional improvement in the output per worker at time $t$ resulting from productivity change over time caused by individual, team, and organizational learning.

$L$ is exogenously determined by the fixed capital and technology of the plant.[2] P and J are parameters chosen by management, and $S_t$ is endogenously determined according to the decision rule that a start-up is authorized to add another shift once a target level of productivity is achieved through the combined effects of $e(P, J)$ and $E_t(P, J)$.

According to this ramp-up production function, start-ups initially hire $L$ workers whose productivity is raised by $e(P, J)$ and increases over time according to $E_t(P, J)$. Once the target level of productivity is achieved, a second shift of labor is then hired and the ramp-up learning process is repeated (see the employment step-function and corresponding output/worker sawtooth function in Figure 8.1).[3] After three-shift capacity is achieved, productivity growth triggers a second round of investment in plant and equipment and a new ramp-up cycle is generated.

This ramp-up process is common to all the plants in the sample, but there are wide inter-firm differences in the composition of the productivity drivers, P and J, chosen by each start-up. We were unable to obtain the data on productivity or unit costs, or on output, that would allow us to specify the functional forms of $e(P, J)$ and $E_t(P, J)$ because such information was considered proprietary. However, we can still use the ramp-up production function to test for the effects of $e(P, J)$ and $E_t(P, J)$ on firm output. This is because changes in output in start-ups are, by definition, a function of changes in employment and productivity.[4] The case studies show that employment changes are conditional upon achieving productivity benchmarks that then trigger the hiring of additional shifts of $L$ workers. Since growth in output and growth in employment both depend upon productivity increases, they can be used interchangeably as measures of ramp-up rates

**Figure 8.1  Illustrative Ramp-Up of a High Performance Start-Up**

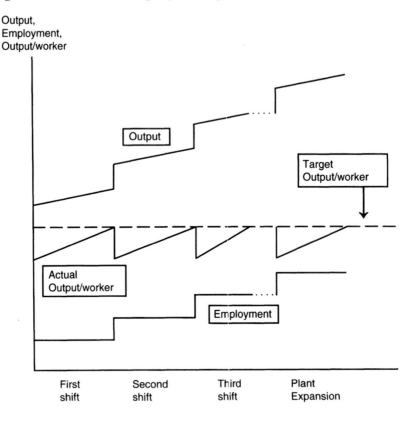

Productivity growth can be caused by technological change, training, increased employee effort, and various kinds of organizational
learning.  We can rule out technological change as a source of productivity growth because technology is fixed in our start-ups during the
period covered by our data.  Because P and J capture the other sources
of productivity change, we can test for a relationship between ramp-up
rates and productivity change by seeing if P and J are related to
employment growth.  Plants where the effects of P and J are strong
should add shifts and invest in new plant and equipment at a faster rate
than those where these effects are weaker (Figure 8.2).

**Figure 8.2  Alternative Ramp-Up Paths**

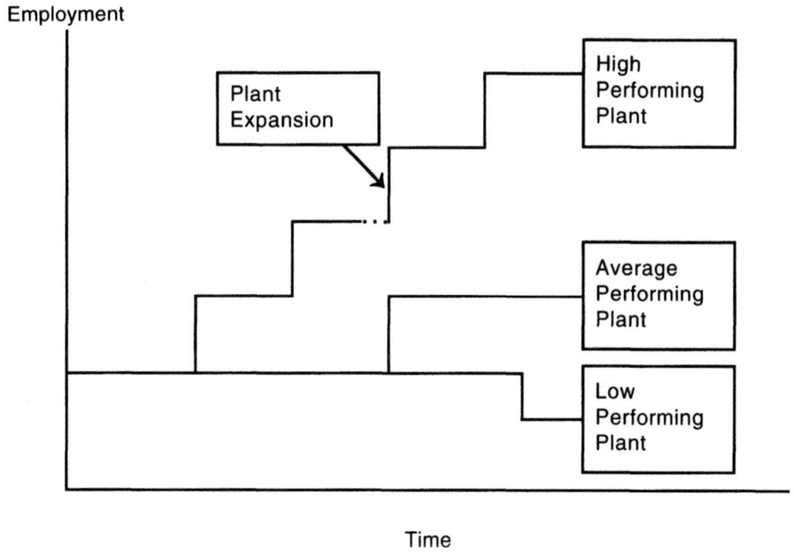

TESTING FOR EFFICIENCY GAINS IN THE RAMP-UP
PRODUCTION FUNCTION

In this section, we test whether differences in the number of high performance practices adopted and the use of particular management regimes affect the speed of the ramp-up cycle through their impact on $e(P, J)$ and $E_t(P, J)$. For these tests, we use ramp-up rates, detailed information on the adoption of high performance management practices, and measures of organizational regimes compiled from the case studies. While the small size of this sample limits our ability to conduct refined tests of the efficiency effects of these organizational factors, we are able to construct a simple model that captures the essence of how management practices affect the speed of the ramp-up cycle.[5] Because the timing of employment changes in the ramp-up production function is determined by productivity growth, the average rate of change in employment over the observed life of the start-up can be used as a measure of the speed of the ramp-up cycle, and therefore as an indicator of productivity improvement. We can then test for whether the intensity of adoption of high performance workplace practices and differences in organizational regimes affects the time it takes for the ramp-up cycles to be completed.

## THE EFFECTS OF HIGH PERFORMANCE MANAGEMENT PRACTICES

The first test looks at how the frequency of adoption of the key high performance management practices affects the ramp-up cycle. This test approximates those in other studies that have measured the effects of high performance management practices on business performance.

The dependent variable in this model (RAMPUP) is the average annual compound growth rate of employment (EMPGRO) between the year of start-up and the year of the case study. RAMPUP represents $dS_tL_i/d_t$ in the ramp-up production function. The explanatory variable of interest is the number of high performance workplace practices (P) adopted. P is specified as either a continuous variable (HIPERFORM) or as a set of binary categorical variables (ONEPRACTICE, TWOPRACTICE, THREEPRACTICE, and FOURPRACTICE). Employment levels in the base year of operation are included as a control for the algebraic effect of differences in the starting size of establishments on estimated rates of employment growth, and industry dummies are added to control for the possibility that the measure of ramp-up rates is an artifact of the firm being in a high-growth industry.

The effects of P are first tested using two models specified as follows:

$$RAMPUP_i = a + b_1HIPERFORM_i + b_2STARTSIZE_i + b_3IND + e$$

and

$$\text{RAMPUP}_i = a + b_1\text{ONEPRACTICE}_i + b_2\text{TWOPRACTICE}_i$$
$$+ b_3\text{THREEPRACTICE}_i + b_4\text{FOURPRACTICE}_i$$
$$+ b_5\text{STARTSIZE}_i + b_6\text{IND}_i + e,$$

where

$\text{RAMPUP}_i$ = average annual compound growth rate of employment in establishment $i$ from year of start-up to the time of case study interview

$\text{HIPERFORM}_i$ = number of high performance practices (from among intensive training, flexible work organization, quality circles, and daily work group meetings or high participation by employees in management decisions adopted by establishment $i$

$\text{ONEPRACTICE}_i$ = binary variable: 1 if establishment $i$ adopts only one practice from among intensive training, flexible work organization, quality circles, and daily work group meetings or high participation by employees in management decisions

$\text{TWOPRACTICE}_i$ = binary variable: 1 if establishment $i$ adopts only two practices from among intensive training, flexible work organization, quality circles, and daily work group meetings or high participation by employees in management decisions

$\text{THREEPRACTICE}_i$ = binary variable: 1 if establishment $i$ adopts only three practices from among intensive training, flexible work organization, quality circles, and daily work group meetings or high participation by employees in management decisions

$\text{FOURPRACTICE}_i$ = binary variable: 1 if establishment $i$ adopts all four practices

$\text{STARTSIZE}_i$ = natural logarithm of employment in the start-up year of establishment $i$

$\text{IND}_i$ = binary variables for SIC 30 (PLAS) and SIC 35 (MACH)

$e$ = random error

The results confirm the basic findings from the field research: the larger the number of high performance practices adopted by a start-up, the faster the long-term ramp-up rate from one shift to the next (columns 1 and 3 of Table 8.1). The coefficient on HIPERFORM implies that each additional practice yields an increase of four and one-half percentage points in the annual ramp-up rate up to a maximum of 18%. This is a relatively strong effect, but it is consistent with the relatively high rates of employment growth of these start-ups. The industry variables are insignificant, which shows that the results are independent of the industries represented in the sample.

The second specification of this model uses binary variables for different numbers of high performance practices adopted in order to test for nonlinear effects of these practices. Firms that adopt one or two high performance practices do not show a statistically significant improvement in their ramp-up rates, but those that adopt three or four practices show significantly faster rates of ramp-up compared with plants that rely exclusively on traditional types of management practices.[6]

### The Effects of Japanese-Style Management Regimes

The case studies also allow us to test for the influences of different organizational regimes. The field research suggests that the effectiveness of high performance practices is enhanced when they are systematically incorporated into a broader Japanese-style management regime. We lack a precise measure of such regimes, but we know from the interviews that they are far more common among Japanese transplants than among domestic start-ups. This correlation between Japanese-style management regimes and Japanese ownership allows us to test for the effects of unobserved management regimes by adding a binary variable, NATJ, representing Japanese ownership, to the ramp-up models.

Reestimating these models with the inclusion of NATJ shows strong evidence of a Japanese-style management effect (columns 2 and 4 of Table 8.1). The coefficients on NATJ are large and significant for both specifications of high performance practices, and a higher fraction of the overall variation in ramp-up rates is explained than in either specification of the first ramp-up model. The NATJ coefficients imply that

**Table 8.1 Estimated Effects of High Performance Practices on Ramp-Up Rates, Case Study Sample**

| Variable | Col. 1 Without NATJ | 2 With NATJ | 3 Without NATJ | 4 With NATJ |
|---|---|---|---|---|
| Constant | 35.33*** | 30.44*** | 32.61** | 31.49** |
| | (3.04) | (2.68) | (2.41) | (2.43) |
| HIPERFORM | 4.56*** | 3.19** | | |
| | (3.26) | (2.16) | | |
| ONEPRACTICE | | | 6.82 | 0.96 |
| | | | (0.85) | (0.12) |
| TWOPRACTICE | | | 12.26 | 0.77 |
| | | | (1.38) | (0.08) |
| THREEPRACTICE | | | 17.50** | 10.06 |
| | | | (2.14) | (1.17) |
| FOURPRACTICE | | | 18.99*** | 10.47 |
| | | | (2.83) | (1.38) |
| NATJ | | 10.11** | | 11.38** |
| | | (2.20) | | (2.14) |
| STARTSIZE | −6.57*** | −6.00*** | −6.41*** | −6.09*** |
| | (3.17) | (3.00) | (2.95) | (2.92) |
| PLAS | −3.90 | −4.27 | −3.30 | −4.02 |
| | (0.71) | (0.82) | (0.55) | (0.69) |
| MACH | −7.17 | −6.92 | −6.75 | −6.11 |
| | (1.24) | (1.26) | (1.08) | (1.02) |
| No. of plants | 48 | 48 | 48 | 48 |
| Adjusted $R^2$ | 0.30 | 0.36 | 0.25 | 0.31 |
| $F$ value | 6.03*** | 6.22*** | 3.25*** | 3.67*** |

NOTE: The dependent variable is RAMPUP. Absolute value of $t$-statistics is in parentheses. *** = Statistically significant at the 0.01 level; ** = statistically significant at the 0.05 level.

SOURCE: Authors' survey.

Japanese-style management increases the speed of the ramp-up cycle by 10–11 percentage points, even after controlling for differences in the frequency of adoption of high performance management practices. This is larger than the estimated effects of high performance practices in the first ramp-up model, suggesting that the overall management strategy is more important than the adoption of individual high performance practices.

## High Performance Management or Incentive Effects?

These results provide dramatic evidence of the power of the combination of high performance management practices and Japanese-style organizational regimes to speed productivity growth. However, many of the start-ups in the sample also adopt productivity-based compensation incentives that could provide an alternative to high performance management as the explanation for faster ramp-up rates.[7] For example, in Chapter 5 it is shown that 23% of the start-ups offer performance bonuses and 21% provide profit-sharing plans to their employees, both of which are intended to provide incentives for increasing labor productivity (Lazear 1998; Black and Lynch 1999). In addition, 8% offer pay-for-knowledge premiums that reward the acquisition of productivity-enhancing human capital. The high wages offered by the sample of start-ups might also explain faster ramp-up rates if they represent the payment of efficiency wage incentives to increase productivity.

This pay incentives hypothesis has already been tested in Chapter 5 using factor analysis. We have also tested a modified version of the preceding ramp-up models in which various wage incentives—high wages, profit sharing, bonuses, and pay for knowledge—were used as independent variables in place of high performance management practices. We also tried a linear measure of incentives (defined as the number of incentive practices used) and a variety of other specifications.

None of these tests showed a significant statistical relationship between RAMPUP and wage incentives.[8] Compensation incentives do not contribute independently to ramp-up performance. These results are consistent with the factor analysis presented in Chapter 5 where it is shown that neither high wages nor performance-based compensation incentives are strongly related to employment growth.

Many of the start-ups in our sample, however, also emphasized that the commitment of employees to the firm was important for reducing turnover and encouraging cooperation with high performance management practices. This was particularly the case among Japanese transplants. Commitment is fostered in a variety of ways, but the most common practices are to provide high levels of job security and to give employees decision-making authority.

We tested for these "commitment incentives" with the same procedures used to test for the performance effects of compensation incentives. Our measures of commitment were job security and employee responsibility for quality control. As with pay incentives, there was no evidence that commitment incentives influenced ramp-up rates.

This result was more problematic than in the case of pay incentives because it contradicted relatively strong interview findings. One possible explanation is that these incentives operate *indirectly* by reinforcing the direct effects of high performance management practices and Japanese-style organizational regimes, rather than having a direct influence on productivity and ramp-up speeds. This raises the possibility that collinearity between various incentives and those variables that *directly* influence ramp-up rates obscures the indirect effects of commitment incentives.[9]

Although the sample size and the limits of the data available make it impossible for us to explicitly estimate these indirect influences, we have already conducted tests for the underlying relationships among commitment incentives, high performance management practices, and ramp-up rates using factor analysis of job quality data presented in Chapter 5. This factor analysis shows a strong relationship among commitment incentives, the cluster of high performance management variables, and the ramp-up rate, particularly for Japanese-owned start-ups (see Table 5.8). The factor loadings in the first "efficiency" factor also show that the commitment incentives are more strongly related to efficiency than are pay incentives.

## CORROBORATING EVIDENCE FROM NATIONAL DATA

Both the case studies and the econometric analyses present detailed and compelling evidence of the contribution of high performance management practices and Japanese-style organizational regimes to ramp-up rates and productivity growth in start-up factories. However, the case studies cover only three manufacturing industries and the sample is too small to allow us to control for other factors, such as business cycle considerations or exchange rates (in the case of Japanese transplants) that might be influencing the results.

To address these limitations, the national panel database of new branch manufacturing plants in the United States (USEEM), discussed in Chapter 7, was combined with corresponding information on Japanese transplants obtained from the Japan Economic Institute and augmented by our own mail and telephone survey of Japanese transplants. Because the USEEM sample of establishments contained only 70 Japanese start-ups for which there were complete employment data, an effort was made to collect additional data directly from the establishments in the JEI directory. Questionnaires were mailed to Japanese plants in the industrial sectors with the largest number of start-ups and follow-up telephone surveys were conducted. Through these direct contacts, responses were obtained from an additional 27 plants, bringing the total Japanese sample to 106.[10] Tables 8.2 and 8.3 describe some of the basic characteristics of the sample.

The national data enable us to replicate the case study ramp-up models that use NATJ as an indicator of firms that use the hybrid model of high performance management practices. These data do not provide us with separate measures of the number of high performance practices used. However, almost two-thirds of all Japanese transplants in the case studies adopted at least two of the key high performance practices, compared with less than one-third of the domestic start-ups, and half of the Japanese transplants adopted three or more practices, in contrast to only one-fifth of their domestic counterparts. Given this highly significant difference in adoption rates, combined with the relative importance of Japanese ownership on productivity growth (as compared with specific high performance practices) in the case study model, Japanese

**Table 8.2  Average Annual Compound Employment Growth Rates
for Japanese and Domestic Start-Ups by Two-Digit
Industry,  1978–88**

| SIC and industry | Domestic | | Japanese | | Distribution of plants (%) | |
|---|---|---|---|---|---|---|
| | No. of plants | Growth rate (%) | No. of plants | Growth rate (%) | Domestic | Japanese |
| 20 Food products | 3,551 | 4 | 11 | 11 | 10.59 | 10.38 |
| 22 Textiles | 824 | 7 | 1 | 60 | 2.46 | 0.94 |
| 23 Apparel | 1,537 | 6 | 1 | 0 | 4.58 | 0.94 |
| 24 Lumber | 1,340 | 8 | 1 | 6 | 4.00 | 0.94 |
| 25 Furniture | 830 | 7 | 3 | 35 | 2.47 | 2.83 |
| 26 Paper | 1,202 | 5 | 1 | 0 | 3.58 | 0.94 |
| 27 Printing | 2,989 | 7 | 0 | — | 8.91 | 0.00 |
| 28 Chemicals | 2,843 | 4 | 5 | 19 | 8.48 | 4.72 |
| 30 Rubber and plastic | 1,729 | 10 | 8 | 54 | 5.15 | 7.55 |
| 32 Stone, clay, glass | 1,761 | 5 | 2 | 18 | 5.25 | 1.89 |
| 33 Primary metals | 1,171 | 6 | 6 | 20 | 3.49 | 5.66 |
| 34 Fabricated metal | 2,946 | 7 | 5 | 50 | 8.78 | 4.72 |
| 35 Non-electrical equip. | 4,321 | 6 | 11 | 53 | 12.88 | 10.38 |
| 36 Electrical equip. | 2,911 | 8 | 26 | 28 | 8.68 | 24.53 |
| 37 Transportation | 1,326 | 9 | 16 | 28 | 3.95 | 15.09 |
| 38 Instruments | 1,406 | 7 | 6 | 13 | 4.19 | 5.66 |
| 39 Miscellaneous | 854 | 5 | 3 | 23 | 2.55 | 2.83 |
| Overall two-digit average | 33,541 | 6 | 106 | 29 | 100.00 | 100.00 |

SOURCE: USEEM panel data, 1978–88; authors' survey.

**Table 8.3  Average Annual Compound Employment
Growth Rates for Japanese and Domestic
Start-Ups by Three-Digit Industry, 1978–88**

| | Domestic | | Japanese | |
|---|---|---|---|---|
| SIC and industry | No. of plants | Growth rate (%) | No. of plants | Growth rate (%) |
| 209 Canned fruit/ veg. | 380 | 7 | 6 | 17 |
| 307 Plastic products n.e.c. | 1,384 | 10 | 5 | 22 |
| 331 Steel | 371 | 7 | 5 | 13 |
| 357 Computers, office equip. | 941 | 8 | 3 | 66 |
| 354 Machine tools | 636 | 5 | 3 | 25 |
| 365 Radio/TV receivers | 109 | 7 | 7 | 37 |
| 367 Electrical components | 945 | 11 | 12 | 19 |
| 371 Auto assembly/ parts | 713 | 8 | 13 | 19 |

SOURCE: USEEM panel data, 1978–88; authors' survey.

ownership can serve as a rough proxy for the combined effects of high
performance practices and Japanese-style management strategy.

### Estimating the Ramp-Up Model from National Data

The national data allow for the testing of the effects of high performance management with control for a number of other effects that
might possibly be influencing ramp-up rates. These include a vector of
industry dummy variables to control for exogenous shifts in product
demand (IND) and a vector of regional dummies (REG) to control for
differences in market access and regional cost structures.[11]   A third

vector of dummy variables, STARTYEAR, is used to control for nonlinear time-varying influences on growth rates, such as cyclical changes in demand, different vintages of technology, and the number of years each plant has been in operation (see Table 8.4 for definitions of the variables used).

The basic model is specified as follows:

$$\text{RAMPUP} = a + b_1\text{NATJ}_i + b_2\text{IND}_i + b_3\text{REG}_i + b_4\text{STARTYEAR}_i + b_5\text{STARTSIZE}_i + e.$$

A variant of this basic model is also tested to see if the estimates of NATJ are biased upward by the presence of Japanese start-ups in industries that are supplying components to rapidly growing Japanese-owned automobile assembly plants. This variant includes both a vector of dummy variables for start-ups in the four-digit industries that supply the automobile industry ($\text{AUTO}_i$) and a variable in which these industries are interacted with Japanese ownership ($\text{AUTO}_i \times \text{NATJ}_i$).[12]

**Table 8.4  Definitions of Variables Used in the National Ramp-Up Models**

| | |
|---|---|
| $\text{AUTO}_i$ = | Binary variable for plant $i$ being in a four-digit SIC industry producing automotive input |
| $\text{AUTO}_i \times \text{NATJ}_i$ = | Binary variable for Japanese-owned plant $i$ being in a four-digit SIC industry producing automotive inputs |
| $\text{IND}_i$ = | Vector of binary variables for the two-digit SIC of establishment $i$ |
| $\text{NATJ}_i$ = | Binary variable for Japanese-owned plants |
| $\text{NATJ}_i \times \text{IND}_j$ = | Vector of binary variables for Japanese plant $i$ being in the two-digit SIC industry $j$ |
| $\text{RAMPUP}_i$ = | Average annual compound growth rate of employment in establishment $i$ from year of start-up to 1988 |
| $\text{REG}_i$ = | Vector of binary variables for regional location of establishment $i$ |
| $\text{STARTSIZE}_i$ = | ln of employment in the start-up year of establishment $i$ |
| $\text{STARTYEAR}_i$ = | Vector of binary variables for starting year (ranging from 1978 to 1986) of establishment $i$ |

Finally, a sectoral model is specified that examines the effects of Japanese ownership on ramp-up rates in different industries by replacing NATJ with a vector of industry-specific interaction terms, $\text{NATJ}_i \times \text{IND}_j$. This sectoral interaction model is specified as

$$\text{RAMPUP} = a + b_1\text{IND}_i + b_2\text{NATJ}_i \times \text{IND}_j + b_3\text{REG}_i + b_4\text{STARTYEAR}_i + b_5\text{STARTSIZE}_i + e.$$

## Empirical Findings

The descriptive statistics in Chapter 3 on growth rates of Japanese transplants and domestic start-ups in the case study sample show that the average annual employment growth rate of the Japanese transplants is over three times that of the domestic start-ups (20% versus 6%). The national start-up database shows a similar pattern in the descriptive statistics (see Table 8.2), and the econometric evidence provides even more compelling evidence of the Japanese growth advantage (Table 8.5).

In the basic model (column 1 of Table 8.5) the coefficient on the NATJ variable implies that the annual growth rates of Japanese start-ups average over 20 percentage points above those of domestic plants after controlling for other factors likely to contribute to firm growth rates.[13] While this is a numerically large impact, it represents the combined influence of Japanese-style organizational regimes and the high performance management practices that Japanese start-ups adopt more frequently than their domestic counterparts.

We can also reject the hypothesis that this NATJ growth advantage is the result of any special circumstances associated with Japanese auto suppliers. The coefficient on AUTO in the auto industry specification (column 2 of Table 8.5) does show that establishments producing for the automotive industry have significantly higher ramp-up rates than other start-ups in the same two-digit industries, but this effect is independent of the nationality of ownership. The estimated effect of Japanese ownership for the entire sample is consistent and robust across both specifications of the basic ramp-up model.[14]

In the sectoral model, where the effects of Japanese ownership in different industries are tested, we find that the effects of Japanese man-

**Table 8.5  Estimated Effects of High Performance Practices on Ramp-Up Rates, National Panel Data 1978–88**

| Variable | Col. 1 Basic model | 2 Basic model with auto interactions | 3 Basic model with sectoral interactions |
|---|---|---|---|
| Constant | 0.20*** (25.32) | 0.20*** (25.35) | 0.20*** (25.34) |
| NATJ | 0.24*** (7.54) | 0.21*** (5.54) | |
| STARTSIZE | –0.04*** (38.96) | –0.04*** (38.96) | –0.04*** (38.96) |
| AUTO | | 0.02** (2.66) | |
| AUTO×NATJ | | 0.11 (1.52) | |
| Industries | | | |
| SIC20 | –0.01 (0.81) | –0.01 (0.80) | 0.00 (0.75) |
| NATJ×SIC20 | | | 0.08 (0.85) |
| SIC22 | 0.04*** (3.59) | 0.04*** (3.56) | 0.04*** (3.57) |
| SIC22 | | | 0.52 (1.69) |
| SIC23 | 0.03*** (2.94) | 0.03*** (2.84) | 0.03*** (2.97) |
| NATJ×SIC23 | | | –0.06 (0.18) |
| SIC24 | 0.03*** (2.60) | 0.03*** (2.61) | 0.03*** (2.62) |
| NATJ×SIC24 | | | 0.05 (0.17) |
| SIC25 | 0.02 (1.34) | 0.02 (1.26) | 0.02 (1.31) |
| NATJ×SIC25 | | | 0.35** (1.97) |

(continued)

**Table 8.5 (continued)**

| Variable | Col. 1<br>Basic model | 2<br>Basic model with<br>auto interactions | 3<br>Basic model<br>with sectoral<br>interactions |
|---|---|---|---|
| SIC26 | 0.02 | 0.02 | 0.02 |
| | (1.47) | (1.48) | (1.49) |
| NATJ×SIC26 | | | 0.06 |
| | | | (0.20) |
| SIC28 | –0.02** | –0.02*** | –0.02** |
| | (2.36) | (2.44) | (2.34) |
| NATJ×SIC28 | | | 0.16 |
| | | | (1.00) |
| SIC30 | 0.05*** | 0.05*** | 0.05*** |
| | (5.37) | (5.13) | (5.26) |
| NATJ×SIC30 | | | 0.49*** |
| | | | (4.11) |
| SIC32 | –0.01 | –0.01 | –0.01 |
| | (1.19) | (1.34) | (1.18) |
| NATJ×SIC32 | | | 0.16 |
| | | | (0.74) |
| SIC33 | 0.02** | 0.02** | 0.02** |
| | (2.02) | (1.98) | (2.09) |
| NATJ×SIC33 | | | 0.11 |
| | | | (0.88) |
| SIC34 | 0.02** | 0.01 | 0.02** |
| | (2.42) | (1.79) | (2.39) |
| NATJ×SIC34 | | | 0.44*** |
| | | | (3.13) |
| SIC35 | 0.00 | 0.00 | 0.00 |
| | (0.15) | (0.14) | (0.07) |
| NATJ×SIC35 | | | 0.49*** |
| | | | (5.00) |
| SIC36 | 0.04 | 0.04*** | 0.04*** |
| | (5.11) | (4.89) | (5.15) |
| NATJ×SIC36 | | | 0.19** |
| | | | (2.79) |

**Table 8.5 (continued)**

| Variable | Col. 1 Basic model | 2 Basic model with auto interactions | 3 Basic model with sectoral interactions |
|---|---|---|---|
| SIC37 | 0.06*** | 0.05*** | 0.06*** |
|  | (5.54) | (4.56) | (5.52) |
| NATJ×SIC37 |  |  | 0.25*** |
|  |  |  | (2.84) |
| SIC38 | 0.02 | 0.02 | 0.02 |
|  | (1.56) | (1.54) | (1.62) |
| NATJ×SIC38 |  |  | 0.07 |
|  |  |  | (0.52) |
| SIC39 | −0.01 | −0.01 | −0.01 |
|  | (0.87) | (0.87) | (0.86) |
| NATJ×SIC39 |  |  | 0.18 |
|  |  |  | (1.00) |
| Regions |  |  |  |
| MTN | 0.01 | 0.01 | 0.00 |
|  | (0.57) | (0.56) | (0.54) |
| WNC | −0.01 | −0.01 | −0.01 |
|  | (0.80) | (0.81) | (0.84) |
| ENC | 0.00 | 0.00 | 0.00 |
|  | (0.19) | (0.34) | (0.25) |
| NNE | 0.00 | 0.00 | 0.00 |
|  | (0.65) | (0.68) | (0.68) |
| WSC | 0.00 | 0.00 | 0.00 |
|  | (0.24) | (0.25) | (0.28) |
| ESC | 0.03*** | 0.03*** | 0.03*** |
|  | (3.98) | (3.89) | (3.88) |
| SAT | 0.02*** | 0.02*** | 0.02** |
|  | (3.83) | (3.80) | (3.76) |
| Starting year cohorts |  |  |  |
| 1978 | −0.04*** | −0.03*** | −0.03*** |
|  | (6.08) | (6.07) | (6.06) |

*(continued)*

**Table 8.5 (continued)**

| Variable | Col. 1<br><br><br>Basic model | 2<br><br>Basic model with<br>auto interactions | 3<br>Basic model<br>with sectoral<br>interactions |
|---|---|---|---|
| 1980 | -0.02*** | -0.02*** | -0.02** |
| | (3.91) | (3.88) | (3.84) |
| 1982 | -0.03*** | -0.03*** | -0.03*** |
| | (5.16) | (5.14) | (5.13) |
| 1984 | -0.02*** | -0.02*** | -0.02*** |
| | (4.62) | (4.60) | (4.63) |
| | | | |
| No. of plants | 33,647 | 33,647 | 33,647 |
| Adj. $R^2$ | 0.05 | 0.05 | 0.05 |
| F value | 61.79*** | 8.15*** | 41.23*** |

NOTE: Dependent variable is RAMPUP. Absolute value $t$-statistics in parentheses. *** = Statistically significant at the 0.01 level; ** = statistically significant at the 0.05 level.

SOURCE: USEEM panel data, 1977–88, and authors' survey.

agement regimes are concentrated in only 6 of the 16 industries examined (column 3 of Table 8.5). The estimated growth advantage of Japanese transplants within this group of industries (furniture [SIC25], rubber and plastics [SIC30], fabricated metals [SIC34], non-electrical equipment [SIC35], electrical equipment [SIC36], and transportation [SIC37]) is even larger than the estimate for the entire sample. It ranges from 25 percentage points per year in transportation to 49 percentage points per year in rubber and plastics and non-electrical equipment.[15] This sectoral model further confirms the case study analyses because all three industries in the case study sample are among those where there is a statistically significant Japanese ownership effect in the national data.

# COMPETING EXPLANATIONS OF THE EFFECT OF JAPANESE-STYLE ORGANIZATIONAL REGIMES

The econometric evidence from both the case study sample and the national panel data strongly supports the conclusion that start-ups adopting high performance management practices have faster ramp-ups than their traditional counterparts. This is not surprising, given the similar findings of other studies.

However, we further conclude that there is a powerful effect of Japanese-style organizational regimes that reinforces the effects of high performance management practices and that has an independent influence on ramp-up rates as well. This organizational regime effect can be seen in the empirical tests of the ramp-up production function and is confirmed independently by reports from managers in the case studies. Since earlier studies have not controlled for these differences in organizational regimes, there is likely to be an upward bias to their estimates of the effects of high performance management practices.

Despite the weight of the econometric and case study evidence, it is possible that our relatively simple ramp-up models omit some important variables or that the results are biased in some way. In order to provide further support for our conclusions, we have examined the most likely competing hypotheses that might explain the growth advantage of Japanese transplants.

## Omitted Variables

The most obvious counterhypothesis is that some variable is omitted from the model that accelerates the ramp-up cycle and is also correlated with Japanese ownership. For example, there could be exogenous differences in technology or worker quality that are associated with growth in employment that are not captured by controls for industry growth and region. There is also the possibility that the high growth rate of Japanese transplants could reflect responses to potential trade restrictions or to exchange rate fluctuations. Some of these potential problems of omitted variables have already been eliminated by the unique features of the sample of start-ups. For example, both Japanese and domestic start-ups adopted the most up-to-date technologies and these technologies remained constant during the period covered by the study. Nor is there evidence of major differences in workforce quality between domestic and Japanese-owned start-ups, as measured by age, education, and experience (Doeringer, Evans-Klock, and Terkla 1998).

The possibility of other omitted variables was also investigated during the interviews with plant managers. Although a large number of different stochastic events that affected growth and performance of specific plants at particular points in time were mentioned by managers, high performance management practices and Japanese-style organizational regimes are the only consistent influence on ramp-up rates that we could identify. Nevertheless, we have examined the most likely candidates for omitted variable bias.

### Import substitution

One potential concern is that the high growth rates of Japanese transplants could result from the substitution of U.S. production for Japanese imports, since import substitution is widely reported to motivate much of the Japanese manufacturing investment in the United States (Kenney and Florida 1993; Caves 1993). It is also the case that investments in Japanese transplants are often predicated on there being a potential market sufficient to absorb output from round-the-clock operations. However, a recent study finds no evidence of production by Japanese transplants substituting for imports from Japan (Lipsey and Ramstetter 2001). In addition, the domestic start-ups in the sample also reported that they served "guaranteed" markets that would otherwise be supplied by less efficient branch plants of the parent company.[16] Since both types of start-ups have somewhat guaranteed markets, and since we control for differences in industry growth rates and cyclical variations in demand, there is no *a priori* reason that import substitution should affect the growth rates of Japanese start-ups any differently than the types of market substitution in which domestic start-ups are engaged.

A second possibility is that growth rates of Japanese transplants reflect import substitution caused by changes in exchange rates. We reject this possibility on two grounds. First, fluctuations in U.S.–Japanese exchange rates do not follow the same pattern as output growth in Japanese transplants and exchange rates are not statistically significant when included as an explanatory variable in the national ramp-up models.[17] The exchange rate hypothesis is also somewhat questionable on theoretical grounds because the positive effect of exchange rates on import-substituting output should be at least partially offset by the negative effect on repatriated profits (McCulloch 1991).

## Survivor Bias

In theory, the results could be biased because the databases only include start-up plants that have survived for a decade or more. If we were trying to estimate *levels* of productivity or employment, survivor biases could be a problem because we do not control for declines in productivity and output in plants that fail. However, our procedure at least partly avoids this problem by testing for relative differences in the ramp-up rates between Japanese transplants and domestic start-ups. If both domestic and Japanese-owned start-ups have similar survival rates, the survival biases should largely cancel out. While we lack comparable data on survivor rates among Japanese and domestic start-ups, Japanese transplants rarely closed during the period under study. Given the high survival rates of Japanese start-ups, our estimates of the Japanese ramp-up advantage could only be biased if the survival rates of domestic start-ups were lower than those of Japanese start-ups. However, this bias would cause the relative differences in ramp-up rates that we observe in our data to be lower, not higher, than what is actually the case.[18]

## Aggregation Bias

Another type of bias might result from having conducted the analysis at the two-digit level of aggregation. The sample of Japanese transplants is too small to conduct a complete analysis of this problem at the three-digit industry level, but ANOVA tests of differences between the mean growth rates of Japanese and domestic start-ups conducted for the handful of three-digit industries for which there are enough observations of Japanese plants (see Table 8.3) show significant differences in growth rates (at the 1% level) for at least three of these industries: SIC 307 (plastic products n.e.c.), SIC 357 (computers, office equipment), and SIC 371 (auto assembly/parts). While aggregation might explain some of the growth differences, the Japanese-style management effect is so large that the basic findings remain valid.

## SUMMARY

Both the case studies and the data from a national panel of new manufacturing plants provide strong and consistent evidence that Japanese-style high performance management practices improve productivity and speed ramp-up rates when compared with start-ups that rely on more traditional U.S.-style management practices. There is a direct correlation between the frequency with which start-ups use high performance workplace practices and the rate at which they increase production to full capacity.

The more important finding, however, is that those start-ups that integrate these practices with Japanese-style organizational regimes have an even more substantial ramp-up advantage when compared with start-ups that rely on more traditional U.S.-style management practices and organizational regimes. Performance incentives, particularly those that build employee commitment, are also associated with faster ramp-up rates. Analysis of a national sample of start-ups further confirms the combined influences of intensive adoption of high performance management practices, commitment incentives, and Japanese-style organizational regimes. The performance advantages from adopting Japanese-style organizational regimes are robust across a number of alternative specifications of the ramp-up model, and the findings also withstand challenges from various alternative hypotheses about why Japanese transplants might have faster ramp-up rates.

The effects of Japanese-style organizational regimes and commitment incentives have been neglected in previous analyses of high performance management practices. To the extent that these studies have included establishments that have adopted such practices, the effectiveness of high performance management practices is overstated. However, ignoring the effects of Japanese-style commitment incentives and organizational regimes in improving productivity and efficiency also means that economists have underestimated the potential for larger reforms in organizational efficiency to improve national productivity.

## Notes

1.  A typical approach would be to posit a production function $Q = AK^a L^b$, where $Q$ is output, $K$ and $L$ are units of capital and labor, $A$ represents a productivity shifter,

in this case as a result of the adoption of high performance practices, and $a$ and $b$ are positive constants. For a review of this literature, see Black and Lynch (1999).

2. Because of the existence of fixed capital and constant technology, there is no need to include capital or technology variables in this production function. The fixed capital and technology determine the amount of labor required per shift.

3. Figure 8.1 posits linear productivity and output growth within each shift for ease of illustration. Output per worker is the average of all shifts. The weighted average productivity for the plant declines by a smaller amount with the addition of each new shift, because newly hired employees (who initially have lower productivity than incumbent workers) constitute a smaller and smaller fraction of the workforce. For illustrative purposes, we have shown linear growth in output per worker in Figure 8.1.

4. Changes in demand for the output of start-ups can be ignored as a source of employment growth because of the special place occupied by start-ups within the overall structure of multiplant firms. Start-ups are expected to be the most-efficient branch plants within their parent companies. Increases in demand are met by adding capacity to start-ups that have met their efficiency benchmarks and declines in demand are absorbed by the least-efficient branch plants.

5. This model is similar to that used by Leonard (1992) in his study of employment growth at the establishment level.

6. The effects of adopting specific practices (such as quality circles) were also tested, but none of these specific practices was statistically significant.

7. For a recent review of the incentives and performance literature, see Prendergast (1999).

8. This result is contrary to that of Black and Lynch (1999), who found that profit sharing matters to productivity.

9. For example, there are relatively high simple correlations between our measure of commitment and high performance practices (i.e., flexible work organization [$R = 0.50$], intensive training [$R = 0.43$], employee involvement [$R = 0.48$], and quality circles [$R = 0.42$]) and with NATJ ($R = 0.46$).

10. Recall the USEEM sample consists of 33,541 plants and this includes non-Japanese foreign-owned plants that cannot be identified because USEEM does not include nationality identifiers. The Japanese plants were identified by matching the addresses of USEEM plants with those in the Japanese Economic Institute listings.

11. Japanese start-ups are more concentrated in the South Atlantic and East Central regions than domestic start-ups. The eight census regions for the continental United States are used as regional controls: MTN = Mountain states, WNC = West North-Central, ENC = East North-Central, NNE = New England and Middle Atlantic, WSC = West South-Central, ESC = East South-Central, and SAT = South Atlantic. The Pacific region is omitted.

12. The four-digit SICs included are 3711 (automobile assembly), 3714 (auto parts fabrication), as well as automotive-related production in plastics and other related

industries such as 3089 (automotive plastic components) and 2399 (seat covers and seat belts).

13. This difference in growth rates might not necessarily continue after the initial start-up period. Regression analysis using number of years in operation, rather than year of start-up, reveals a growth path that declines in a nonlinear way over time for both Japanese and U.S. start-ups.

14. When the region dummies are omitted from the basic growth model, the estimated coefficient on NATJ is 0.22, nearly identical to that in the full model. Similarly, alternative ways of adjusting for differences in start-up sizes—using the second year of operation as the base year, dropping all establishments reporting fewer than 20 employees in the first year of operation, and dropping U.S. establishments in small, multi-plant firms with fewer than 2,500 employees—left the estimated Japanese growth advantage substantially unchanged. Replacing the cohort dummies with a variable representing the age of the firm also did not change the results. In addition, we independently estimated the starting size of start-ups and found that there is no statistically significant difference between the starting sizes of Japanese transplants and their U.S. counterparts.

15. These industries are mainly in the durable goods sector that manufactures relatively high-value-added products with variable demand, exactly the sectors for which Aoki (1990) predicted that Japanese-style organizational regimes are likely to matter the most.

16. The allocation of production among branch plants depends on a complicated set of marginal cost calculations and company-specific transfer pricing decisions (Scherer 1975). Domestic start-ups have substantial market guarantees because they are intended to serve markets already established by less efficient branch plants within the parent company, as well as new markets with high growth potential. Japanese plants that come to the United States for reasons other than export substitution face demand curves that are steeper than export-substituting plants. These plants are analogous to domestic start-ups that are entering new markets, as opposed to markets previously served by outdated branch plants that they are replacing.

17. We looked for the effect of the Japanese/U.S. exchange rate using two different specifications. In one case, we included the percentage change in the exchange rate over the lifetime of the firm interacted with NATJ as an independent variable. This was insignificant and did not substantially change the coefficients in the original regression. We also tried including this interacted exchange rate without the NATJ dummy and this too proved to be insignificant. Exchange rates were taken from the *Economic Report of the President*, 1996.

18. It could also be argued that the performance advantage of Japanese transplants is affected by self-selection biases. If Japanese companies that make direct investments in the United States are better managed than those that do not, we might be comparing a self-selected group of exceptionally well-managed transplants with a group of domestic start-ups that have a wider distribution of management ability. However, since we are trying to identify the management practices that contribute

to higher productivity growth, any self-selection bias would occur along the precise dimensions that are of interest to our study. Our research design allows us to compare "representative" U.S. start-ups with transplants that are most likely to adopt state-of-the-art high performance management practices.

# 9
# Conclusions

Previous chapters have examined the workplace practices, location decisions, and growth experiences of new manufacturing plants in the United States. Manufacturing start-ups were chosen for study because they should provide a leading indicator of what will constitute "best" manufacturing practices in the future. The results of this study show that this assumption is largely correct. Many of these new manufacturing plants embody leading-edge technologies, they adopt innovative, high performance management practices to operate this technology efficiently, and they select locations based upon both standard cost considerations and workforce qualities that complement their choices of technology and management practices.

A review of the theoretical and empirical literature on economic organizations and high performance management practices shows that practices such as quality circles, intensive training, and production teams can raise productivity. However, this literature provides little guidance about how and why these practices contribute to productivity growth. Nor did the wide range of theoretical perspectives—economic theories of organizations, behavioral theories of motivation and productivity, and theories emphasizing the balance of workplace power between labor and management—point to conclusive explanations of productivity growth. We therefore turned to field research to gain first-hand knowledge of why innovative management practices are being adopted, how they operate, and what benefits they bring to employers and workers.

Our field research was focused on providing answers to six basic questions:

1) To what extent do the newest and technologically most advanced manufacturing plants adopt high performance management practices?

2) Are there complementarities among these practices?

3) Is there a single "best practice" model of high performance management being used in these plants?

4) Do high performance management practices contribute to jobs of high quality?

5) Are there unique regional characteristics that reinforce high performance workplace practices?

6) How large a competitive advantage can be generated by factories that combine state-of-the-art technologies with comprehensive high performance management strategies?

The field research provides us with a rich set of answers to these questions, almost all of which are confirmed through quantitative tests. These findings sharpen our understanding of how high performance management strategies interact with technological and labor market environments. They also contribute to the development of more informed theories of high performance management practices. As a result, we see new possibilities for improving business productivity and the well-being of workers and offer some fresh proposals for action by managers, labor organizations, and policymakers.

## THE HIGH PERFORMANCE MANAGEMENT PRACTICES OF START-UP FACTORIES

Our field interviews with managers reveal that the parent corporations of new branch plants devote considerable effort to identifying the most profitable locations. From these interviews and from our shop-floor observations, we also know that similar emphasis is placed on installing advanced technologies. Managers are then expected to bring this technology to full production capacity as quickly as possible by adopting state-of-the-art workplace management practices for raising labor productivity and improving plant efficiency. The result is that these new factories are adopting high performance management practices at higher rates than are established U.S. manufacturing plants, and output and employment in these plants is growing faster than the average rate for their industries.

However, not all start-ups are equally adept at implementing these high performance strategies. Plant managers embrace high performance management practices to varying degrees.  Some adopt many of these practices, pay considerable attention to complementarities among practices, and seek to create highly integrated systems of high performance management strategies, while others do not.

The criterion that comes closest to distinguishing between those start-up factories in our sample that frequently, systematically, and successfully adopt high performance practices and those that do not is the nationality of ownership.  Japanese-owned transplants typically adopt clusters of high performance management policies that are designed to interact with plant location decisions, operations management practices, and supply logistics.  In contrast, most domestic start-ups adopt high performance practices less frequently and they combine them less systematically with other high performance management strategies. The result is often a piecemeal model of workplace organization that retains many of the features of traditional command and control management.  This piecemeal model does not exploit the workforce's problem-solving capabilities, and it neglects the attention to complementarities that give coherency to the Japanese hybrid model of management.

This is not to say that there are no domestic start-ups in our sample that assembled such coherent hybrid models; there are several that rival the best of the Japanese transplants.  Nor does it mean that Japanese transplants are uniformly successful in adopting hybrid models of management.  We found examples of successes and failures among both types of new plants.  However, it is clear from the case studies and quantitative analyses that the average Japanese transplant adopts a different and richer set of high performance practices than its domestic counterpart.

These differences between the hybrid management practices of Japanese transplants and the piecemeal approach to high performance management taken by domestic start-ups are most apparent in the interview materials from our case studies.  Japanese transplants recruit employees who can work in teams, control quality, and solve operating and quality-control problems.  They strengthen these workforce qualities through intensive training and then draw upon them in a variety of problem-solving situations.  Domestic plants often try to mimic these Japanese practices, but they do so less frequently, with less reliance on employee problem solving, less concern with teamwork skills of potential new hires, and less commitment to identifying interactions among practices.

## HIGH PERFORMANCE PRACTICES AND GOOD JOBS

Almost all the start-ups in our sample provide well-paying and otherwise good jobs that are typically filled by high school graduates. A substantial fraction, however, provides truly excellent jobs for high school graduates in terms of very high wages, substantial job security, opportunities for employee voice, and practices that empower employees.

The interviews reveal that this job excellence is not intended to compensate for dangerous, stressful, or otherwise adverse working conditions. Instead, high wages and secure jobs augment good working conditions and often complement the efficiency effects of other high performance management practices. For example, unusually high compensation helps to recruit a pool of job applicants who will respond positively to high performance management practices, as when teamwork and problem-solving skills are used for selection criteria. High job quality can also reduce quit rates that might otherwise erode employer returns to intensive training.

Similarly, the subset of job quality components relating to pay, high wages, and wage supplements that are contingent upon performance can be explained as a means of stimulating higher productivity. Efficiency wages can reduce shirking, bonuses can inspire greater effort, and pay for gaining skills and knowledge can provide incentives for learning. The evidence of this incentive aspect of good jobs, however, is mixed. Adopting some form of contingent compensation yields only modest performance gains. However, our interviews suggest that high wages and wage supplements may also operate indirectly on performance through their effect on the probability of adopting high performance management practices. In contrast, there are strong performance improvements associated with practices such as job security that foster workforce commitment.

Finally, we find provocative evidence that worker power is quite influential in leading to good jobs in start-ups. This power effect is not derived as much from formal bargaining by unions (which is rare among the start-ups in our sample) as from the informal sources of power that come from fostering work groups and empowering these groups to make decisions and solve problems. Informal power is strongly associated with both the adoption of high performance management practices and with job excellence.

## HIGH PERFORMANCE MANAGEMENT AND REGIONAL LOCATION ADVANTAGES

All of the start-ups in our sample see business location as central to strong business performance. The field interviews show that location decisions are influenced by factors that are typically found in the literature on business location strategies. This conclusion is further confirmed by econometric analyses. Apart from some occasional differences affecting auto and high-technology factories, both Japanese transplants and domestic start-ups are significantly influenced in their location decisions by physical characteristics such as proximity to markets, access to good transportation networks, and agglomeration economies. They both regard the prospects of being unionized as a negative location factor, and they value the presence of large pools of workers who are high school graduates. Neither type of start-up is influenced by corporate taxes or development incentives.

However, beyond this common set of factors, the location strategies of Japanese transplants and domestic start-ups diverge in ways that further highlight differences in the adoption and implementation of high performance management practices. The biggest differences are that Japanese transplants seek locations that offer a labor force that is particularly amenable to working under the hybrid model of workplace organization and where there are supportive governmental institutions. Japanese firms see a rural workforce as an indicator of a pool of labor that will cooperate with high performance management practices and that can become broadly skilled and flexible through in-plant learning. Similarly, avoidance of unionized locations is emblematic of the importance of cooperative workforce attitudes and freedom from interference with workforce commitment to the company. More generally, Japanese transplants seek labor pools with attitudinal qualifications—such as the ability to work in teams, to solve workplace production and quality-control problems, and to be loyal and committed to the firm—that complement other high performance management practices.

The case study interviews also point to characteristics of state and local governments that attract Japanese transplants, such as enthusiasm for having a Japanese business presence and evidence that government will be supportive of Japanese transplants should legal or regulatory problems arise. While we lack direct empirical measures of these governmental qualities, the field research shows that the presence of a state recruiting office in Japan is widely interpreted by Japanese transplants as symbolic evidence of such a supportive governmental environment. The national econometric evidence on business location confirms the importance of such recruiting offices for the location of Japanese transplants.

In contrast, when domestic start-ups hire high school labor, they often rank qualities that are related to knowledge and skill higher than those related to flexibility and the ability to learn and problem-solve. Consequently, they pay far less attention than Japanese transplants to careful workforce recruitment and selection. Like the Japanese transplants, domestic start-ups try to avoid areas where there are unions. However, union avoidance is motivated more by concerns with future wage costs and inefficient work rules than by the possibility of reduced cooperation, loyalty, and commitment, and this union avoidance is less intense than among Japanese transplants. Domestic start-ups have no particular preference for rural workers, and they are also largely indifferent to the qualities of supportive government that are valued by Japanese plants.

## HIGH PERFORMANCE MANAGEMENT STRATEGIES AND BUSINESS PERFORMANCE

While our research findings demonstrate pervasive differences in the management practices, quality of jobs, and location choices between high performance and traditional start-ups, what ultimately matters is which of these clusters of management strategies performs better.  Even if high performance management practices contribute to stronger business performance, these benefits might simply be offsetting the higher costs of such practices.  It is even plausible to argue that Japanese transplants might have to adopt additional practices that contribute to productivity to offset disadvantages that they may experience from having less knowledge than domestic start-ups of how to operate efficiently in U.S. market environments.

There was, however, no mention in our interviews of high performance management practices being unusually costly or of Japanese transplants operating at a disadvantage in U.S. markets except among auto industry suppliers, who felt that U.S. automobile companies might exclude them from competing with domestic suppliers.  What we did seem to find was a conviction that complementarities among high performance management practices are as important as the individual effects of such practices.  Training in teamwork and problem-solving skills complements the careful selection of workers with problem-solving skills and cooperative work attitudes.  Instruction in statistical process control can improve problem solving, and performance bonuses can provide an incentive to employees to participate in problem solving and productivity-enhancing efforts.

The highest performance benefits, however, were reported to come from incorporating clusters of complementary practices into an overall framework of strategic management.  These larger strategies include siting facilities where there are abundant labor pools of workers with cooperative attitudes (as well as good transportation networks and other standard location advantages); openness to sharing power and authority with workers through employee voice mechanisms; and the provision of economic incentives and job benefits that allow employees to share in the gains from increased productivity.

The tests of these propositions through econometric analyses reveal a significant association between the adoption of high performance management practices and growth in employment and productivity.  There is moderate evidence of complementarities among clusters of high performance practices and much stronger evidence of complementarities associated with strategies of continuous improvement, employee involvement, and the employment of workers with attitudes that support high performance practices commonly found in Japanese transplants.

While the qualitative evidence from a small sample of case studies is too limited to support a definitive judgment about these performance differences, the national econometric evidence provides very compelling confirmation of the field research findings. The positive effects on growth of adopting a cluster of high performance management practices in tandem with other high performance strategies are further confirmed with the analysis of a national panel of manufacturing start-ups.

### Educating Managers about the Hybrid Model

The evidence from this and other studies is unequivocal. The hybrid model of high performance workplace practices is not simply another management fad. Managers can be confident that adopting an appropriate version of this model can lead to higher productivity and stronger business growth. If our assessment of the benefits of high performance management is correct, traditional management practices and attitudes will eventually give way to competition from firms that adopt hybrid models of high performance management strategies. The increased diffusion of high performance practices throughout the U.S. economy during the 1990s is evidence that this process of replacing traditional with more innovative management practices is already under way (Osterman 2000).

Nevertheless, there are signs that this diffusion of practices may represent their incorporation into piecemeal models of high performance management, rather than the prevalence of Japanese-style hybrid models that perform so much better in start-up plants. While the available data do not allow us to distinguish between these two approaches, the fact that these practices are being adopted without a corresponding sharing of efficiency gains with workers through higher wages and greater job security provides circumstantial evidence that we are observing the growth of piecemeal strategies.

This suggests that management education and management consultants have effectively promoted the benefits of high performance management practices without sufficiently advocating the importance of utilizing the complementarities among these practices within the framework of an integrated hybrid model of high performance management. Management education and training programs need to give more attention to understanding what the full hybrid model entails in terms of adjustments in existing management practices.

Moreover, the full benefits of high performance cannot be achieved without a greater sharing of decision-making authority with workers than has been the norm in the United States, as well as a greater sharing of the economic gains of high performance management than is presently occurring. Failure to share power and efficiency gains may be as widespread a stumbling block to faster growth for U.S. managers today as it was for those who managed the domestic start-ups in our field research.

### The Role of Theories of High Performance Management

In the case of advancing the use of high performance management strategies, an understanding of the theories that underlie these strategies can be an important tool for educating managers and unions. For example, the findings from our high performance start-ups demonstrate that high wages, which have been the focus of many efficiency-wage theories, are not by themselves necessarily the best instrument for achieving labor efficiency. Nor is the threat of discharge from a high-wage job likely to be the best means of motivating labor productivity. The primary sources of effort and motivation are in recruiting workers with attitudes that support training, teamwork, and problem solving and in securing commitment and loyalty by providing job security, opportunities for voice, and involvement in decision making.

High wages and otherwise good job qualities, of course, do help to attract large pools of the kinds of high-ability labor with good work attitudes that contribute to the performance of start-ups, and the form that compensation takes can also contribute to productivity. We show, for example, that group bonuses, profit sharing, and pay for knowledge are important performance incentives and encourage the learning of new skills and abilities.

Once workers with the appropriate attitudes are hired and given incentives to be productive and well trained, the start-ups in our sample secure the commitment by reinforcing worker preferences and attitudes. Operant conditioning and behavioral modification have traditionally been the most common approaches among U.S. companies for modifying preferences and attitudes at the workplace, but there is no evidence of the widespread adoption of such techniques among the start-ups in the sample. Instead, we find evidence that "gift" and "fairness" theories of labor efficiency characterize the preferred approach to modifying attitudes and improving productivity.

Organizational learning and continuous productivity improvement in start-ups that adopt hybrid models of high performance management seem most strongly linked to the reduction of principal–agent conflicts between production workers and managers. Careful selection, intensive training, and compensation incentives all contribute to cooperative workforce behavior that is aligned with the objectives of the firm. However, the most important elements that contribute to high performance are gifts, such as employment guarantees and workforce empowerment, that are not explicitly conditioned upon performance. Egalitarian employee participation mechanisms also contribute to a sense that employment relationships are fair and equitable.

### Unions and High Performance Management

Our analysis also carries implications for trade union strategies. Unions need to be aware of how they are perceived by start-ups and what these perceptions mean for organizing and bargaining strategies. The preference of at least some start-up factories for avoiding unions can be traced more to a concern with the constraints that unions may impose on flexibility and cooperation than to a resistance to paying union wages or a fear of employee power. High performance management start-ups routinely pay wages that are at least equal to union rates, and they often deliberately empower their employees. Concerns about the flexibility and cooperativeness of unionized workforces were particularly strong among domestic start-ups that had previous experience with unions at other branch plants. Our interviews showed little awareness among start-ups of the possibility that unionization might be able to contribute to the kinds of constructive employee voice that high performance management start-ups value and for which they often adopt non-union forms of employee involvement.

Even though the threat of unionization represents a large influence on the location choices made by start-ups, it is likely that other locations would be preferred if start-ups perceived a more positive balance between the costs and benefits of union organizing and bargaining. To the extent that unions choose to accommodate their bargaining and representation goals to the new high performance management models that are being adopted by start-ups, it is not inconceivable that both employers and workers could gain from reduced incentives to locate in states where unions are weakest.

## IMPLICATIONS FOR ECONOMIC DEVELOPMENT POLICY

The most important implications for public policy relate to state and local economic development policy. The conventional wisdom is that state and local economic development policy is largely a zero-sum game when viewed nationally. For every state that successfully uses industrial recruitment incentives to attract new businesses, there is an equivalent loss for some other state. To the extent that development incentives succeed in altering the relative location advantages among states, there will be counterpart distortions of market efficiency and public revenues will not be used in the most effective way.

This book provides no evidence, either from the case studies or the econometric analysis of start-ups nationally, that taxes or traditional economic development incentives have a significant influence on plant location. This confirms that state-level financial incentives for new plants are ineffective at best and may simply represent the transfer of resources from taxpayers to firms.

The distinction between high performance and traditional workplaces, however, points to new ways in which state governments and local communities can leverage growth while avoiding traditional, zero-sum development policies. Partly, this involves making investments in infrastructure such as transportation networks and schools that have long been part of the core location incentives for business. However, the larger implication of this book is that economic development policies should be targeted at encouraging new and existing companies to adopt the full hybrid model of high performance management. Such policies are likely to yield higher rates of growth in productivity and jobs than those that simply promote general business investment without regard to the types of management strategies being adopted.

One policy approach available to state and local governments is to help develop labor pools that can contribute to the effectiveness of the hybrid model. The availability of a strong labor pool that appears likely to be receptive to teamwork production practices and the development of flexible job skills should be particularly attractive to high performance firms. State and local governments can also try to encourage constructive labor–management relations. In the case of Japanese transplants, visible, concerted efforts by state and local governments to develop the mediation and troubleshooting capacities that can reduce the risks of starting factories in an unfamiliar political environment can also be a location advantage.

**Building Efficiency Labor Pools**

Some states already have an edge in these intangible regional advantages because they have large rural populations or low levels of unionization. However, there are other ways that states can generate high performance regional advantages. One way is to use education and training to foster problem solving and teamwork as well as traditional production skills. High performance management start-ups are attracted by the quantity of high school graduates, and start-ups in high-technology sectors also value relatively higher expenditures on education by states and localities. Many states are already involved in strengthening postsecondary technical education to provide larger pools of trained labor that will attract new industry. This study supports the wisdom of such a policy for attracting both domestic start-ups and Japanese transplants, but only those in high-technology sectors.

What really matters, however, are "efficiency" labor pools that contain the types of workforce qualities valued by high performance management plants. The labor force skills that are more generally important to start-ups are attitudinal rather than vocational. Teamwork and problem-solving skills are particularly important to high performance management practices and can be made part of the primary and secondary school curricula.

Efficiency labor pools are also often built through informal learning in social and family environments, which explains much of the attraction that rural areas hold for high performance start-ups. In addition, efficiency labor comes from the organizational learning that occurs in companies that engage in substantial job training, pay high wages, and motivate commitment and productivity. This accounts for the preference of high performance start-ups for locating in states where efficiency-wage payments lead to higher average wages for production workers.

The importance of the existing industrial base for building efficiency labor pools means that states should be seeking to upgrade the performance of their newer companies, as well as ensuring that they recruit new companies that have high performance management systems and a commitment to developing efficiency labor. It also means a regional development strategy that refrains from assisting low-wage, low-performance companies.

### Fostering Labor–Management Cooperation

In addition to building a labor force likely to attract high performance management firms, state and local governments should also focus on the quality of labor–management relationships. Currently, start-ups are attracted to states with low levels of unionization. For high performance start-ups, the main disadvantages of unions are not the wage costs or threat of strikes per se, but rather that collective bargaining may weaken employee commitment to the firm and may foster adversarial employee attitudes that are incompatible with cooperation.

States can attract high performance start-ups by enacting right-to-work laws and promoting employment-at-will policies that limit unionization, but such policies may result in hostile labor–management relations if unions organize workers and gain bargaining rights. Adversarial relationships, lower cooperation, and lessened commitment, however, are not the only outcomes of unionization. Unions can also be an important source of employee voice that can strengthen the participatory role of workers.

An alternative to development policies that restrict unions is for states to establish mechanisms to encourage cooperative labor–management relations and to help reduce workplace conflict. One example of such an effort is found in Jamestown, New York, where strikes and difficult labor relations were threatening the industrial base of the community until civic leaders formed a series of community and plant-level labor–management committees, which succeeded in slowing job loss by reducing labor conflict (Gittell 1992).

### Encouraging Mediation and Problem Solving

The Japanese transplants in particular place considerable weight on the willingness of states and communities to accommodate to their presence. For example, Japanese transplants value governments that can mobilize public and private support to smooth the introduction of new plants and their assimilation into the social and economic fabric of the community. This includes help in understanding the norms and values about the treatment of employees, the networks of political and social contacts that are essential for effective community relationships, and which private and public sector officials have the authority to respond to the company's needs. It also means an ability to anticipate and to help mediate problems that may arise in business–government and business–community relationships.

These participation and mediation skills often represent a departure from the traditional mode in which many governments operate and in which economic development incentives are usually conceived. These governmental capacities are most important to foreign-owned start-ups that have less experience with U.S. political and social institutions. However, they are also capacities that should be valuable to business generally.

## HIGH PERFORMANCE MANAGEMENT AND THE NATIONAL ECONOMY

For over two decades, the economics profession has been puzzled by a slowdown in national productivity growth that only briefly recovered during the late 1990s. None of the traditional explanations of a long-term decline in productivity growth, such as oil shocks, a slowdown in capital investment, a decline in research and development, imperfect markets, a stricter regulatory environment, or a deterioration in the quality of human capital, is able to account for this slowdown.

By default, the discussion has turned to ad hoc explanations invoking technology frontiers that have become more difficult to tap through R&D, deficiencies in corporate governance, and a loss of business dynamism. These are plausible hypotheses, but there is little evidence to support them.

This book offers an alternative set of explanations, backed by concrete evidence from case studies and econometric analyses, for these productivity trends. For example, at least some of the slowdown in national productivity growth might be traced to the persistence of outmoded managerial practices in American industry. Conversely, the recovery in productivity growth after 1996 could be partially attributed to the substantial spread of high performance management practices in the 1990s (Osterman 2000). Finally, the failure of productivity growth to fully regain its postwar highs is consistent with high performance management practices being adopted piecemeal, and with the reluctance of American managers to foster commitment, share workplace power with employees, and reward productivity gains with higher real wages.

The hybrid model of high performance management can yield high rates of growth in jobs that pay well, offer job security, and are otherwise of high quality, in addition to increasing productivity. Integrating advances in management practices with complementary improvements in efficiency labor pools can create a trickle-up chain of growth from the workplace, to the region, to the national level. The case studies show that managers of start-ups are universally aware of what constitutes high performance management practices. In the case of Japanese transplants, there is a conviction that high performance management practices work best when fully integrated into all aspects of management strategy and adapted to local circumstances through systematic experimentation.

We encountered much more skepticism among domestic start-ups about the extent of the benefits from these high performance management practices. This skepticism may explain why the rates of adoption of high performance practices are lower among domestic start-ups and why there is less evidence of domestic start-ups seeking to integrate these practices into their overall management strategies or systematically experiment with ways of improving performance. Resistance to the adoption of high performance practices seems to be associated with the reluctance of managers of domestic start-ups to share power and authority at the workplace.

We are, however, optimistic about the prospects for U.S. industry eventually adopting the Japanese-style hybrid model of high performance management. Our case studies do not reveal any type of high performance management practice or strategy that cannot be learned or otherwise imitated by domestic start-ups. Nor do we observe any economic disadvantages from the sharing of power at the workplace or providing jobs of high quality. Moreover, there is evidence of increased adoption of these practices nationwide since the period of our interviews (Osterman 2000). However, translating this increased adoption of high performance workplace practices into maximum firm benefits may require the reeducation of the current generation of U.S. managers in the benefits of power sharing, as well as in how to develop management strategies that most effectively utilize these practices.

# Appendix

## Supplementary Tables for Chapter 7

## Table 7A.1  Labor Market Data – State Rankings

| | WAGE | | UNION | | RURAL | | HSGRAD | |
|---|---|---|---|---|---|---|---|---|
| Rank | State | ($) | State | (%) | State | (%) | State | (%) |
| 1 | Mich. | 12.64 | Mich. | 51.60 | Idaho | 80.9 | Iowa | 40.70 |
| 2 | Wash. | 11.63 | N.Y. | 50.60 | Vt. | 77.2 | Ind. | 40.00 |
| 3 | Ohio | 11.38 | Ohio | 42.20 | Mont. | 75.7 | Pa. | 39.50 |
| 4 | Mont. | 10.95 | Pa. | 42.00 | S.Dak. | 72.1 | Wis. | 38.75 |
| 5 | Ind. | 10.71 | Ind. | 41.40 | Wyo. | 71.4 | Ohio | 38.40 |
| 6 | Ore. | 10.50 | Mo. | 38.10 | Miss. | 70.6 | Me. | 38.20 |
| 7 | La. | 10.43 | Ill. | 37.80 | Me. | 63.9 | Nebr. | 37.65 |
| 8 | Ill. | 10.37 | W.Va. | 36.30 | N.Dak. | 63.6 | Wyo. | 36.60 |
| 9 | Iowa | 10.32 | Wash. | 33.50 | W. Va. | 63.3 | W.Va. | 36.10 |
| 10 | Wis. | 10.26 | Md. | 31.90 | Ark. | 60.9 | Nev. | 35.95 |
| 11 | W.Va. | 10.24 | Wis. | 29.50 | Iowa | 57.7 | Kan. | 35.95 |
| 12 | Calif. | 10.12 | Iowa | 28.60 | Ky. | 54.5 | Minn. | 35.80 |
| 13 | Minn. | 10.05 | Ky. | 26.50 | Nebr. | 53.5 | Mont. | 35.70 |
| 14 | Del. | 9.86 | Mont. | 25.20 | N.M. | 52.7 | Vt. | 35.45 |
| 15 | Okla. | 9.86 | Ore. | 24.50 | Kan. | 49.9 | Mich. | 35.15 |
| 16 | N.J. | 9.86 | Calif. | 24.30 | N.C. | 45.1 | S.Dak. | 34.95 |
| 17 | Md. | 9.73 | N.J. | 23.20 | N.H. | 43.8 | Mo. | 34.70 |
| 18 | N.Y. | 9.67 | Minn. | 23.00 | Okla. | 41.7 | N.H. | 34.45 |
| 19 | Utah | 9.64 | La. | 20.80 | S.C. | 40.0 | Del. | 34.45 |
| 20 | Wyo. | 9.64 | Me. | 20.70 | Ala. | 36.4 | N.J. | 33.50 |
| 21 | Pa. | 9.57 | Del. | 20.40 | Ga. | 36.1 | Idaho | 33.45 |
| 22 | Conn. | 9.57 | Wyo. | 19.50 | Minn. | 34.6 | Mass. | 33.05 |
| 23 | Mo. | 9.57 | Mass. | 19.10 | Mo. | 34.4 | Ore. | 33.00 |
| 24 | Ky. | 9.53 | Ala. | 18.80 | Del. | 33.7 | Ark. | 32.95 |
| 25 | Colo. | 9.52 | Okla. | 17.50 | Wis. | 33.5 | Okla. | 32.65 |
| 26 | Ariz. | 9.48 | Conn. | 16.20 | Tenn. | 33.4 | Wash. | 32.65 |
| 27 | Kan. | 9.45 | Tex. | 15.60 | Ore. | 32.8 | Fla. | 32.60 |
| 28 | Tex. | 9.41 | Tenn. | 15.20 | Ind. | 32.0 | Ill. | 32.55 |
| 29 | Idaho | 9.41 | Ga. | 13.60 | La. | 30.9 | Ariz. | 32.50 |
| 30 | Nev. | 9.15 | Ark. | 13.50 | Va. | 28.7 | Conn. | 31.95 |
| 31 | Nebr. | 9.02 | N.M. | 13.50 | Ariz. | 23.7 | N.Y. | 31.80 |
| 32 | Mass. | 9.00 | N.Dak. | 12.90 | Utah | 23.2 | Ky. | 31.55 |
| 33 | Va. | 8.51 | Kan. | 12.70 | Ohio | 21.2 | Utah | 31.55 |
| 34 | Ala. | 8.48 | Idaho | 11.90 | Mich. | 19.8 | N.M. | 31.45 |

(continued)

**Table 7A.1 (continued)**

| | WAGE | | UNION | | RURAL | | HSGRAD | |
|---|---|---|---|---|---|---|---|---|
| Rank | State | ($) | State | (%) | State | (%) | State | (%) |
| 35 | N.M. | 8.41 | Va. | 11.90 | Tex. | 19.5 | La. | 31.35 |
| 36 | Vt. | 8.41 | Nebr. | 11.50 | Wash. | 19.1 | R.I. | 31.15 |
| 37 | Me. | 8.40 | R.I. | 11.00 | Colo. | 18.8 | Tenn. | 30.85 |
| 38 | N.H. | 8.39 | Colo. | 10.80 | Ill. | 17.7 | Ala. | 30.60 |
| 39 | Tenn. | 8.29 | Vt. | 10.30 | Nev. | 17.3 | Colo. | 30.50 |
| 40 | Ga. | 8.10 | Miss. | 8.80 | Pa. | 15.4 | Md. | 30.30 |
| 41 | N.Dak. | 8.05 | Fla. | 8.80 | N.Y. | 9.5 | N.Dak. | 29.65 |
| 42 | Fla. | 7.86 | N.H. | 7.70 | Mass. | 9.1 | Ga. | 29.50 |
| 43 | S.C. | 7.61 | Nev. | 7.60 | Fla. | 9.0 | N.C. | 28.40 |
| 44 | R.I. | 7.59 | Utah | 6.50 | R.I. | 7.5 | Miss. | 28.35 |
| 45 | Ark. | 7.57 | N.C. | 5.00 | Conn. | 7.4 | S.C. | 28.25 |
| 46 | S.Dak. | 7.43 | Ariz. | 4.80 | Md. | 7.1 | Va. | 27.50 |
| 47 | N.C. | 7.29 | S.C. | 3.80 | Calif. | 4.3 | Tx. | 27.20 |
| 48 | Miss. | 7.22 | S.Dak. | 3.70 | N.J. | 0.1 | Calif. | 26.90 |
| | | | | | | | | |
| Avg. | | 9.34 | | 20.51 | | 36.76 | | 33.25 |
| Std. dev. | | 11.8 | | 12.4 | | 22.1 | | 3.4 |

**Table 7A.2 Market and Transportation Data—State Rankings**

| | | Market | | AIRPORT | | HIGHWAY |
|---|---|---|---|---|---|---|
| Rank | State | $/mi.$^2$ | State | pass./yr. (000) | State | (mi./mi.$^2$) |
| 1 | Calif. | 424.063 | Ill. | 22,775.4 | Mass. | 0.072 |
| 2 | N.Y. | 289.861 | Ga. | 20,236.1 | Conn. | 0.070 |
| 3 | Tex. | 223.731 | Tex. | 18,348.3 | R.I. | 0.066 |
| 4 | Ill. | 175.163 | Calif. | 18,006.0 | N.J. | 0.052 |
| 5 | Pa. | 166.568 | N.Y. | 14,951.4 | Md. | 0.039 |
| 6 | Fla. | 161.251 | Colo. | 12,921.5 | Ohio | 0.038 |
| 7 | N.J. | 148.413 | Fla. | 9,702.5 | Vt. | 0.035 |
| 8 | Ohio | 147.546 | N.J. | 9,569.2 | Pa. | 0.034 |
| 9 | Mich. | 132.192 | Mass. | 9,092.9 | Ill. | 0.033 |
| 10 | Mass. | 100.446 | Mo. | 8,685.2 | N.Y. | 0.032 |
| 11 | Md. | 88.117 | Ariz. | 7,127.9 | Ind. | 0.031 |
| 12 | Va. | 87.508 | Mich. | 7,050.1 | Va. | 0.026 |
| 13 | Ga. | 79.916 | Minn. | 6,976.3 | S.C. | 0.026 |
| 14 | N.C. | 77.761 | Pa. | 6,961.7 | Tenn. | 0.025 |
| 15 | Ind. | 74.498 | Del. | 6,961.7 | Fla. | 0.024 |
| 16 | Mo. | 70.967 | Wash. | 5,890.8 | N.H. | 0.024 |
| 17 | Wis. | 68.687 | Nev. | 5,726.8 | Del. | 0.021 |
| 18 | Conn. | 65.252 | N.C. | 5,191.9 | Ga. | 0.021 |
| 19 | Wash. | 63.849 | Utah | 3,983.7 | W.Va. | 0.021 |
| 20 | Minn. | 62.833 | Tenn. | 3,446.2 | Mich. | 0.021 |
| 21 | Tenn. | 58.648 | Md. | 3,333.3 | Ky. | 0.019 |
| 22 | La. | 54.143 | Ohio | 3,086.8 | Ala. | 0.017 |
| 23 | Colo. | 50.318 | La. | 3,034.5 | Mo. | 0.017 |
| 24 | Ala. | 47.701 | Ore. | 2,448.9 | N.C. | 0.016 |
| 25 | Ky. | 46.047 | Conn. | 1,871.4 | La. | 0.016 |
| 26 | Okla. | 44.383 | Ind. | 1,853.1 | Calif. | 0.015 |
| 27 | Ariz. | 43.467 | N.M. | 1,804.7 | Miss. | 0.015 |
| 28 | Iowa | 40.537 | Wis. | 1,565.5 | Iowa | 0.014 |
| 29 | S.C. | 40.438 | Va. | 1,443.6 | Okla. | 0.014 |
| 30 | Kan. | 37.707 | Okla. | 1,378.6 | Tex. | 0.012 |
| 31 | Ore. | 36.109 | Nebr. | 990.3 | Wis. | 0.011 |
| 32 | Ark. | 29.050 | Ky. | 935.0 | Minn. | 0.011 |
| 33 | Miss. | 28.348 | Ala. | 797.6 | Wash. | 0.011 |

(continued)

**Table 7A.2 (continued)**

| | | Market | | AIRPORT | | HIGHWAY |
| --- | --- | --- | --- | --- | --- | --- |
| Rank | State | $/mi.$^2$ | State | pass./yr. (000) | State | (mi./mi.$^2$) |
| 34 | W.Va. | 25.102 | Ark. | 676.2 | Me. | 0.011 |
| 35 | Nebr. | 24.816 | R.I. | 629.8 | Utah | 0.011 |
| 36 | N.H. | 20.898 | Iowa | 613.2 | Ark. | 0.010 |
| 37 | R.I. | 20.802 | Kan. | 572.5 | Kan. | 0.010 |
| 38 | Utah | 20.007 | S.C. | 534.5 | Ariz. | 0.010 |
| 39 | N.M. | 18.978 | Me. | 472.1 | Wyo. | 0.009 |
| 40 | Me. | 18.823 | Idaho | 468.0 | Colo. | 0.009 |
| 41 | Del. | 17.207 | Miss. | 374.9 | S.Dak. | 0.009 |
| 42 | Nev. | 16.551 | Vt. | 342.4 | N.Dak. | 0.008 |
| 43 | Idaho | 13.166 | Mont. | 285.3 | N.M. | 0.008 |
| 44 | Mont. | 11.424 | S.Dak. | 220.0 | Mont. | 0.008 |
| 45 | Vt. | 11.293 | W.Va. | 205.2 | Ore. | 0.008 |
| 46 | N.Dak. | 11.255 | N.Dak. | 189.0 | Idaho | 0.007 |
| 47 | S.Dak. | 10.529 | N.H. | 169.0 | Nebr. | 0.006 |
| 48 | Wyo. | 9.683 | Wyo. | 93.0 | Nev. | 0.005 |
| | | | | | | |
| Avg. | | 73.251 | | 4,874.9 | | 0.021 |
| Std. dev. | | 78.655 | | 5,789.4 | | 0.016 |

## Table 7A.3  Fiscal Policy Data—State Rankings

| Rank | CORPTAX State | (100−% tax rate) | EXPEDUC State | ($) | JOF State | (1 = yes) | UNITARY State | (1 = yes) |
|------|-------|-------|-------|-------|-------|-------|-------|-------|
| 1 | Tex. | 100.0 | N.Y. | 0.420 | Ala. | 1 | Calif. | 1 |
| 2 | Wyo. | 100.0 | Mass. | 0.407 | Conn. | 1 | Colo. | 1 |
| 3 | Nev. | 100.0 | N.J. | 0.352 | Fla. | 1 | Idaho | 1 |
| 4 | Wash. | 100.0 | Me. | 0.325 | Ga. | 1 | Ill. | 1 |
| 5 | S.Dak. | 96.8 | Conn. | 0.320 | Ill. | 1 | Me. | 1 |
| 6 | Colo. | 96.4 | Vt. | 0.305 | Ind. | 1 | Mass. | 1 |
| 7 | Mo. | 96.2 | Ore. | 0.298 | Ky. | 1 | Minn. | 1 |
| 8 | Okla. | 96.1 | Del. | 0.292 | Md. | 1 | Mont. | 1 |
| 9 | Ind. | 96.0 | R.I. | 0.290 | Mich. | 1 | Nebr. | 1 |
| 10 | Utah | 95.2 | Ky. | 0.290 | Minn. | 1 | N.Y. | 1 |
| 11 | Ohio | 94.9 | Wyo. | 0.283 | Mo. | 1 | N.Dak. | 1 |
| 12 | Miss. | 94.8 | Md. | 0.281 | N.C. | 1 | Ore. | 1 |
| 13 | Va. | 94.7 | Fla. | 0.281 | Nebr. | 1 | Utah | 1 |
| 14 | Nebr. | 94.6 | N.H. | 0.266 | N.Y. | 1 | Ala. | 0 |
| 15 | Ala. | 94.4 | Mont. | 0.252 | Ohio | 1 | Ariz. | 0 |
| 16 | Me. | 94.1 | Pa. | 0.252 | Pa. | 1 | Ark. | 0 |
| 17 | Ark. | 93.8 | Va. | 0.247 | S.C. | 1 | Conn. | 0 |
| 18 | Fla. | 93.7 | Kan. | 0.245 | Va. | 1 | Del. | 0 |
| 19 | S.C. | 93.6 | Minn. | 0.238 | Wash. | 1 | Fla. | 0 |
| 20 | Ga. | 93.3 | Mo. | 0.236 | Ark. | 0 | Ga. | 0 |
| 21 | Md. | 93.3 | La. | 0.236 | Ariz. | 0 | Ind. | 0 |
| 22 | Idaho | 93.2 | Wash. | 0.235 | Calif. | 0 | Kan. | 0 |
| 23 | Del. | 93.1 | Nebr. | 0.230 | Colo. | 0 | Ky. | 0 |
| 24 | N.M. | 93.1 | N.M. | 0.225 | Del. | 0 | La. | 0 |
| 25 | Ore. | 92.9 | Ill. | 0.224 | Iowa | 0 | Md. | 0 |
| 26 | Ill. | 92.9 | W.Va. | 0.221 | Idaho | 0 | Mich. | 0 |
| 27 | Tenn. | 92.7 | Ohio | 0.220 | Kan. | 0 | Miss. | 0 |
| 28 | Iowa | 92.7 | Okla. | 0.220 | La. | 0 | Mo. | 0 |
| 29 | Ky. | 92.4 | Wis. | 0.211 | Mass. | 0 | Nev. | 0 |
| 30 | La. | 92.4 | S.Dak. | 0.209 | Me. | 0 | N.H. | 0 |
| 31 | R.I. | 92.2 | Mich. | 0.206 | Miss. | 0 | N.J. | 0 |
| 32 | N.Dak. | 92.1 | Iowa | 0.205 | Mont. | 0 | N.M. | 0 |

(continued)

**Table 7A.3 (continued)**

| Rank | CORPTAX State | (100–% tax rate) | EXPEDUC State | ($) | JOF State | (1 = yes) | UNITARY State | (1 = yes) |
|------|-------|------|-------|------|-------|------|-------|------|
| 33 | Mont. | 92.1 | Ark. | 0.201 | N.Dak. | 0 | N.Y. | 0 |
| 34 | W.Va. | 92.0 | Colo. | 0.197 | N.H. | 0 | N.C. | 0 |
| 35 | Ariz. | 91.9 | Nev. | 0.188 | N.J. | 0 | Ohio | 0 |
| 36 | Kan. | 91.6 | Ind. | 0.187 | N.M. | 0 | Okla. | 0 |
| 37 | N.C. | 91.5 | N.Dak. | 0.187 | Nev. | 0 | Pa. | 0 |
| 38 | Minn. | 91.5 | Tex. | 0.186 | Okla. | 0 | R.I. | 0 |
| 39 | Vt. | 91.4 | Ga. | 0.186 | Ore. | 0 | S.C. | 0 |
| 40 | Pa. | 91.1 | S.C. | 0.184 | R.I. | 0 | S.Dak. | 0 |
| 41 | Wis. | 90.2 | N.C. | 0.174 | S.Dak. | 0 | Tenn. | 0 |
| 42 | N.Y. | 90.0 | Ariz. | 0.173 | Tenn. | 0 | Tex. | 0 |
| 43 | N.J. | 89.7 | Tenn. | 0.166 | Tex. | 0 | Vt. | 0 |
| 44 | N.H. | 88.3 | Calif. | 0.159 | Utah | 0 | Va. | 0 |
| 45 | Conn. | 86.4 | Miss. | 0.147 | Vt. | 0 | Wash. | 0 |
| 46 | Calif. | 85.5 | Idaho | 0.145 | Wis. | 0 | W.Va. | 0 |
| 47 | Mass. | 84.9 | Ala. | 0.144 | W.Va. | 0 | Wis. | 0 |
| 48 | Mich. | 84.6 | Utah | 0.123 | Wyo. | 0 | Wyo. | 0 |
| Avg. | | 93.0 | | 0.235 | | 0.38 | | 0.25 |
| Std. dev. | | 3.5 | | 0.064 | | 0.48 | | 0.43 |

**Table 7A.4  Miscellaneous Data—State Rankings**

| | AGGLOM | | JTEMP | | LAND | |
|---|---|---|---|---|---|---|
| Rank | State | (prod. hr./ acre) | State | (°F) | State | Acres (000s) |
| 1 | R.I. | 0.2342 | Fla. | 60.2 | Tex. | 164,948 |
| 2 | N.J. | 0.1745 | La. | 52.4 | Mont. | 64,815 |
| 3 | Mass. | 0.1545 | Ariz. | 52.3 | Calif. | 53,742 |
| 4 | Conn. | 0.1530 | Ala. | 50.8 | N.M. | 53,425 |
| 5 | N.Y. | 0.0554 | Calif. | 49.9 | Kan. | 51,929 |
| 6 | Ohio | 0.0513 | Miss. | 45.7 | Nebr. | 48,318 |
| 7 | Pa. | 0.0510 | S.C. | 44.7 | Minn. | 47,746 |
| 8 | Del. | 0.0489 | Tex. | 44.1 | S.Dak. | 46,150 |
| 9 | Md. | 0.0442 | Ga. | 41.9 | Okla. | 43,265 |
| 10 | Calif. | 0.0431 | N.C. | 40.1 | N.Dak. | 42,505 |
| 11 | N.C. | 0.0407 | Ark. | 39.9 | Colo. | 42,440 |
| 12 | Ill. | 0.0356 | Ore. | 38.9 | Mo. | 42,180 |
| 13 | Ind. | 0.0334 | Tenn. | 38.4 | Ariz. | 41,384 |
| 14 | Mich. | 0.0331 | Va. | 38.3 | Iowa | 35,700 |
| 15 | N.H. | 0.0288 | Okla. | 35.9 | Ill. | 35,295 |
| 16 | S.C. | 0.0287 | N.M. | 34.8 | Ga. | 35,266 |
| 17 | Tenn. | 0.0253 | W.Va. | 32.9 | Wis. | 33,181 |
| 18 | Va. | 0.0248 | Md. | 32.7 | Mich. | 32,964 |
| 19 | Ga. | 0.0200 | Ky. | 32.5 | Ore. | 31,628 |
| 20 | Wis. | 0.0187 | Nev. | 32.2 | Ala. | 31,587 |
| 21 | Fla. | 0.0186 | N.J. | 31.8 | Wyo. | 31,465 |
| 22 | Ala. | 0.0152 | Del. | 31.2 | Fla. | 30,460 |
| 23 | Ky. | 0.0133 | Idaho | 29.9 | Ark. | 30,275 |
| 24 | Mo. | 0.0113 | Mass. | 29.6 | Wash. | 30,214 |
| 25 | Wash. | 0.0108 | Kan. | 29.6 | N.C. | 29,193 |
| 26 | Miss. | 0.0105 | Colo. | 29.5 | N.Y. | 29,126 |
| 27 | Vt. | 0.0102 | Pa. | 29.0 | Miss. | 28,546 |
| 28 | La. | 0.0101 | Utah | 28.6 | Pa. | 28,163 |
| 29 | Ark. | 0.0092 | R.I. | 28.2 | La. | 27,726 |
| 30 | W.Va. | 0.0085 | Ohio | 27.6 | Ohio | 25,904 |

(continued)

**Table 7A.4 (continued)**

| Rank | AGGLOM State | (prod. hr./ acre) | JTEMP State | (°F) | LAND State | Acres (000s) |
|------|-------|-------|-------|------|-------|------|
| 31 | Me. | 0.0084 | Wash. | 27.4 | Tenn. | 24,852 |
| 32 | Tex. | 0.0079 | Mo. | 27.4 | Ky. | 24,111 |
| 33 | Minn. | 0.0079 | Wyo. | 26.1 | Va. | 23,031 |
| 34 | Ore. | 0.0075 | Ind. | 26.0 | Ind. | 22,721 |
| 35 | Iowa | 0.0073 | N.Y. | 25.5 | Me. | 19,697 |
| 36 | Utah | 0.0054 | Conn. | 25.2 | Idaho | 19,217 |
| 37 | Okla. | 0.0054 | Mich. | 23.4 | Utah | 19,162 |
| 38 | Colo. | 0.0049 | Ill. | 21.5 | S.C. | 18,213 |
| 39 | Kan. | 0.0042 | Me. | 21.5 | W.Va. | 14,243 |
| 40 | Ariz. | 0.0040 | Nebr. | 20.2 | Nev. | 10,474 |
| 41 | Idaho | 0.0033 | N.H. | 19.9 | Md. | 6,121 |
| 42 | Nebr. | 0.0026 | Mont. | 18.7 | Vt. | 5,615 |
| 43 | Nev. | 0.0024 | Wis. | 18.7 | N.H. | 5,029 |
| 44 | N.M. | 0.0008 | Iowa | 18.6 | Mass. | 4,952 |
| 45 | S.Dak. | 0.0007 | Vt. | 16.6 | N.J. | 4,653 |
| 46 | N.Dak. | 0.0004 | S.Dak. | 12.4 | Conn. | 3,122 |
| 47 | Mont. | 0.0004 | Minn. | 8.8 | Del. | 1,236 |
| 48 | Wyo. | 0.0004 | N.Dak. | 6.7 | R.I. | 672 |
| | | | | | | |
| Avg. | | 0.0311 | | 31.2 | | 31,180 |
| Std. dev. | | 0.0482 | | 11.5 | | 24,794 |

# Reference List

Abernathy, Frederick H., John T. Dunlop, Janice H. Hammond, and David Weil. 1999. *A Stitch In Time*. New York: Oxford University Press.

Abo, Tetsuo, ed. 1994. *Hybrid Factory: The Japanese Production System in the United States*. New York: Oxford University Press.

Adams, J. Stacy. 1988. "Towards an Understanding of Inequity." *Journal of Abnormal and Social Psychology* 67(May): 422–436.

Adler, Paul S. 2001. "Crossroads—Market, Hierarchy, and Trust: The Knowledge Economy and the Future of Capitalism." *Organization Science* 12(2): 214 (21 pp).

Advisory Commission on Intergovernmental Relations. 1986. *Tax Capacity of the States*. ACIR.

―――. 1990. *Tax Capacity of the States*. ACIR.

Ady, Robert M. 1997. "'Taxation and Economic Development: The State of the Economic Literature' and 'The Effects of State and Local Public Services on Economic Development': Discussion." *New England Economic Review* (March/April): 77–82.

Aitken, Hugh G.J. 1985. *Scientific Management in Action: Taylorism at the Watertown Arsenal, 1908–1915*. Cambridge, Massachusetts: Harvard University Press.

Akerlof, George. 1982. "Labor Contracts as a Partial Gift Exchange." *Quarterly Journal of Economics* 97(4): 543–570.

―――. 1984. "Gift Exchange and Efficiency Wages: Four Views." *American Economic Review* 74(May): 79–83.

Akerlof, George, and Janet L. Yellen. 1990. "The Fair Wage–Effort Hypothesis and Unemployment." *Quarterly Journal of Economics* 105(2): 255–283.

Allen, Steven G. 1984. "Unionized Construction Workers Are More Productive." *Quarterly Journal of Economics* 99(May): 251–274.

Aoki, Masahiko. 1990. "Toward an Economic Model of the Japanese Firm." *Journal of Economic Literature* 27(March): 1–27.

Appelbaum, Eileen, and Rosemary Batt. 1994. *The New American Workplace: Transforming Work Systems in the United States*. Ithaca, New York: ILR Press.

Appelbaum, Eileen, Thomas Bailey, Peter Berg, and Arne L. Kalleberg. 2000. *Manufacturing Advantage: Why High-Performance Work Systems Pay Off*. Ithaca, New York: ILR Press.

Argyris, Chris. 1957. *Personality and the Organization*. New York: Harper and Row.

————. 1964. *Integrating the Individual and the Organization.* New York: Harper and Row.

Baily, Martin N., and Alok K. Chakrabarti. 1988. *Innovation and the Productivity Crisis.* Washington, D.C.: Brookings Institution.

Baker, George P., Michael Gibbs, and Bengt Holmstrom. 1994. "The Internal Economics of the Firm: Evidence from Personnel Data." *Quarterly Journal of Economics* 109(4): 881–919.

Bandura, Albert. 1969. *Principles of Behavior Modification.* New York: Holt, Rinehart, and Winston.

————. 1977. *Social Learning Theory.* Englewood Cliffs, New Jersey: Prentice Hall.

Bartel, Ann. 1995. "Training, Wage Growth, and Job Performance: Evidence from a Company Data Base." *Journal of Labor Economics* 13(3): 401–425.

Bartik, Timothy J. 1985. "Business Location Decisions in the United States: Estimates of the Effects of Unionization, Taxes, and Other Characteristics of States." *Journal of Business & Economic Statistics* 3(1): 14–22.

————. 1989. "Small Business Start-Ups in the United States: Estimates of the Effects of the Characteristics of States." *Southern Economic Journal* 55: 1004–1018.

————. 1991. *Who Benefits from State and Local Economic Development Policies?* Kalamazoo, Michigan: W.E. Upjohn Institute for Employment Research.

————. 1997. "'Taxation and Economic Development: The State of the Economic Literature' and 'The Effects of State and Local Public Services on Economic Development': Discussion." *New England Economic Review* (March/April): 67–70.

Becker, Brian, and Barry Gerhart. 1996. "The Impact of Human Resource Management Practices on Organizational Performance: Progress and Report." *Academy of Management Journal* 39(4): 779–801.

Bendix, Reinhart. 1956. *Work and Authority in Industry.* New York: John Wiley.

Berman, Eli, John Bound, and Zvi Griliches. 1994. "Changes in the Demand for Skilled Labor within the U.S. Manufacturing: Evidence from the Annual Survey of Manufactures." *Quarterly Journal of Economics* 109(2): 367–397.

Berman, Eli, John Bound, and Stephen Machin. 1998. "Implications of Skill-Biased Technological Change: International Evidence." *Quarterly Journal of Economics* 113(4): 1245–1279.

Black, Sandra E., and Lisa M. Lynch. 1996. "Human Capital Investment and Productivity." *American Economic Review* 86(2): 263–267.

————. 1997. "How To Compete: The Impact of Workplace Practices and Information Technology on Productivity." Working paper no. 6120, National Bureau of Economic Research, Cambridge, Massachusetts, August.

————. 1999. "What's Driving the New Economy: The Benefits of Workplace Innovation." Photocopy, November.

Blakemore, Arthur, ed. 1987. "Supplement: The New Economics of Personnel." *Journal of Labor Economics* 5(4), Part 2: entire issue (189 pp.).

Bluestone, B., and Bennett Harrison. 1982. *The Deindustrialization of America.* New York: Basic Books.

Borjas, George J., Richard B. Freeman, and Lawrence F. Katz. 1997. "How Much Do Immigration and Trade Affect Labor Market Outcomes?" *Brookings Papers on Economic Activity* 1: 1–67.

Bound, John, and George Johnson. 1992. "Changes in the Structure of Wages in the 1980's: An Evaluation of Alternative Explanations." *American Economic Review* 82(3): 371–392.

Bowey, Angela M., and Richard Thorpe. 1986. *Payment Systems and Productivity.* New York: St. Martin's Press.

Brandes, Stuart D. 1970. *American Welfare Capitalism 1880–1940.* Chicago: University of Chicago Press.

Braverman, Harry. 1974. *Labor and Monopoly Capital.* New York: Monthly Review Press.

Brody, David. 1980. *Workers in Industrial America.* Oxford: Oxford University Press.

Brown, Charles, James Hamilton, and James Medoff. 1990. *Employers Large and Small.* Cambridge, Massachusetts: Harvard University Press.

Bulow, Jeremy J., and Lawrence H. Summers. 1986. "A Theory of Dual Labor Markets with Application to Industrial Policy, Discrimination, and Keynesian Unemployment." *Journal of Labor Economics* 4(3), Part 1: 376–414.

Burawoy, Michael. 1979. *Manufacturing Consent.* Chicago: University of Chicago Press.

————. 1985. *The Politics of Production.* London: Verso.

Burtless, Gary A. 1990. "Introduction." In *A Future of Lousy Jobs*, Gary A. Burtless, ed. Washington, D.C.: Brookings Institution, pp. 1–30.

Cappelli, Peter. 1999. *The New Deal at Work.* Boston: Harvard Business School Press.

Cappelli, Peter, and David Neumark. 1999. "Do 'High Performance' Work Practices Improve Establishment Level Outcomes?" Working paper no. 7374, National Bureau of Economic Research, Cambridge, Massachusetts, October.

Carlton, Dennis W. 1983. "The Location and Employment Choices of New Firms: An Econometric Model with Discrete and Continuous Endogenous Variables." *Review of Economics and Statistics* 65(3): 440–449.

Caroli, Eve, and John Van Reenen. 2001. "Skill-Biased Organizational Change? Evidence from a Panel of British and French Establishments." *Quarterly Journal of Economics* 116(4): 1449–1492.

Carroll, Robert, and Michael Wasylenko. 1994. "Do State Business Climates Still Matter? Evidence of a Structural Change." *National Tax Journal* 47: 19–38.

Carson, Paula P., Patricia A. Lanice, Kerry D. Carson, and Brandi N. Guidry. 2000. "Clearing a Path through the Management Fashion Jungle: Some Preliminary Trailblazing." *Academy of Management Journal* 43(6): 1143–1158.

Cartwright, Dorwin, and Ronald Lippit. 1976. "Group Dynamics and the Individual." In *People and Productivity*, third edition, Robert A. Sutermeister, ed. New York: McGraw-Hill.

Caves, Richard E. 1993. "Japanese Investment in the United States: Lessons for the Economic Analysis of Foreign Investment." *The World Economy* 16(3): 279–300.

Chandler, Alfred D. 1992. "Organizational Capabilities and Economic History of the Industrial Firm." *Journal of Economic Perspectives* 6(3): 79–100.

Chapman, Keith, and David Walker. 1987. *Industrial Location, Principles and Policies.* New York: Basil Blackwell.

Chernotsky, Harry I. 1983. "Selecting U.S. Sites: A Case Study of German and Japanese Firms." *Management International Review* 23(2): 45–55.

Coch, L., and J.P. French, Jr. 1948. "Overcoming Resistance to Change." *Human Relations* 1: 512–532.

Cole, Robert E. 1971. *Japanese Blue Collar: The Changing Tradition.* Berkeley: University of California Press.

Cole, Robert E., and Donald R. Deskins, Jr. 1988. "Racial Factors in Site Location and Employment Patterns of Japanese Auto Firms in America." *California Management Review* (Fall): 9–22.

Commission on the Future of Worker-Management Relations. 1994. *Fact Finding Report.* Washington, D.C.: U.S. Department of Labor and U.S. Department of Commerce, May.

Council of Economic Advisers. 1999. *Economic Report of the President.* Washington, D.C.: Government Printing Office.

———. 1996. *Economic Report of the President.* Washington, D.C.: Government Printing Office.

————. 2000. *Economic Report of the President.* Washington, D.C.: Government Printing Office.

————. 2001. *Economic Report of the President.* Washington, D.C.: Government Printing Office.

Crandall, Robert W. 1993. *Manufacturing on the Move.* Washington, D.C.: Brookings Institution.

Daft, Richard L. 1998. *Essentials of Organization Theory and Diffusion.* Cincinnati: Southwestern College Publishers.

Dalton, Melville. 1959. *Men Who Manage.* New York: John Wiley.

Davis, Paul. 1987. "Managerial Compensation in Theory and Practice." Unpublished doctoral dissertation, Boston University.

Delery, J.E., and D. Harold Doty. 1996. "Modes of Theorizing in Strategic Human Resources Management." *Academy of Management Journal* 39(4): 802–835.

Denison, Edward F. 1985. *Trends in American Economic Growth 1929–1982.* Washington, D.C.: Brookings Institution.

Dertouzos, Michael L., Richard K. Lester, and Robert M. Solow. 1989. *Made in America.* Cambridge, Massachusetts: MIT Press.

DeWolfe, Pieter, ed. 1965. *Wages and Labour Mobility.* Paris: Organisation for Economic Co-operation and Development.

Dickens, William T., Lawrence Katz, and Kevin Lang. 1986. "Are Efficiency Wages Efficient?" Working paper no. 1935, National Bureau of Economic Research, Cambridge, Massachusetts.

Doeringer, Peter B. 1984. "Internal Labor Markets and Paternalism in Rural Areas." In *Internal Labor Markets*, Paul Osterman, ed. Cambridge, Massachusetts: MIT Press, pp. 271–289.

————. 1991. "The Socio-Economics of Labor Productivity." In *Morality, Rationality, and Efficiency: New Perspectives on Socio-Economics*, Richard M. Coughlin, ed. New York: M.E. Sharpe, pp. 103–118.

Doeringer, Peter B., and Michael J. Piore. 1971. *Internal Labor Markets and Manpower Analysis.* Lexington, Massachusetts: D.C. Heath

Doeringer, Peter B., and David G. Terkla. 1995. *Troubled Waters: Economic Structure, Regulatory Reform, and Fisheries Trade.* Toronto: University of Toronto Press.

Doeringer, Peter B., and Audrey Watson. 1999. "Apparel." In *U.S. Industry in 2000: Studies in Competitive Performance*, David C. Mowery, ed. Washington, D.C.: National Academy Press, pp. 329–362.

Doeringer, Peter B., Christine Evans-Klock, and David G. Terkla. 1998. "Hybrids or Hodgepodges? Workplace Practices of Japanese and Domestic Startups in the United States." *Industrial and Labor Relations Review* 51(2): 171–186.

Doeringer, Peter B., David G. Terkla, and Gregory C. Topakian. 1987. *Invisible Factors in Local Economic Development.* New York and Oxford: Oxford University Press.

Doeringer, Peter B., Kathleen Christenson, Patricia M. Flynn, Douglas T. Hall, Harry C. Katz, Jeffrey H. Keefe, Christopher J. Ruhm, Andrew M. Sum, and Michael Useem. 1991. *Turbulence in the American Workplace.* New York: Oxford University Press.

Dore, Ronald. 1973. *Japanese Factory, British Factory.* Berkeley: University of California Press.

Economic Policy Institute. 2000. "Quarterly Wage and Employment Series." EPI, Washington, D.C.

Edwards, Richard C. 1979. *Contested Terrain: The Transformation of the Workplace in the Twentieth Century.* New York: Basic Books.

Ehrenberg, Ronald G., and George T. Milkovich. 1987. "Compensation and Firm Performance." In *Human Resources and the Performance of the Firm,* Morris M. Kleiner, Richard N. Block, Myron Roomkin, and Sidney W. Salsburg, eds. Madison, Wisconsin: Industrial Relations Research Association, pp. 87–122.

Evans-Klock, Christine. In preparation. "Japanese Manufacturers in the U.S.: Human Resource Strategies and Investment Location Decisions." Ph.D. dissertation, Boston University.

Farber, Henry S. 1998. "Has the Rate of Job Loss Increased in the Nineties?" *IRRA 50th Annual Proceedings*, Industrial Relations Research Association, pp. 88–97.

Fisher, Ronald C. 1997. "The Effects of State and Local Public Services on Economic Development." *New England Economic Review* (April): 53–66.

Fisher, Peter S., and Alan H. Peters. 1998. *Industrial Incentives: Competition among American States and Cities.* Kalamazoo, Michigan: W.E. Upjohn Institute for Employment Research.

Foulkes, Fred K. 1980. *Personnel Policies in Large Nonunion Companies.* Englewood Cliffs, New Jersey: Prentice Hall.

Frazis, Harley, Maury Gittleman, Michael Horrigan, and Mary Joyce. 1998. "Results from the 1995 Survey of Employer-Provided Training." *Monthly Labor Review* (June): 3–13.

Freed, Shervin. 1990. "Locating Japanese Manufacturing Facilities in the United States." *Industrial Development and Site Selection* 159(3): 23–26.

Freeman, Richard B., and Lawrence F. Katz. 1994. "Rising Wage Inequality: The United States vs. Other Advanced Countries." In *Working under Different Rules*, Richard B. Freeman, ed. New York: Russel Sage, pp. 29–62.

Freeman, Richard B., and Morris M. Kleiner. 2000. "Who Benefits Most from Employee Involvement: Firms or Workers?" *American Economic Review* 90(3): 219–223.

Freeman, Richard B., and James L. Medoff. 1984. *What Do Unions Do?* New York: Basic Books.

Freeman, Richard B., and Joel Rogers. 1999. *What Workers Want.* Ithaca, New York: ILR Press.

Friedman, Joseph, Daniel A Gerlowski, and Jonathan Silberman. 1992. "What Attracts Foreign Multinational Corporations? Evidence from Branch Plant Location in the United States." *Journal of Regional Science* 34(4): 403–418.

Fruin, W. Mark. 1999. "Site-Specific Organizational Learning in International Technology Transfer: Example from Toshiba." In *Remade in America: Transplanting and Transforming Japanese Management Systems*, Jeffrey K. Liker, W. Mark Fruin, and Paul S. Adler, eds. New York: Oxford University Press.

Fucini, Joseph, and Susan Fucini. 1990. *Working for the Japanese: Inside Mazda's American Auto Plant.* New York: Free Press.

Gibbons, Robert, and Michael Waldman. 1999a. "Careers In Organizations: Theory and Evidence." In *Handbook of Labor Economics*, Vol. 3B, Orley Ashenfelter and David Card, eds. Amsterdam and New York: Elsevier, pp. 2372–2437.

———. 1999b. "A Theory of Wage and Promotion Dynamics within Firms." *Quarterly Journal of Economics* 114(4): 1321–1358.

Gittell, Ross. 1992. *Renewing Cities.* Princeton, New Jersey: Princeton University Press.

Goldberg, Victor. 1980. "Bridges over Contested Terrain." *Journal of Economic Behavior and Organization* 1(3): 274–279.

Gordon, David M. 1997. "Econometric Tests for the Transition between Productivity Regimes." *Industrial Relations* 36(2): 125–159.

Gouldner, Alvin W. 1954. *Patterns of Industrial Bureaucracy.* Glencoe, Illinois: Free Press.

Graham, Edward M., and Paul R. Krugman. 1989. *Foreign Direct Investment in the United States.* Washington: Institute for International Economics.

Grant Thornton. 1989. *Manufacturing Climate Study.* Chicago: Grant Thornton LLP, July.

Greene, William H. 1993. *Econometric Analysis.* Englewood Cliffs, New Jersey: Prentice Hall.

Habermas, Jurgens. 1970. *Toward a Rational Society.* Boston: Beacon Press.

———. 1975. *Legitimation Crisis.* Boston: Beacon Press.

Hackman, J. Richard, and Greg R. Oldham. 1980. *Work Redesign*. Reading, Massachusetts: Addison-Wesley.

Hackman, J. Richard, Edward E. Lawler, and Lyman W. Porter. 1983. *Perspectives on Behavior in Organizations*. 2nd ed. New York: McGraw-Hill.

Haigh, Robert. 1990. "Selecting a U.S. Plant Location: The Management Decision Process in Foreign Companies." *Columbia Journal of World Business* 25(3): 22–31.

Haitani, Kanji, and Charles T. Marquis. 1990. "Japanese Investment in the Southeast United States: Factors, Obstacles, and Opportunities." *Economic Development Review* (Summer): 42–48.

Hammner, W. Clay, and Ellen Hammner. 1983. "Behavior Modification on the Bottom Line." In *Perspectives on Organizational Behavior*, J. Richard Hackman, Edward E. Lawler, III, and Lyman W. Porter, eds. New York: McGraw-Hill.

Harman, H.H. 1976. *Modern Factor Analysis*. Third ed. Chicago: University of Chicago Press.

Harrison, Bennett, and Barry Bluestone. 1988. *The Great U-Turn: Corporate Restructuring and the Polarizing of America*. New York: Basic Books.

Head, Keith, John Ries, and Deborah Swenson. 1995. "Agglomeration Benefits and Location Choice: Evidence from Japanese Manufacturing Investments in the United States." *Journal of International Economics* 38: 223–247.

Helms, L. Jay. 1985. "The Effect of State and Local Taxes on Economic Growth: A Time Series–Cross Section Approach." *Review of Economics and Statistics* 67(February): 574–582.

Herzberg, Frederick, Bernard Mausner, and Barbara Bloch Snyderman. 1959. *The Motivation to Work*. New York: Wiley.

Herzog, Henry W., Jr., and Alan M. Schlottmann, eds. 1991. *Industry Location and Public Policy*. Knoxville: University of Tennessee Press.

Hilgard, Ernest R., and Donald G. Marquis. 1961. *Conditioning and Learning*. New York: Appleton Century Crofts.

Holmstrom, Bengt, and Paul Milgrom. 1994. "The Firm as an Incentive System." *American Economic Review* 84(4): 972–991.

Holzer, Harry J., Lawrence F. Katz, and Alan B. Krueger. 1988. "Job Queues and Wages." Working paper, Department of Economics, Harvard University, September.

Huselid, M.A. 1995. "The Impact of Human Resource Management Practices on Turnover, Productivity, and Corporate Financial Performance." *Academy of Management Journal* 38(June): 635–672.

Hwang, Margaret Y., and David Weil. 1997. "Production Complementarities and the Diffusion of Modern Manufacturing Practices: Evidence from the

U.S. Apparel Industry." Photocopy, Harvard Center for Textile and Apparel Research, February.

Hyman, Richard, and Ian Brough. 1975. *Social Values and Industrial Relations.* Oxford: Basil Blackwell.

Ichniowski, Casey. 1990. "Human Resources Management Systems and the Performance of U.S. Manufacturing Businesses." Working paper no. 3449, National Bureau of Economic Research, Cambridge, Massachusetts.

Ichniowski, Casey, Katherine Shaw, and Giovanna Prennushi. 1997. "The Effects of Human Resource Management Practices on Productivity: A Study of Steel Finishing Lines." *American Economic Review* 87(3): 291–313.

Ichniowski, Casey, David I. Levine, Craig Olson, and George Strauss. 2000. *The American Workplace: Skills, Compensation, and Employee Involvement.* New York: Cambridge University Press.

Jackson, J.E. 1991. *A User's Guide to Principal Components.* New York: John Wiley.

Jacobson, Louis S., Robert J. LaLonde, and Daniel G. Sullivan. 1993. "Earnings Losses of Displaced Workers." *American Economic Review* 83(4): 685–709.

Jacoby, Sanford M. 1985. *Employing Bureaucracy: Managers, Unions and the Transformation of Work in American Industry.* New York: Columbia University Press.

———. 1997. *Modern Manors: Welfare Capitalism since the New Deal.* Princeton, New Jersey: Princeton University Press.

Jenkins, Davis, and Richard Florida. 1999. "Work System Innovation among Japanese Transplants in the United States." In *Remade in America: Transplanting and Transforming Japanese Management Systems*, Jeffrey K. Liker, W. Mark Fruin, and Paul S. Adler, eds. New York: Oxford University Press, pp. 331–360.

Kaboolian, Linda. 1990. "Shifting Gears: Auto Workers Assess the Transformation of Their Industry." Unpublished Ph.D. dissertation, University of Michigan, Ann Arbor.

Kandel, Edward, and Edward P. Lazear. 1992. "Peer Pressure and Partnership." *Journal of Political Economy* 100: 801–817.

Katz, Harry, Thomas Kochan, and Kenneth R. Gobeille. 1983. "Industrial Relations Performance, Economic Performance, and QWL Programs: An Interplant Analysis." *Industrial and Labor Relations Review* 37(October): 3–17.

Katz, Lawrence F., and Lawrence H. Summers. 1989. "Industry Rents: Evidence and Implications." *Brookings Papers on Economic Activity, Microeconomics*, pp. 209–250.

Kenney, Martin. 1999. "Transplantation? A Comparison of Japanese Television Assembly Plants in Japan and the United States." In *Remade in America: Transplanting and Transforming Japanese Management Systems,* Jeffrey K. Liker, W. Mark Fruin, and Paul S. Adler, eds. New York: Oxford University Press, pp. 256–293.

Kenney, Martin, and Richard Florida. 1993. *Beyond Mass Production: The Japanese System and Its Transfer to the U.S.* New York: Oxford University Press.

Kieschnick, M. 1981. *Taxes and Growth: Business Incentives and Development.* Washington, D.C.: Council of State Planning Agencies.

Kleiner, Morris, and Marvin Bouillon. 1988. "Providing Business Information to Production Workers: Correlates of Compensation and Profitability." *Industrial and Labor Relations Review* 41(4): 606–617.

Kleiner, Morris M., Richard N. Block, Myron Roomkin, and Sidney W. Salsburg, eds. 1987. *Human Resources and the Performance of the Firm.* Madison, Wisconsin: Industrial Relations Research Association.

Kletzer, Lori. 1998. "Job Displacement." *Journal of Economic Perspectives* 12(1): 115–136.

Kochan, Thomas, and Paul Osterman. 1994. *The Mutual Gains Enterprise.* Boston: Harvard Business School Press.

Kochan, Thomas, Harry Katz, and Richard B. McKersie. 1986. *The Transformation of American Industrial Relations.* New York: Basic Books.

Kruse, Douglas L. 1993. *Profit Sharing: Does It Make a Difference?* Kalamazoo, Michigan: W.E. Upjohn Institute for Employment Research.

Kujawa, Duane. 1986. *Japanese Multinationals in the United States.* New York: Praeger.

Lang, Kevin, Jonathan Leonard, and David M. Lilien. 1987. "Labor Markets Structure, Wages, and Unemployment." In *Unemployment and the Structure of Labor Markets*, Kevin Lang and Jonathan S. Leonard, eds. New York: Basil Blackwell, pp. 1–16.

Lawler, Edward E., III. 1971. *Pay and Organizational Effectiveness: A Psychological View.* New York: McGraw-Hill.

———. 1978. "The New Plant Revolution." *Organizational Dynamics* 6(3): 2–12.

———. 1981a. "Whatever Happened to Incentive Pay?" In *Productivity through People*, William B. Werther, Jr., William A. Ruch, and Lynne McLure, eds. St. Paul: West Publishing.

———. 1981b. *Pay and Organization Development.* Reading, Massachusetts: Addison-Wesley.

———. 1996. *From the Ground Up.* San Francisco: Jossey-Bass.

———. 2000. *Rewarding Excellence: Pay Strategies for the New Economy.* San Francisco: Jossey-Bass.

Lawler, Edward E., III, and Paul W. O'Gara. 1967. "Effects of Inequality Produced by Underpayment in Work Output, Work Quality and Attitudes toward Work." *Journal of Applied Psychology* 51: 403–410.

Lazear, Edward P. 1981. "Agency, Earnings Profiles, Productivity, and Hours Restrictions." *American Economic Review* 71(14): 606–620.

———. 1998. *Personnel Economics for Managers.* New York: John Wiley.

Lazear, Edward P., and Sherwin Rosen. 1981. "Rank Order Tournaments as Optimum Labor Contracts." *Journal of Political Economy* 89(October): 841–868.

Lee, Charles. 1987. "The New Employment Contract." *Training* (December 4): 45–46.

Leonard, Jonathan S. 1987. "Carrots and Sticks: Pay Supervision and Turnover." *Journal of Labor Economics* 5(4), Part 2: S136–S152.

Leonard, Jonathan. 1992. "Unions and Employment Growth." *Industrial Relations* 31(3): 80–94.

Levinson, Arik. 1996. "Environmental Regulations and Manufacturers' Location Choices: Evidence from the Census of Manufactures." *Journal of Public Economics* 62(1–2): 5–26.

Lewin, Kurt. 1947. "Frontiers in Group Dynamics." *Human Relations* 1: 5–41.

———. 1951. *Field Theory in Social Science.* New York: Harper and Row.

Liker, Jeffrey K., W. Mark Fruin, and Paul S. Adler, eds. 1999. *Remade in America: Transplanting and Transforming Japanese Management Systems.* New York: Oxford University Press.

Likert, Rensis. 1958. "Measuring Organizational Performance." *Harvard Business Review* 36(2): 41–51.

———. 1967. *The Human Organization.* New York: McGraw Hill.

Lincoln, James R., and Arne L. Kalleberg. 1990. *Culture, Control, and Commitment.* New York: Cambridge University Press.

Lipsey, Robert E., and Eric Ramstetter. 2001. "Affiliate Activity in Japanese and U.S. Multinationals and Japanese Exports, 1986–1995." NBER working paper no. W8581, November.

Locke, Edwin A., Dena B. Feren, Vickie M. McCaleb, Karyll N. Shaw, and Anne T. Denny. 1980. "The Relative Effectiveness of Four Methods of Motivating Employee Performance." In *Changes in Working Life*, K.D. Duncan, Michael M. Gruneberg, and Don Wallis, eds. Chichester, U.K.: John Wiley.

Luger, Michael I. 1987. "The States and Industrial Development: Program Mix and Policy Effectiveness." In *Perspectives on Local Public Finance and Public Policy*, John M. Quigley, ed. Greenwich, Connecticut: JAI Press, pp. 29–63.

Luthans, Fred, and Robert Kreitner. 1984. *Organizational Behavior Modification and Beyond: An Operant and Social Learning Approach.* Glencoe, Illinois: Scott Foresman.

Luthans, Fred, and David Lyman. 1976. "Training Supervisors to Use Organizational Behavior Modification." In *People and Productivity*, third edition, Robert A. Sutermeister, ed. New York: McGraw-Hill, pp. 333–338.

MacDuffie, John Paul. 1995. "Human Resource Bundles and Manufacturing Performance: Organizational Logic and Flexible Production Systems in the World Auto Industry." *Industrial and Labor Relations Review* 48(2): 197–221.

MacDuffie, John Paul, and Susan Helper. 1999. "Creating Lean Suppliers: Diffusing Lean Production through the Supply Chain." In *Remade in America: Transplanting and Transforming Japanese Management Systems*, Jeffrey K. Liker, W. Mark Fruin, and Paul S. Adler, eds. New York: Oxford University Press, pp. 154–200.

MacKnight, Susan. 1989. *Japan's Expanding Manufacturing Presence in the United States: An Update.* Washington, D.C.: Japan Economic Institute, October.

MacLeod, W. Bentley, and James M. Malcomson. 1998. "Motivation and Markets." *American Economic Review* 88(3): 388–411.

Maddala, G.S. 1983. *Limited-Dependent and Qualitative Variables in Econometrics.* Cambridge, U.K.: Cambridge University Press.

Mair, Andrew, Richard Florida, and Martin Kenney. 1988. "The New Geography of Automobile Production: Japanese Transplants in North America." *Economic Geography* (October): 352–373.

Markusen, Ann, Peter Hall, and Amy Glasmeier. 1986. *High Tech America.* Boston: Allen & Unwin.

Maslow, Abraham H. 1954. *Motivation and Personality.* New York: Harper and Row.

Mathewson, Stanley B. 1931. *Restricting Output among Organized Workers.* New York: Viking Press.

Maurice, Marc, Francois Sellier, and Jean-Jacques Silvestre. 1984. "The Search for a Societal Effect in the Production of Company Hierarchy: A Comparison of France and Germany." In *Internal Labor Markets*, Paul Osterman, ed. Cambridge, Massachusetts: MIT Press, pp. 231–270.

Maurice, Marc, Arndt Sorge, and Malcolm Warner. 1980. "Societal Differences in Organizing Manufacturing Units: A Comparison of France, West Germany, and Great Britain." *Organization Studies* 1: 59–86.

Mayo, Elton. 1933. *The Human Problems of Industrial Civilization.* New York: MacMillan.

McConnell, Virginia D., and Robert M. Schwab. 1990. "The Impact of Environmental Regulation on Industry Location Decisions: The Motor Vehicle Industry." *Land Economics* 66(1): 67–81.

McCulloch, Rachel. 1991. "Why Foreign Corporations Are Buying into U.S. Businesses." *Annals of the American Academy on Political and Social Science* 516(July): 162–182.

McFadden, Daniel. 1974. "Conditional Logit Analysis of Qualitative Choice Behavior." In *Frontiers in Econometrics*, Paul Zarembka, ed. New York: Academic Press, pp. 105–142.

———. 1981. "Econometric Models of Probabalistic Choice." In *Structural Analysis of Discrete Data with Econometric Application*, Charles Manksi and D. MacFadden, eds. Cambridge, Massachusetts: MIT Press, pp. 198–272.

McGregor, Douglas M. 1960. *The Human Side of Enterprise.* New York: McGraw-Hill.

McGuire, Therese J., and Michael Wasylenko. 1987. *Employment Growth and State Fiscal Behavior: A Report on Economic Development for States from 1973 to 1984.* Report prepared for the New Jersey State and Local Expenditure, Revenue and Policy Commission, July.

Milgrom, Paul, and John Roberts. 1990. "The Economics of Modern Manufacuring: Technology, Strategy and Organization." *American Economic Review* 80(3): 511–528.

———. 1992. *Economics, Organizations, and Management.* Englewood Cliffs, New Jersey: Prentice Hall.

Milkman, Ruth. 1991. *Japan's California Factories: Labor Relations and Economic Globalization.* Los Angeles: University of California Institute of Industrial Relations.

Milward, H. Brinton, and Heidi Hosbach Newman. 1989. "State Incentive Packages and the Industrial Location Decision." *Economic Development Quarterly* 3(3): 203–222.

Mishel, Lawrence, Jared Bernstein, and John Schmitt. 1999. *The State of Working America, 1998–99.* Ithaca, New York: ILR Press.

———. *The State of Working America, 2000–2001.* 2001. Ithaca, New York: ILR Press.

Mitchell, Daniel J.B. 1994. "A Decade of Concession Bargaining." In *Labor Economics and Industrial Relations*, Clark Kerr and Paul Staudohar, eds. Cambridge, Massachusetts: Harvard University Press, pp. 435–474.

Mohr, Michael F. 1983. "Diagnosing the Productivity Problem and Developing an Rx for Improving the Prognosis." Working paper on Productivity and Economic Growth, Cabinet Council on Economic Affairs, Washington, D.C., October.

Mohrman, Susan A. 1999. "Top Management Viewed from Below." In *The Leaders Change Handbook*, Jay A. Conger, Gretchen M. Spreitzer, and Edward E. Lawler, III, eds. San Francisco: Jossey-Bass.

Mohrman, Susan A., Jay R. Galbraith, Edward E. Lawler, III, and associates. 1998. *Tomorrow's Organization: Crafting Winning Capabilities in a Dynamic World*. San Francisco: Jossey-Bass.

Montgomery, David. 1987. *The Fall of the House of Labor*. Cambridge, U.K.: Cambridge University Press.

Moore, Michael, Bert Steece, and Charles Swenson. 1987. "An Analysis of the Impact of State Income Rates and Bases on Foreign Investment." *Accounting Review* 62: 671–685.

Mowday, Richard T., Lyman W. Porter, and Richard M. Steers. 1982. *Employee-Organizational Linkages: The Psychology of Commitment, Absenteeism and Turnover*. New York: Academic Press.

Mowery, David, ed. 1999. *U.S. Industry 2000*. Washington, D.C.: National Academy Press.

Nakabayashi, Takeshi. 1987. "A Study on Locational Choices of Japanese Manufacturing Companies in the U.S.: Guidelines for State and Local Governments in Attracting Japanese Firms' Investments." Photocopy, policy analysis exercise, John F. Kennedy School of Government, Harvard University, April.

Neumark, David, Daniel Polsky, and Daniel Hanson. 1999. "Has Job Stability Declined Yet? New Evidence for the 1990s." *Journal of Labor Economics* 17(4), Part 2: S29–S64.

Newby, Howard. 1977. "Paternalism and Capitalism." In *Industrial Society: Class Cleavage and Control*, Richard Scase, ed. New York: St. Martin's Press.

———. 1979. *The Deferential Workers*. Madison: University of Wisconsin Press.

Newman, Robert J., and Dennis H. Sullivan. 1988. "Econometric Analysis of Business Tax Impacts on Industrial Location: What Do We Know, and How Do We Know It?" *Journal of Urban Economics* 23: 215–234.

Ondrich, Jan, and Michael Wasylenko 1993. *Foreign Direct Investment in the United States*. Kalamazoo, Michigan: W.E. Upjohn Institute for Employment Research.

Osterman, Paul. 1994. "How Common Is Workplace Transformation and Who Adopts It?" *Industrial and Labor Relations Review* 47(2): 173–188.

————. 2000. "Work Reorganization in an Era of Restructuring: Trends in Diffusion and Effects on Employee Welfare." *Industrial and Labor Relations Review* 53(2): 179–196.

Ouchi, William. 1984. *The M-Form Society.* Reading, Massachusetts: Addison Wesley.

Ouchi, William G., and Raymond L. Price. 1983. "Hierarchies, Clans and Theory: A New Perspective on Organizational Development." In *Perspectives on Organizational Behavior*, J. Richard Hackman, Edward E. Lawler, III, and Lyman W. Porter, eds. New York: McGraw-Hill, pp. 564–577.

Papke, Leslie E. 1991. "Interstate Business Tax Differentials and New Firm Location." *Journal of Public Economics* 45: 47–68.

Parker, Mike, and Jane Slaughter. 1988. *Choosing Sides: Unions and the Team Concept.* Boston: South End Press.

Pascal, Richard. 1986. "Fitting New Employees into the Company Culture." In *Productivity through People*, William B. Werther, Jr., William A. Ruch, and Lynne McLure, eds. St. Paul: West Publishing.

Pfeffer, Jeffrey. 1982. *Organizations and Organization Theory.* Marshfield, Massachusetts: Pitman.

Pil, Frits K., and John Paul MacDuffie. 1999. "Transferring Competitive Advantage across Borders: A Study of Japanese Auto Transplants in North America." In *Remade in America; Transplanting and Transforming Japanese Management Systems*, Jeffrey K. Liker, W. Mark Fruin, and Paul S. Adler, eds. New York: Oxford University Press, pp. 39–74.

Piore, Michael J., and Charles Sabel. 1984. *The Second Industrial Divide.* New York: Basic Books.

Plaut, Thomas R., and Joseph E. Pluta. 1983. "Business Climate, Taxes and Expenditures, and State Industrial Growth in the United States." *Southern Economic Journal* 50(1): 99–119.

Prendergast, Canice. 1999. "The Provision of Incentives in Firms." *Journal of Economic Literature* 37(1): 7–63.

Quan, Nguyen, and John Beck. 1987. "Public Education Expenditures and State Economic Growth—Northeast and Sunbelt Regions." *Southern Economic Journal* 54: 361–376.

Raff, Daniel M. 1991. "Ford Welfare Capitalism in Its Economic Context." In *Masters to Managers*, Sanford M. Jacoby, ed. New York: Columbia University Press.

Raysey, Harvey, Dore Scholerious, and Bill Harley. 2000. "Employers and High Performance Work Systems: Testing inside the Black Box." *British Journal of Industrial Relations* 38(4): 501–532.

Reid, Neil. 1989. "Spatial Patterns of Japanese Investment in the U.S. Automobile Industry." *Industrial Relations Journal* 20(August): 49–59.

Rencher, A.C. 1998. *Multivariate Statistical Inference and Applications.* New York: John Wiley.

Roethlisberger, Fritz J., and William J. Dickson. 1939. *Management and the Worker.* Cambridge, Massachusetts: Harvard University Press.

Rousseau, Denise M. 1995. *Psychological Contracts in Organizations: Understanding Written and Unwritten Agreements.* Thousand Oaks, California: Sage.

Salop, Steven. 1979. "A Model of the Natural Rate of Unemployment." *American Economic Review* 69(March): 117–125.

Saltzman, Gregory M. 1994. "Job Applicant Screening by a Japanese Transplant: A Union-Avoidance Tactic." *Workplace Topics* 4(1): 61–82.

Schein, Edgar H. 1985. *Organizational Culture and Leadership.* San Francisco, California: Jossey-Bass.

Scherer, F.M. 1975. *The Economics of Multi-Plant Operation.* Cambridge, Massachusetts: Harvard University Press.

Schmenner, Roger W. 1982. *Making Location Decisions.* Englewood Cliffs, New Jersey: Prentice-Hall.

Schmenner, Roger W., Joel C. Huber, and Randall L. Cook. 1987. "Geographic Differences and the Location of New Manufacturing Facilities." *Journal of Urban Economics* 21(1): 83–104.

Schneider, Benjamin. 1984. "Industrial and Organizational Psychology Perspective." In *Productivity Research in the Behavioral and Social Sciences*, Arthur P. Brief, ed. New York: Praeger, pp. 174–206.

Simon, Herbert A. 1991. "Organizations and Markets." *Journal of Economic Perspectives* 5(2): 25–44.

Skinner, Burris F. 1953. *Science and Human Behavior.* New York: MacMillan.

Smith, Donald F., Jr., and Richard Florida. 1994. "Agglomeration and Industrial Location: An Econometric Analysis of Japanese-Affiliated Manufacturing Establishments in Automotive-Related Industries." *Journal of Urban Economics* 35: 1–19.

Stajkovic, Alexander D., and Fred Luthans. 1997. "A Meta Analysis of the Effects of Organizational Behavior Modifications on Task Performance: 1975–1995." *Academy of Management Journal* 40(5): 1122–1149.

Stiglitz, Joseph E. 1974. "Wage Determination and Unemployment in L.D.C.'s: The Labor Turnover Model." *Quarterly Journal of Economics* 88: 194–227.

Stone, Katherine. 1975. "The Origins of Job Structures in the Steel Industry." In *Labor Market Segmentation*, Richard C. Edwards, Michael Reich, and David M. Gordon, eds. Lexington, Massachusetts: D.C. Heath, pp. 27–84.

Strauss, George. 1977. "Managerial Practices." In *Improving Life at Work*, J. Richard Hackman and J. Lloyd Suttle, eds. Santa Monica, California: Goodyear Publishing, pp. 297–363.

Sutermeister, Robert A. 1976. *People and Productivity.* Third edition. New York: McGraw-Hill.

Tannenwald, Robert. 1984. "The Pros and Cons of Worldwide Unitary Taxation." *New England Economic Review* (July/August): 17–28.

Taylor, Frederic W. 1911. *The Principles of Scientific Management.* New York: Harper and Brothers.

Ulgado, Francis M. 1996. "Location Characteristics of Manufacturing Investments in the U.S.: A Comparison of American and Foreign-Based Firms." *Management International Review* 36(1): 7–26.

U.S. Department of Commerce. Various years. *County and City Data Book.* Bureau of the Census, Washington, D.C.

U.S. Department of Education. 1982. *Digest of Education Statistics.* Washington, D.C.

Viteles, Morris S. 1953. *Motivation and Morale in Industry.* New York: Norton.

Vroom, Victor H. 1964. *Work and Motivation.* New York: Wiley.

Walton, Richard E. 1985. "From Control to Commitment: Transformation of Workforce Management Strategies in the Unites States." In *The Uneasy Alliance: Managing the Productivity–Technology Dilemma*, Kim B. Clark, Robert H. Hayes, and Christopher Lorenz, eds. Boston: Harvard Business School Press, pp. 237–265.

Wasylenko, Michael. 1997. "Taxation and Economic Development: The State of the Economic Literature." *New England Economic Review* (March/April): 37–52.

Wasylenko, Michael, and Therese McGuire. 1985. "Jobs and Taxes: The Effect of Business Climate on States' Employment Growth Rates." *National Tax Journal* 38(4): 497–511.

Weiss, Andrew. 1980. "Job Queues and Layoffs in Labor Markets with Flexible Wages." *Journal of Political Economy* 88(June): 526–538.

———. 1990. *Efficiency Wages: Models of Unemployment, Layoffs and Wage Dispersion.* New York: Harwood Academic.

Weitzman, Martin. 1989. "A Theory of Wage Dispersion and Job Market Segmentation." *Quarterly Journal of Economics* (February): 121–138.

Westney, D. Eleanor. 1999. "Organizational Perspectives on the Cross-Border Transfer of Organizational Patterns." In *Remade in America; Transplanting and Transforming Japanese Management Systems*, Jeffrey K. Liker, W. Mark Fruin, and Paul S. Adler, eds. New York: Oxford University Press, pp. 385–408.

Whyte, William F., ed. 1955. *Money and Motivation*. New York: Harper and Row.

Williamson, Oliver E. 1975. *Markets and Hierarchies: Analysis and Antitrust Implications*. New York: Free Press.

———. 1985. *The Economic Institutions of Capitalism*. New York: Free Press.

Williamson, Oliver E., Michael L. Wachter, and Jeffrey E. Harris. 1975. "Understanding the Employment Relation: The Analysis of Idiosyncratic Exchange." *Bell Journal of Economics* 6: 250–280.

Winship, Christopher, and Sherwin Rosen. 1988. "Introduction: Sociological and Economic Approaches to the Analysis of Social Structure." *American Journal of Sociology* 94(supplement): S1–S17.

Woodward, Douglas P. 1992. "Locational Determinants of Japanese Manufacturing Start-Ups in the United States." *Southern Economic Journal* 58(3): 690–708.

Wyatt Company. 1990. *A Report on the Survey of Human Resource Management in Japanese-Owned Companies in the United States*. Washington, D.C.

Yanarella, Ernest J., and William C. Green. 1990. *The Politics of Industrial Recruitment: Japanese Automobile Investment and Economic Development in the American States*. New York: Greenwood Press.

Yoshida, Mamoru. 1987. *Japanese Direct Manufacturing Investment in the United States*. New York: Praeger.

# The Authors

Peter B. Doeringer is a Professor of Economics at Boston University and has taught at Harvard University, the London School of Economics, and the University of Paris. His research interests include labor markets, collective bargaining, industry economics, and regional economic development. He is a consultant and adviser to government agencies, and to international organizations such as the ILO. His most recent public service was as Research Director for the Commonwealth of Massachusetts Blue Ribbon Commission on Older Workers. Professor Doeringer is also a practicing labor arbitrator.

David G. Terkla is a Professor in the Economics Department and a member of the Environmental Coastal and Ocean Sciences Department at the University of Massachusetts Boston. His research interests include local and regional economic development and industry studies and he currently directs the Greater Boston regional economic development project at the University of Massachusetts. He is also a specialist on the New England fishing industry and is a member of the Social Science Advisory Committee for the New England Fisheries Management Council and of the Lobster Socioeconomic Sub-Committee of the Atlantic States Marine Fisheries Commission

Christine Evans-Klock currently works for the International Labour Organization as Director of the InFocus Programme on Boosting Employment through Small Enterprise Development. While at the ILO she has published papers on employment and enterprise restructuring in CIS countries and on policy responses to worker retrenchment. Ms. Evans-Klock participated in the research for this book as a doctoral student at Boston University, prior to joining the ILO. She currently lives in Geneva, Switzerland, with her husband and twin sons.

# Cited Author Index

The italic letters *f*, *n*, *t* following a page number indicate that the cited name is within a figure, note, or table respectively, on that page.

# Subject Index

The italic letters *f*, *n*, *t* following a page number indicate that the subject information is within a figure, note, or table respectively, on that page.

259

# About the Institute

The W.E. Upjohn Institute for Employment Research is a nonprofit research organization devoted to finding and promoting solutions to employment-related problems at the national, state, and local levels. It is an activity of the W.E. Upjohn Unemployment Trustee Corporation, which was established in 1932 to administer a fund set aside by the late Dr. W.E. Upjohn, founder of The Upjohn Company, to seek ways to counteract the loss of employment income during economic downturns.

The Institute is funded largely by income from the W.E. Upjohn Unemployment Trust, supplemented by outside grants, contracts, and sales of publications. Activities of the Institute comprise the following elements: 1) a research program conducted by a resident staff of professional social scientists; 2) a competitive grant program, which expands and complements the internal research program by providing financial support to researchers outside the Institute; 3) a publications program, which provides the major vehicle for disseminating the research of staff and grantees, as well as other selected works in the field; and 4) an Employment Management Services division, which manages most of the publicly funded employment and training programs in the local area.

The broad objectives of the Institute's research, grant, and publication programs are to 1) promote scholarship and experimentation on issues of public and private employment and unemployment policy, and 2) make knowledge and scholarship relevant and useful to policymakers in their pursuit of solutions to employment and unemployment problems.

Current areas of concentration for these programs include causes, consequences, and measures to alleviate unemployment; social insurance and income maintenance programs; compensation; workforce quality; work arrangements; family labor issues; labor-management relations; and regional economic development and local labor markets.

Lightning Source UK Ltd.
Milton Keynes UK
03 September 2009

143340UK00004B/15/A